Baseball in Broome County

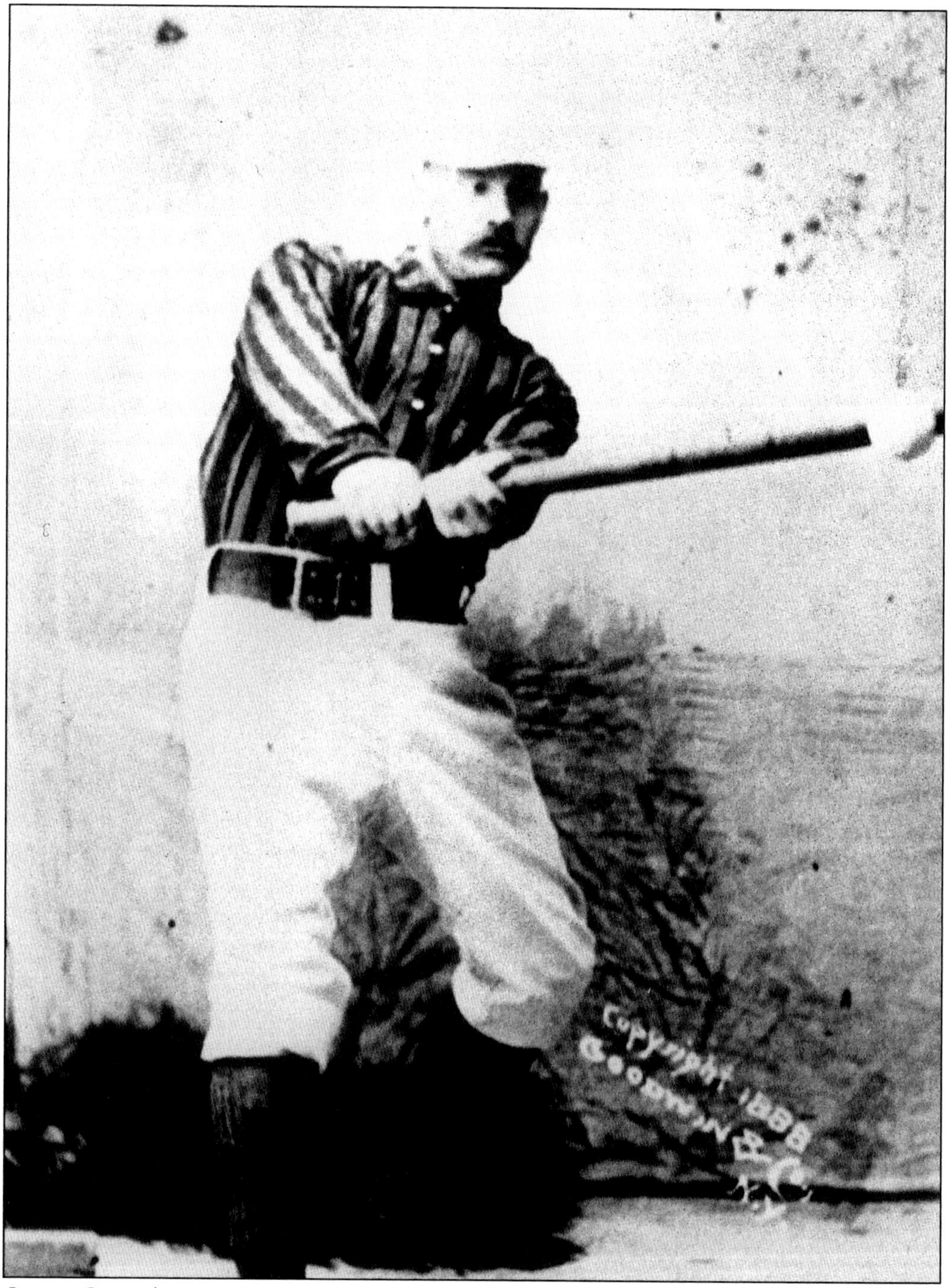

George Gore, the center fielder for the Chicago White Stockings in the old National League from 1879 to 1886, was known for his speed and hitting ability. Born in Saccarappa, Maine, in 1857, he was as difficult off the field—being excessively enamored of wine and women—as he was valuable on it. Chicago finally traded him to the Giants, where he hit .348 in 1887. Gore hit .319 for Binghamton in 1894 and promptly retired. (Courtesy of the National Baseball Hall of Fame Library, Cooperstown, New York.)

BASEBALL IN BROOME COUNTY

Marvin A. Cohen and Michael J. McCann

ARCADIA PUBLISHING

ISBN 978-0-7385-3484-8

Published by Arcadia Publishing
Charleston, South Carolina

Printed in the United States of America

Library of Congress Catalog Card Number: 2003112424

For all general information contact Arcadia Publishing at:
Telephone 843-853-2070
Fax 843-853-0044
E-mail sales@arcadiapublishing.com
For customer service and orders:
Toll-Free 1-888-313-2665

Visit us on the Internet at www.arcadiapublishing.com

Contents

ACKNOWLEDGMENTS

Photographs are courtesy of the National Baseball Hall of Fame Library in Cooperstown, New York; the Binghamton Mets; the Broome County Historical Society; Your Home Public Library in Johnson City, New York; the Farrell family; Fran Gennarelli; Steve Kraly; Joe Lukasik; Michael and Susan McCann; the John Nuzzela family; Fred Perry; "Plumlily;" Frank Saraceno; the George Trencansky family; and Colleen (DeClercq) Zuhone. The 1947 scorecard cover is courtesy of American Legion Post 758 in Johnson City, New York.

Special thanks go to Bill Burdick, Charles Brown, Richard O'Donnell, and Janet Ottman for their research. Special thanks also go to the people at the Binghamton Mets for giving the authors full access to their organization's photograph archives: Michael Urda, president; Bill Terlecky, general manager; and Scott Brown, assistant general manager.

Baseball cards are included with the permission of Crowley Foods LLC and the Topps Company Inc., with additional permissions from Frank Keetz, owner of the Crowley card set, Fred Norman for his card, and Sara Raschi for Vic Raschi's card.

The following people provided valuable information and editorial assistance: John "Jack" Cahill, Cay Cohen, John W. Fox and his wife, Terri, Ken Gilchrist (the "Voice of the Triplets"), Joseph C. McCann, Charlotte Sauve, and Jerry Toman.

Without the help of everyone mentioned above, this book could not have been written.

INTRODUCTION

The baseball history of Broome County, New York, had its beginnings in its largest city, Binghamton, in 1871. On August 25 of that year, the hometown Crickets played the Norwich Comets. Playing without gloves, as was the custom in those early days, and with batters requesting specific locations of pitches to hit, Binghamton lost that inaugural game with a score of 35-33.

In 1885, Binghamton was awarded a franchise in the New York State League and won its first game as Bingos, beating Oswego 8-1. By 1892, the Bingos were in the International League and winning the league championship, with the help of a third baseman named "Wee Willie" Keeler.

The baseball spotlight then moved from Binghamton to Johnson City (still called Lestershire) in 1899, with ownership of that village's semiprofessional team belonging to George F. Johnson of Endicott-Johnson fame. He loved the game and eventually bought the Bingos, a professional team, in 1913. In that same year, he built Johnson Field for them to play on, and the club rewarded him with a pennant.

When the Eastern League was formed in 1923, three American Legion posts from Binghamton, Johnson City, and Endicott bought the franchise. The ownership arrangement was unique for baseball anywhere in the United States and led to the team becoming known as "Triple Cities" or "Triplets." Its glory years came a bit later as a franchise associated with the New York Yankees that produced many of its great stars.

Unfortunately, Johnson Field was demolished after the 1968 season to make way for a frontage road for Route 17, a major New York artery. From 1969 to 1991, professional baseball simply disappeared from the area. However, it would return with a flourish in 1992, when after years of effort led by former Binghamton mayor Juanita Crabb and local business leaders, plus a $6 million rescue effort by the New York Mets, a new stadium was built and the Binghamton Mets were born.

Professional baseball was back not only in Broome County but also in Binghamton, where its first game had been played 121 years earlier. Here in pictures and captions are the people, places, and events that have made Broome County such a great home for our national pastime.

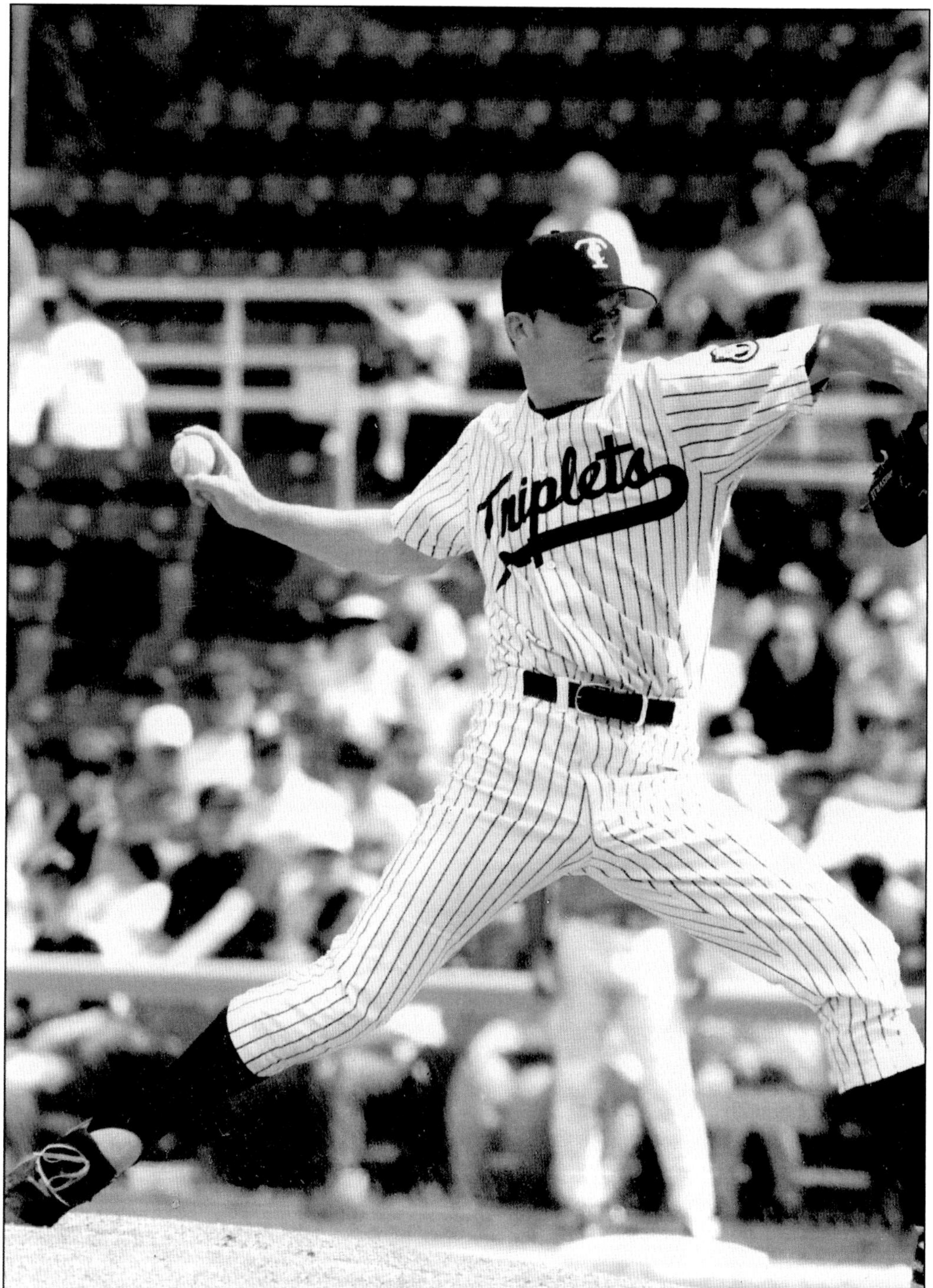

The Triplets may be gone from the Triple Cities, but they are not forgotten. A favorite promotion of the B-Mets is the "Turn Back the Clock" game. The B-Mets don Triplets uniforms for the occasion and play an official game. Here, in a 1996 rendition, hurler Cory Lidle prepares to fire the ball. He led the B-Mets that year with 14 wins.

One

The Early Days

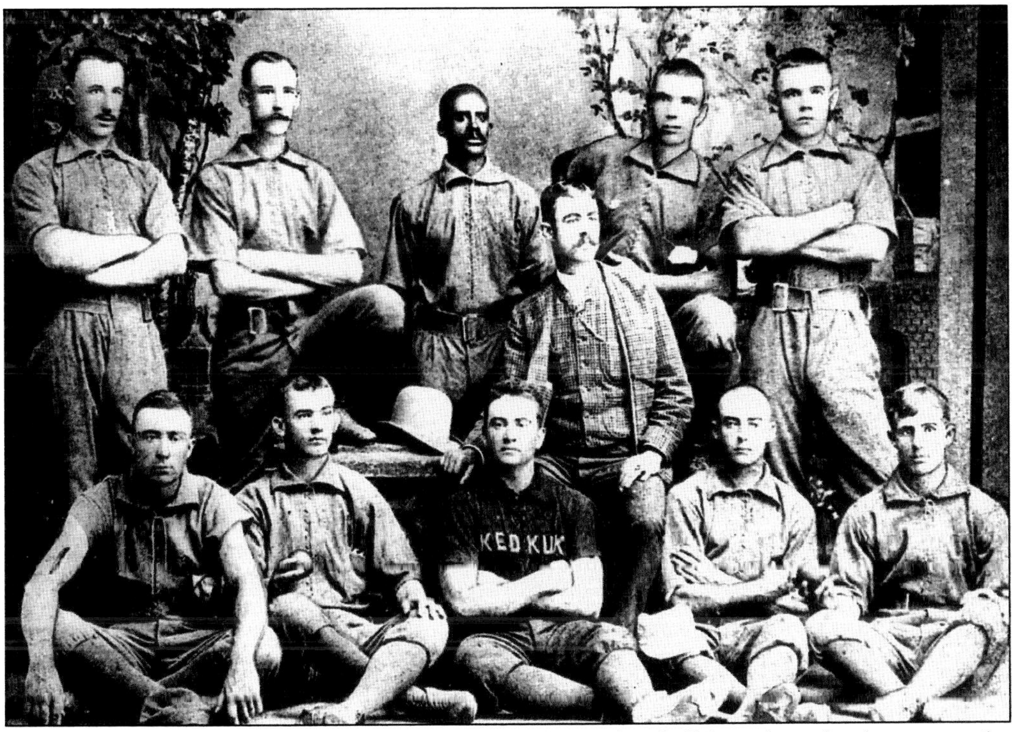

The 1885 Keokuk Baseball Club might have been lost in baseball lore if not for the man in the center of the back row. John (Bud) Fowler is recognized as professional baseball's first known black player. His stay with Binghamton in 1887 was shortened because both teammates and opponents refused to play if he was in the lineup. At the time of his release, Fowler was hitting .350. (Courtesy of the National Baseball Hall of Fame Library, Cooperstown, New York.)

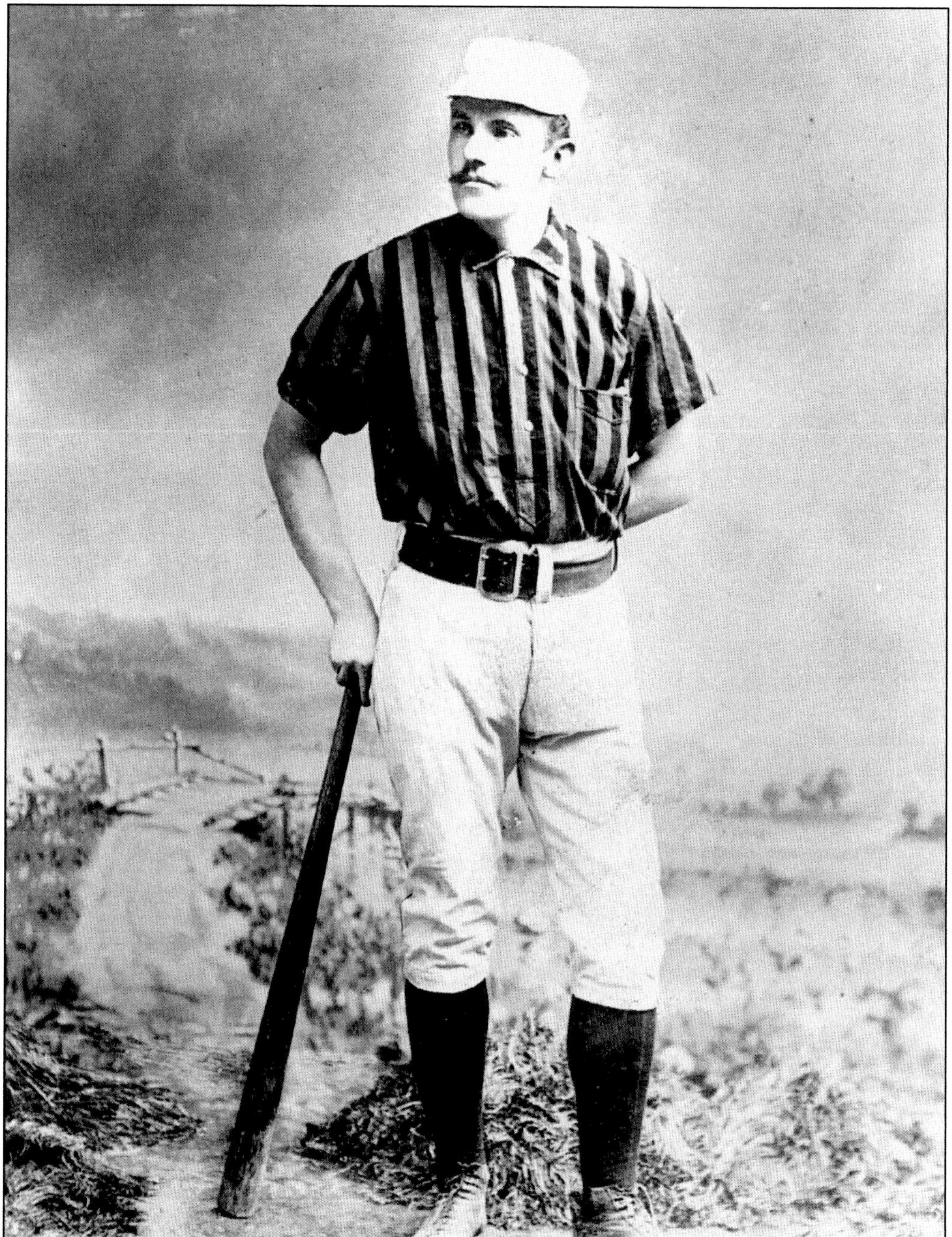

On June 12, 1880, John Lee Richmond threw the first complete, perfect game in National League history. Five days later, future Hall of Famer John Montgomery Ward (shown here), a former Binghamton Cricket, now pitching for Providence, hurled the second. Another such gem would not occur in the National League for 84 years, when Jim Bunning did it against the New York Mets. Ward, at age 20, the youngest ever to pitch a perfect game, is also credited with inventing the pitcher's mound and the intentional walk. (Courtesy of the National Baseball Hall of Fame Library, Cooperstown, New York.)

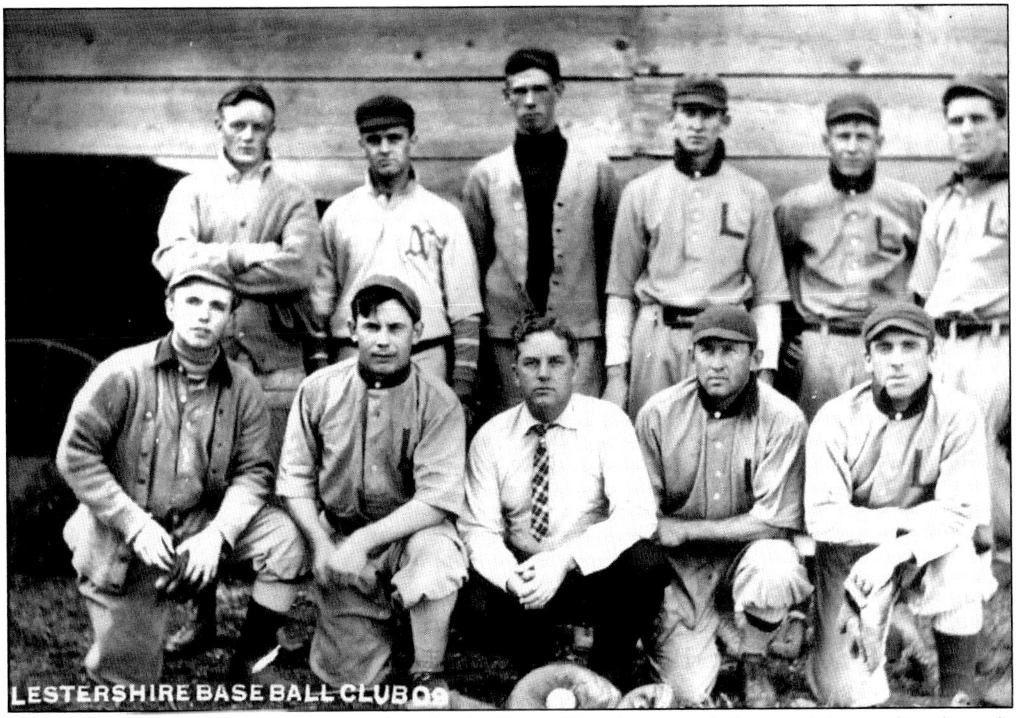

Baseball has always been popular in the Triple Cities (Binghamton, Johnson City, and Endicott), and many private teams formed. Competition was often intense, and local pride was at stake each time teams met. The Village of Lestershire, later to become Johnson City, is represented here by two squads. Most teams in the early 1900s had rosters no larger than 10 players; the extra man provided for a loss due to injury. Mascots were ineligible.

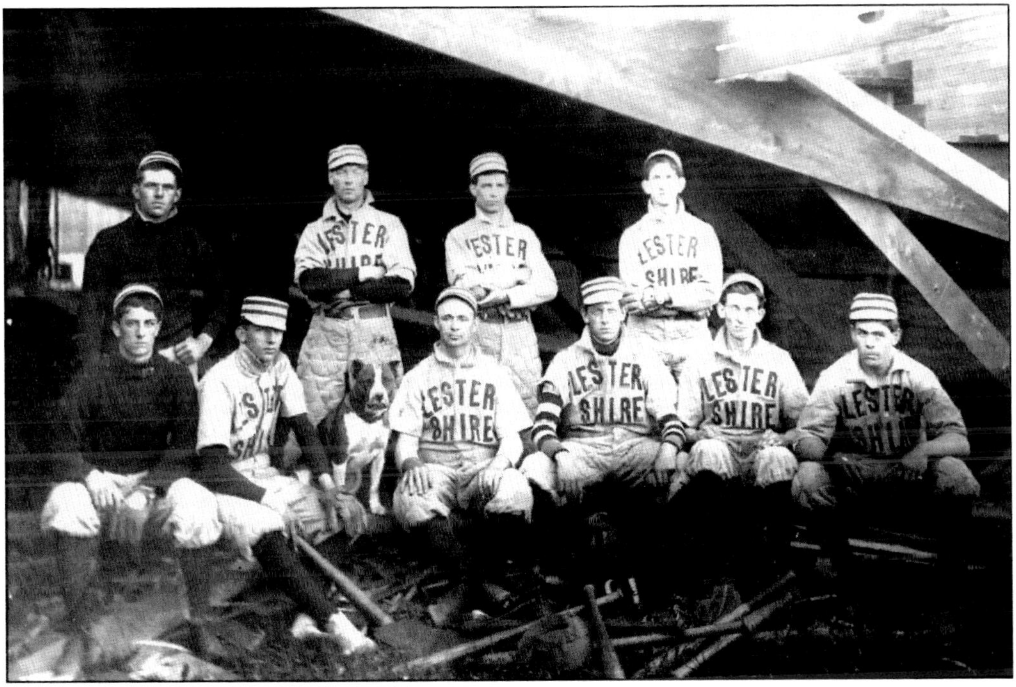

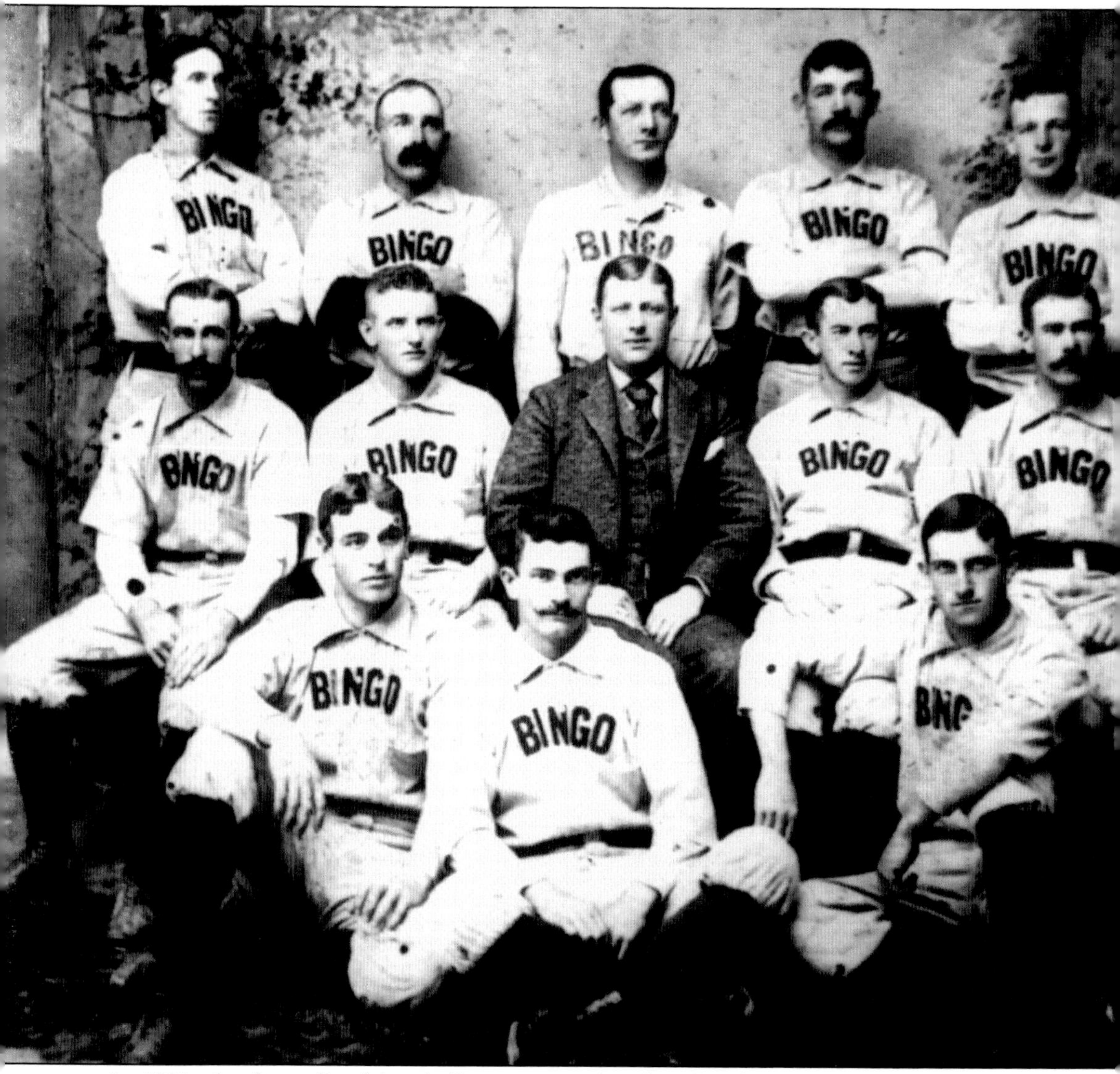

In 1871, the first official baseball game was played in Binghamton. On that occasion, the hometown Crickets lost to the Norwich Comets 35-33. In 1885, Binghamton was awarded a franchise in the New York State League, and the team became the Bingos. Seven years later, it was in the International League, and its 1892 club, featuring Wee Willie Keeler, won the championship. Keeler is shown in the second row, second from right, seated next to manager Herman Doescher, who recruited him for the team.

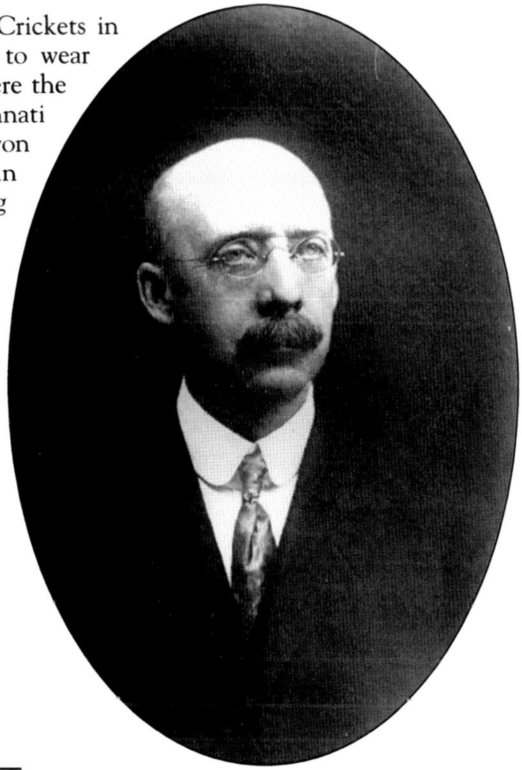

William Henry White, who played for the Crickets in 1876, was not only the first major-leaguer to wear glasses, but he and his older brother, Jim, were the first brother battery. That was with Cincinnati from 1878 to 1880. In seven seasons, White won 226 games and lost only 161. He set a record in 1879, which may never be broken, by starting and finishing 75 games. He won 43 of them. (Courtesy of the National Baseball Hall of Fame Library, Cooperstown, New York.)

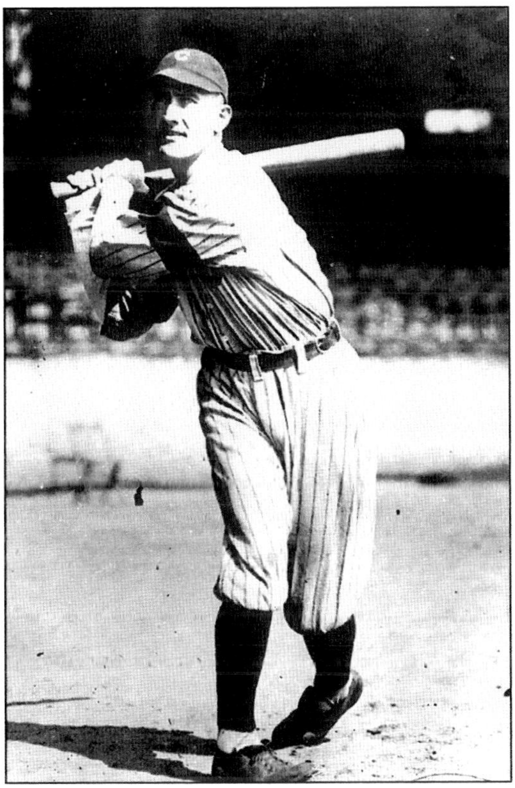

At age 19, Elmer Smith won 34 games for Cincinnati in 1887. After two more seasons of 20-plus wins, his arm went dead. Undaunted, he went on to spend 10 years as an outfielder in the National League. In 1906, at age 37, now playing with the Binghamton Bingos of the New York State League, he hit .313. He was born in 1868 in Allegheny, Pennsylvania, once part of Pittsburgh, and died there in 1945. (Courtesy of the National Baseball Hall of Fame Library, Cooperstown, New York.)

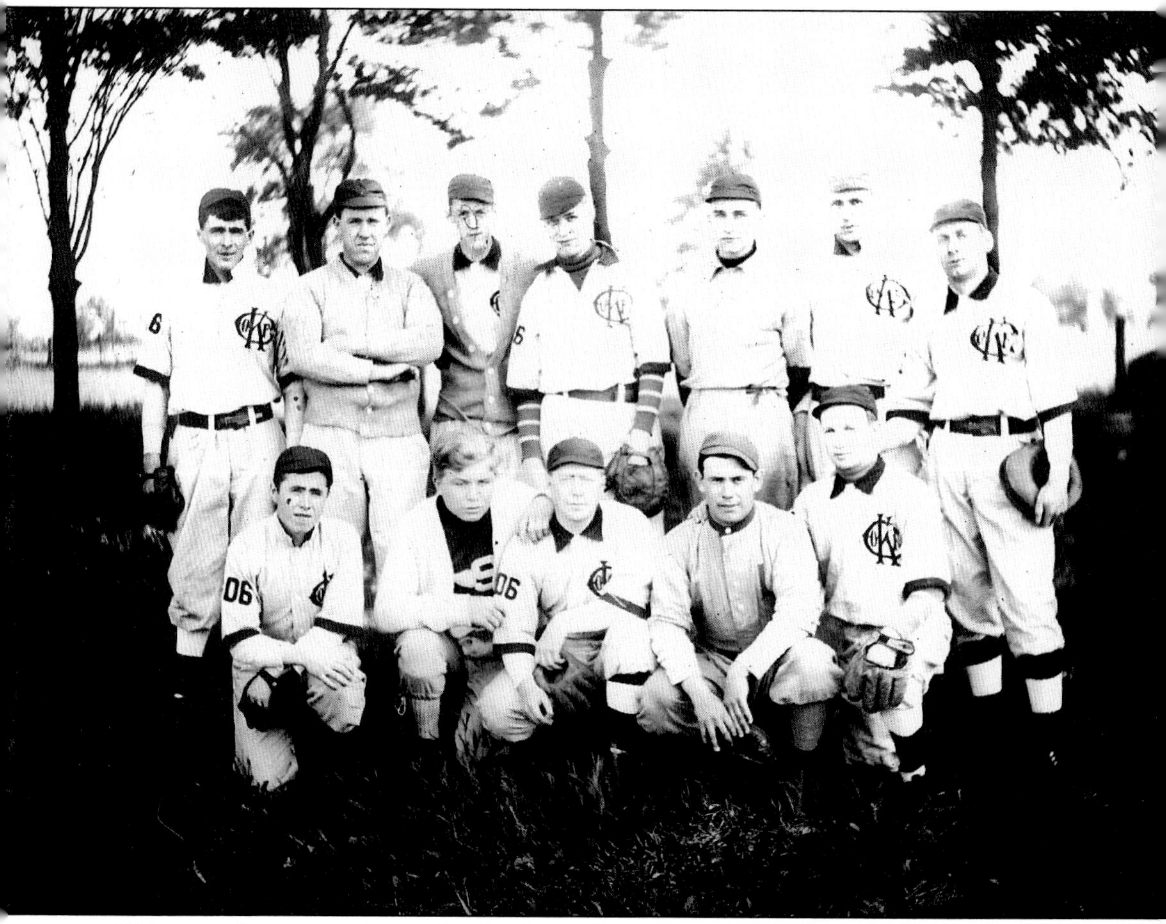

This team photograph of the 1886 Knights of Columbus squad is of interest because of the gloves used at that time. Baseball had been played barehanded for decades in the 1800s, and even at this time, some purists disdained the use of them. Here, the catcher (back row, right) and the first baseman (back row, center), as well as some of the fielders, display their equipment.

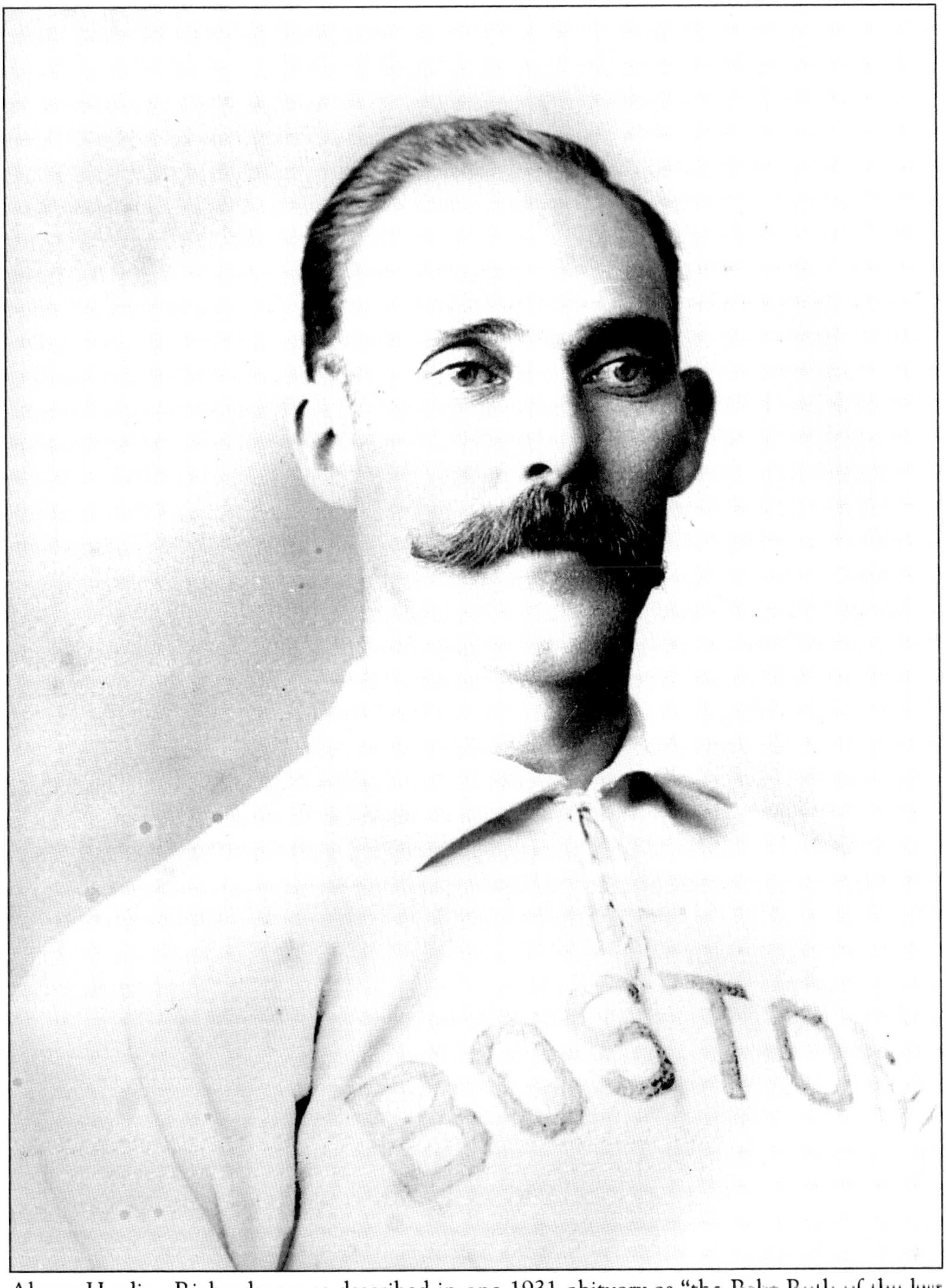

Abram Harding Richardson was described in one 1931 obituary as "the Babe Ruth of the last century." In 14 National League seasons, he hit 73 home runs. That was a lot for the dead-ball era. He began his career with the Binghamton Crickets in baseball's pioneer minor league, the International Association. A versatile performer who played all nine positions, he ended his career with the Giants in 1892. (Courtesy of the National Baseball Hall of Fame Library, Cooperstown, New York.)

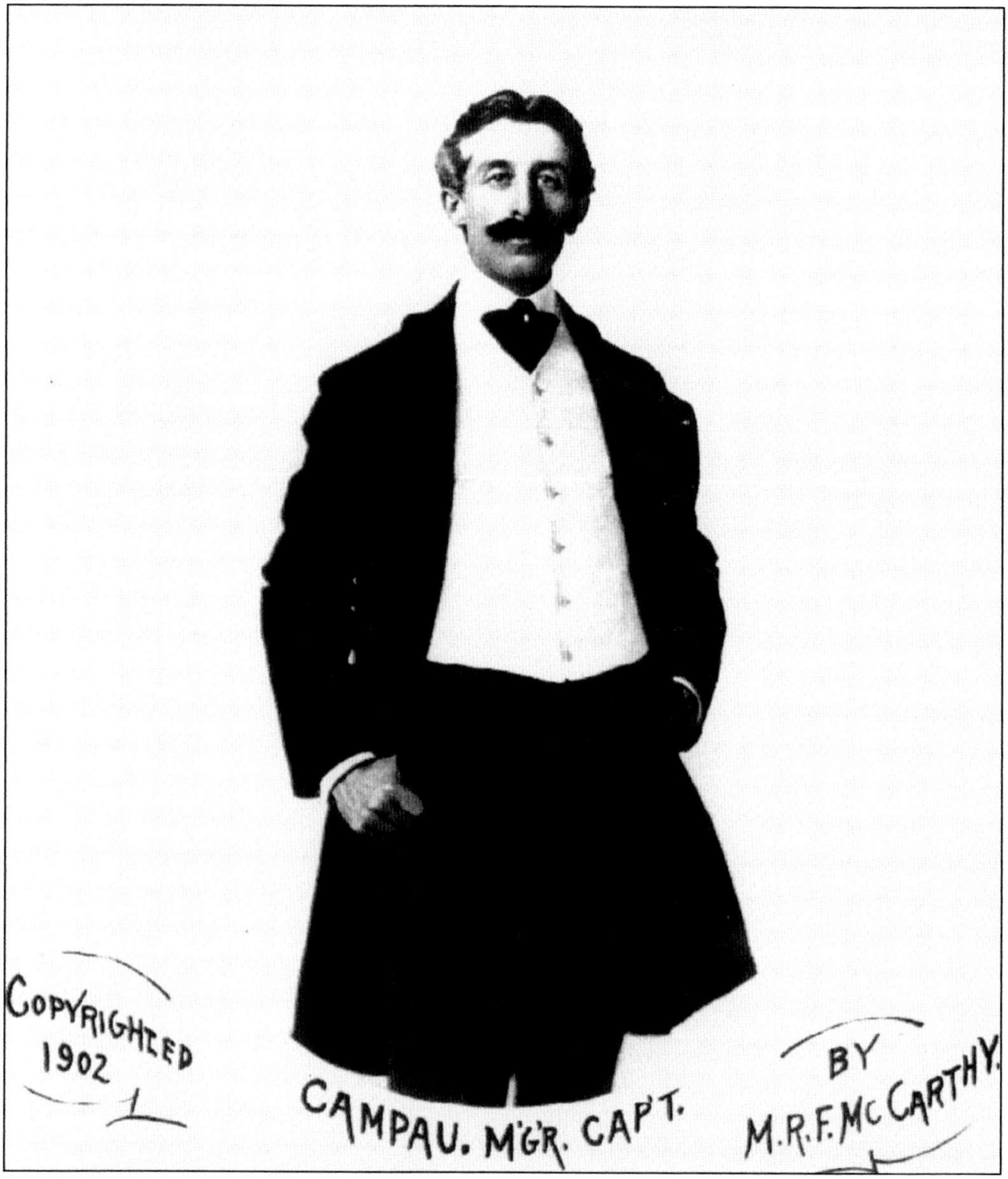

Charles "Count" Campau was that rare kind of player who can both hit for power and steal bases. A descendant of one of the original founding families of the city of Detroit, he combined style with the ability to fashion a (mostly minor-league) career that lasted for more than two decades. Campau came to the Bingos in 1901 and finished his career there at the age of 41 in 1905. He hit over .300 for them in both 1901 and 1903. Despite his slight 160-pound build, in 1887, he slammed 17 home runs in that dead-ball era while stealing 100 bases. When he hit three homers in one game that year, the appreciative fans showered him with coins totaling $60—a pretty penny in those days.

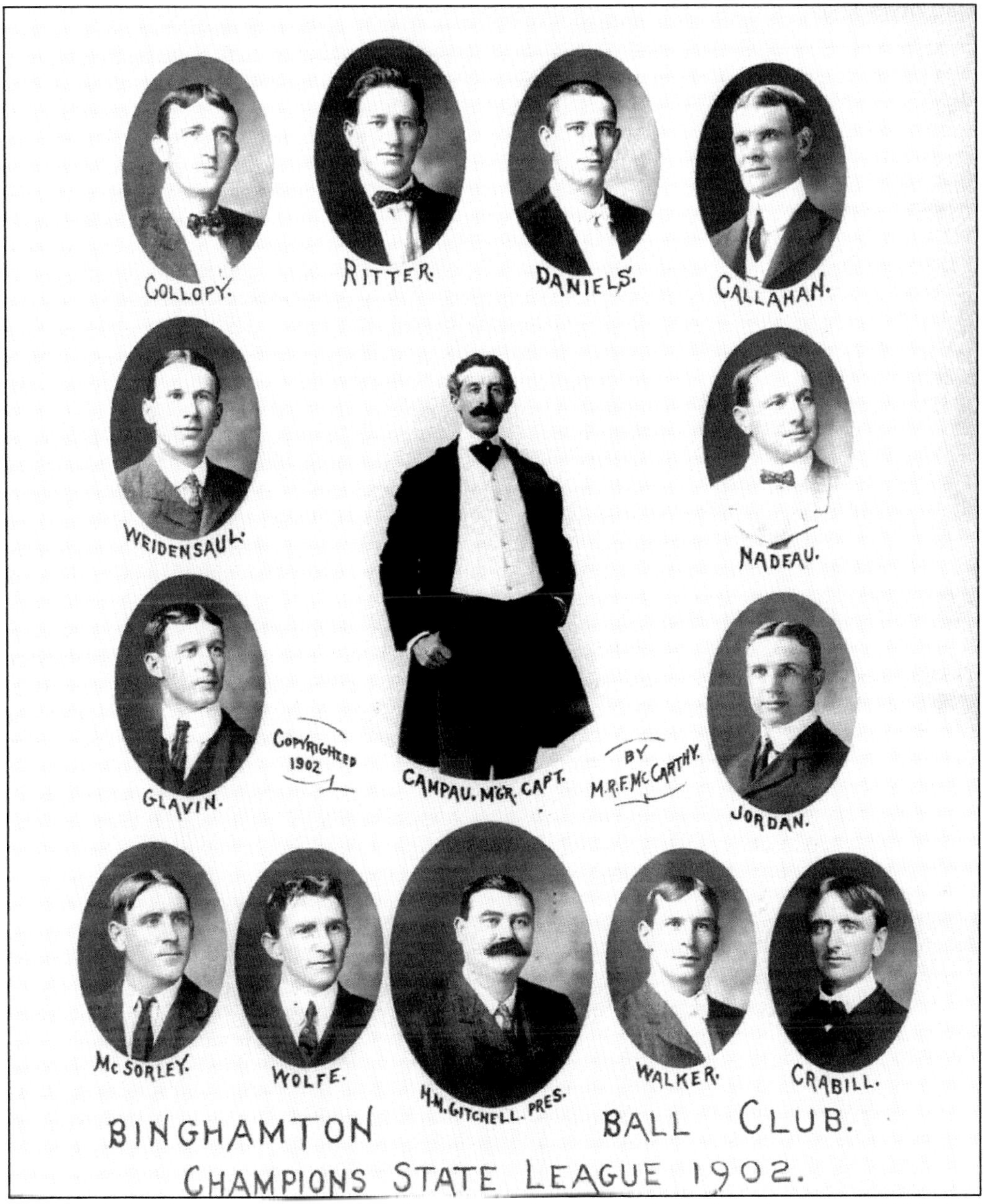

The 1902 Binghamton Bingos were champions of the New York State League in 1902. Led by their dashing player-manager-captain, Charles Columbus Campau, they had captured the imagination and support of the Triple Cities. The club had a sentimental side too. When Campau retired from active play in 1905, as a tribute to his popularity with the players, as well as the fans, he was presented with an elk's head ring by his teammates.

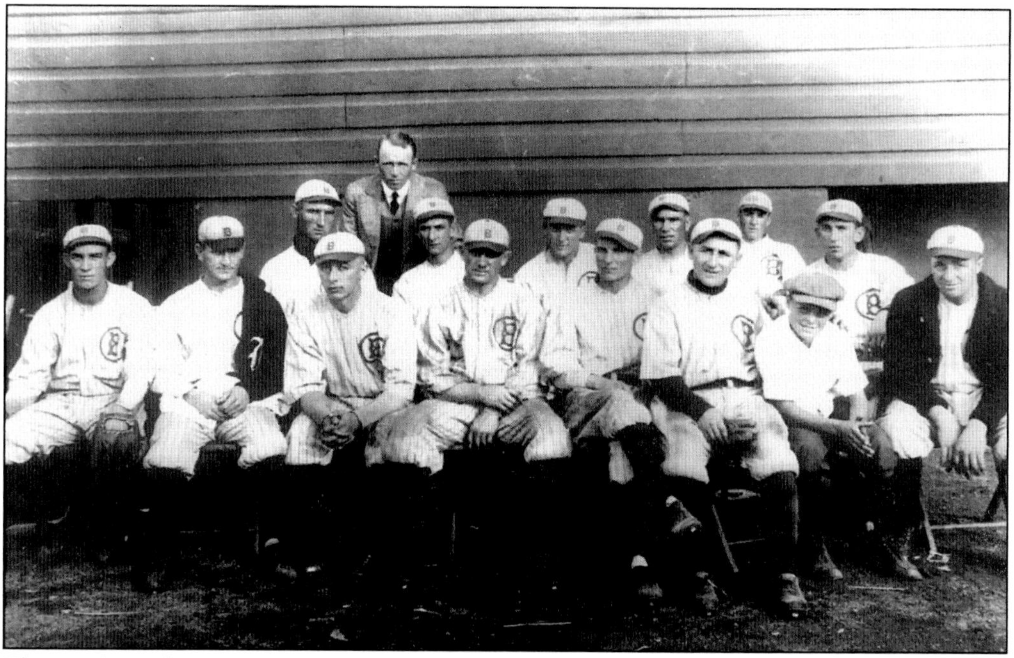

The 1915 Binghamton Bingos pose for their team picture. While World War I was raging in Europe, the Triple Cities were enjoying a period of prosperity. Baseball also flourished in this business climate. The batboy is none other than Edward Farrell. Ten years later, as Doc Farrell, a recent graduate of dental school, he was summoned directly to John McGraw's New York Giants. Farrell would later be a member of the Yankees' 1932 world championship club.

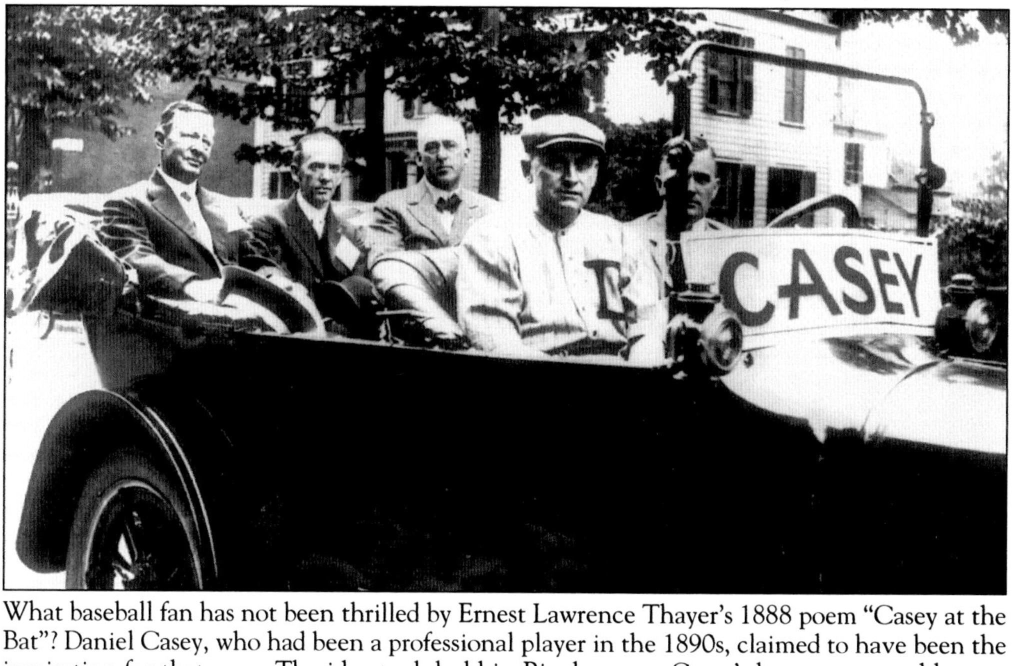

What baseball fan has not been thrilled by Ernest Lawrence Thayer's 1888 poem "Casey at the Bat"? Daniel Casey, who had been a professional player in the 1890s, claimed to have been the inspiration for that opus. The idea took hold in Binghamton, Casey's hometown, and he was honored in 1915 with a "Casey Day." Casey, wearing the cap and baseball shirt, later returned to Binghamton, less glamorously, as a streetcar conductor.

Two

The Triplets Take the Field

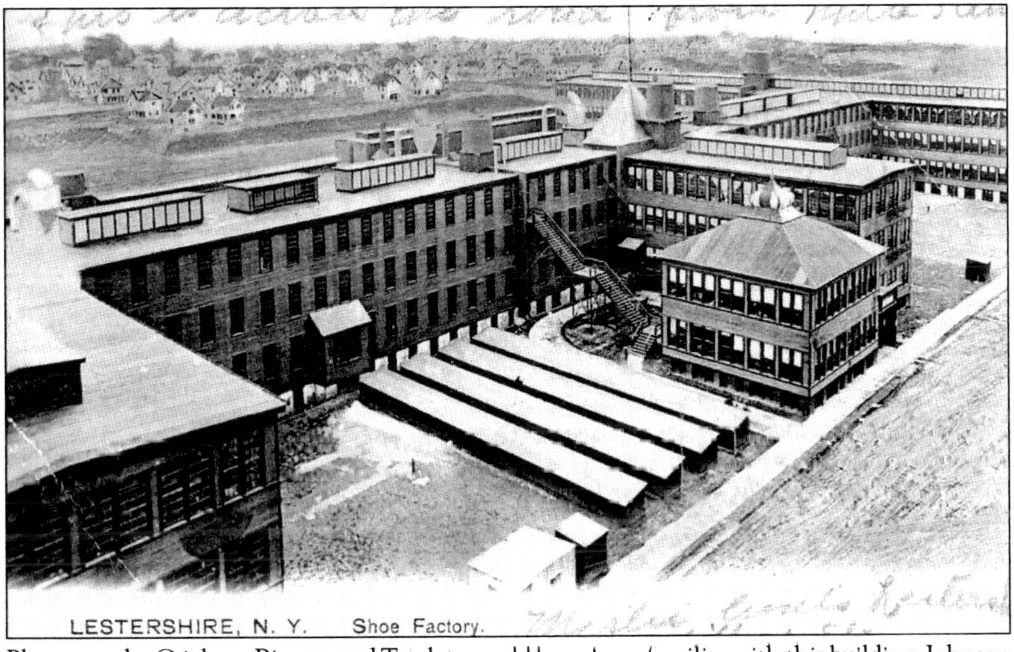

Players on the Crickets, Bingos, and Triplets would have been familiar with this building. Johnson City (one of the Triple Cities) was originally called Lestershire, before George F. Johnson arrived and created the success of Endicott-Johnson. Dating from the first decade of the 20th century, this view shows the factory that gave the area its nickname, "Shoetown."

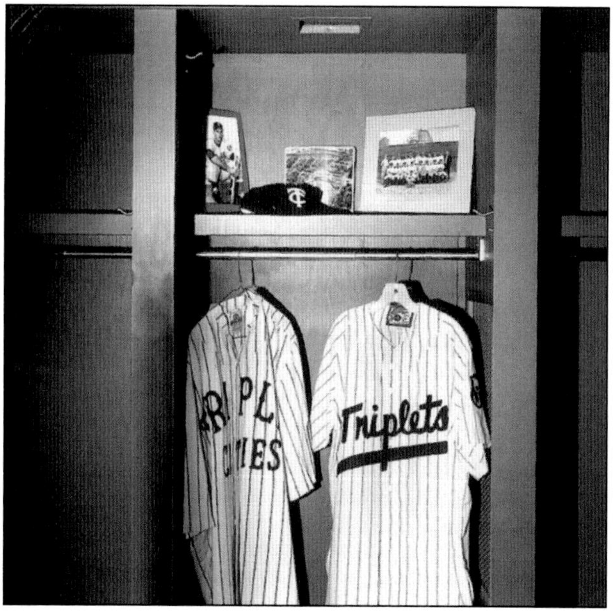

From 1923 to 1968, the Triplets played their home games at Johnson Field and wore Triplets uniforms. However, since few fans outside of Binghamton knew what "Triplets" stood for, road uniforms carried the words "Triple Cities." Even some hometown fans may not have known that the name derived from the fact that the original owners of the club were American Legion posts located in Binghamton, Johnson City, and Endicott. That arrangement was unique for all of organized baseball at the time.

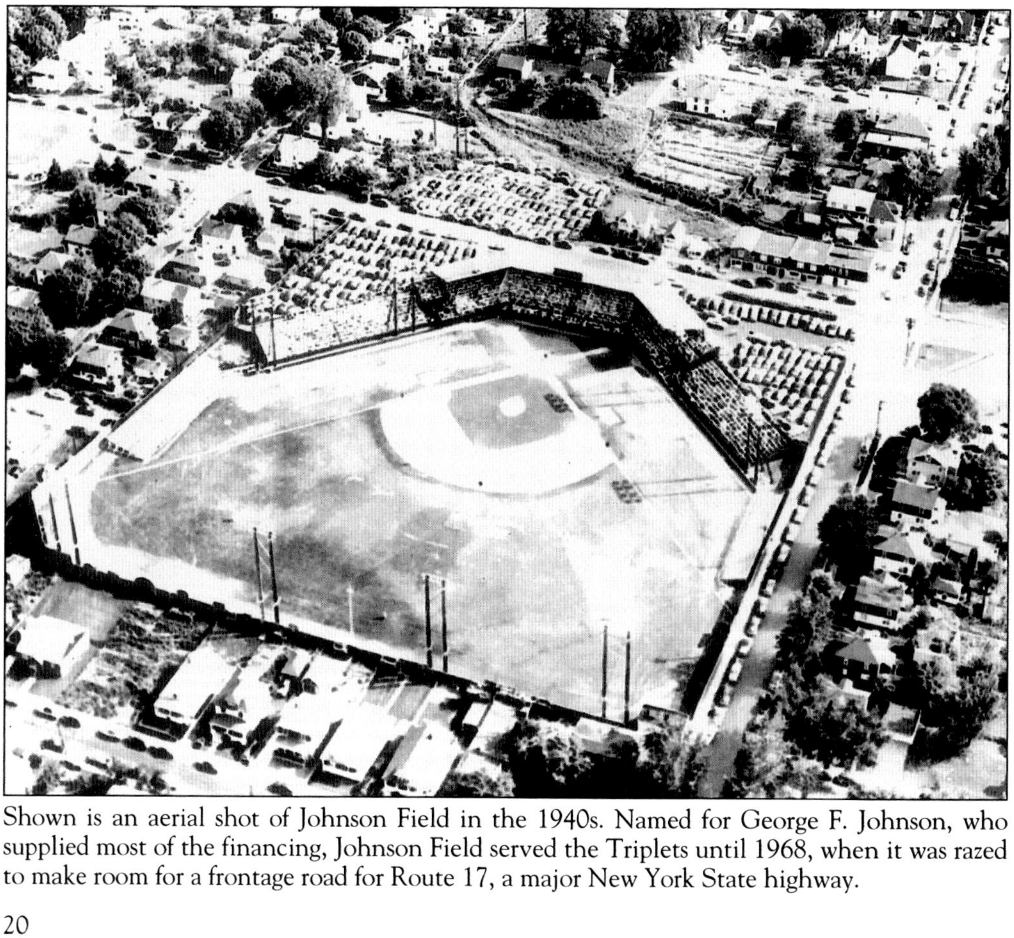

Shown is an aerial shot of Johnson Field in the 1940s. Named for George F. Johnson, who supplied most of the financing, Johnson Field served the Triplets until 1968, when it was razed to make room for a frontage road for Route 17, a major New York State highway.

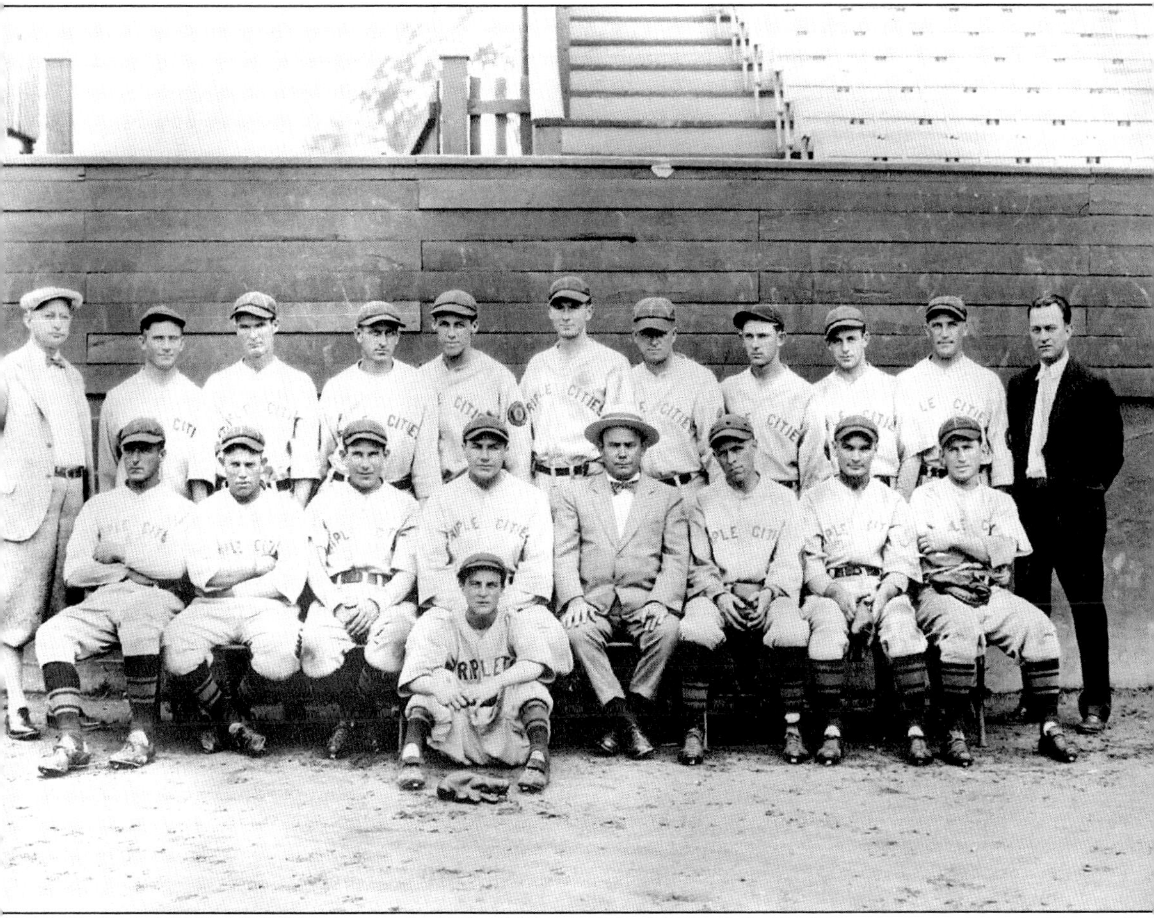

Mike McNally became manager of the Triplets in 1927. In an 11-year career as a utility infielder, he had played on six pennant-winning teams with the Red Sox, the Yankees, and the Senators. A teammate of Babe Ruth on both the Red Sox and the Yankees, he brought enthusiasm and experience to the Triplets. It took just two years for him to lead the club from seventh place in 1927 to the Eastern League Championship with this 1929 team.

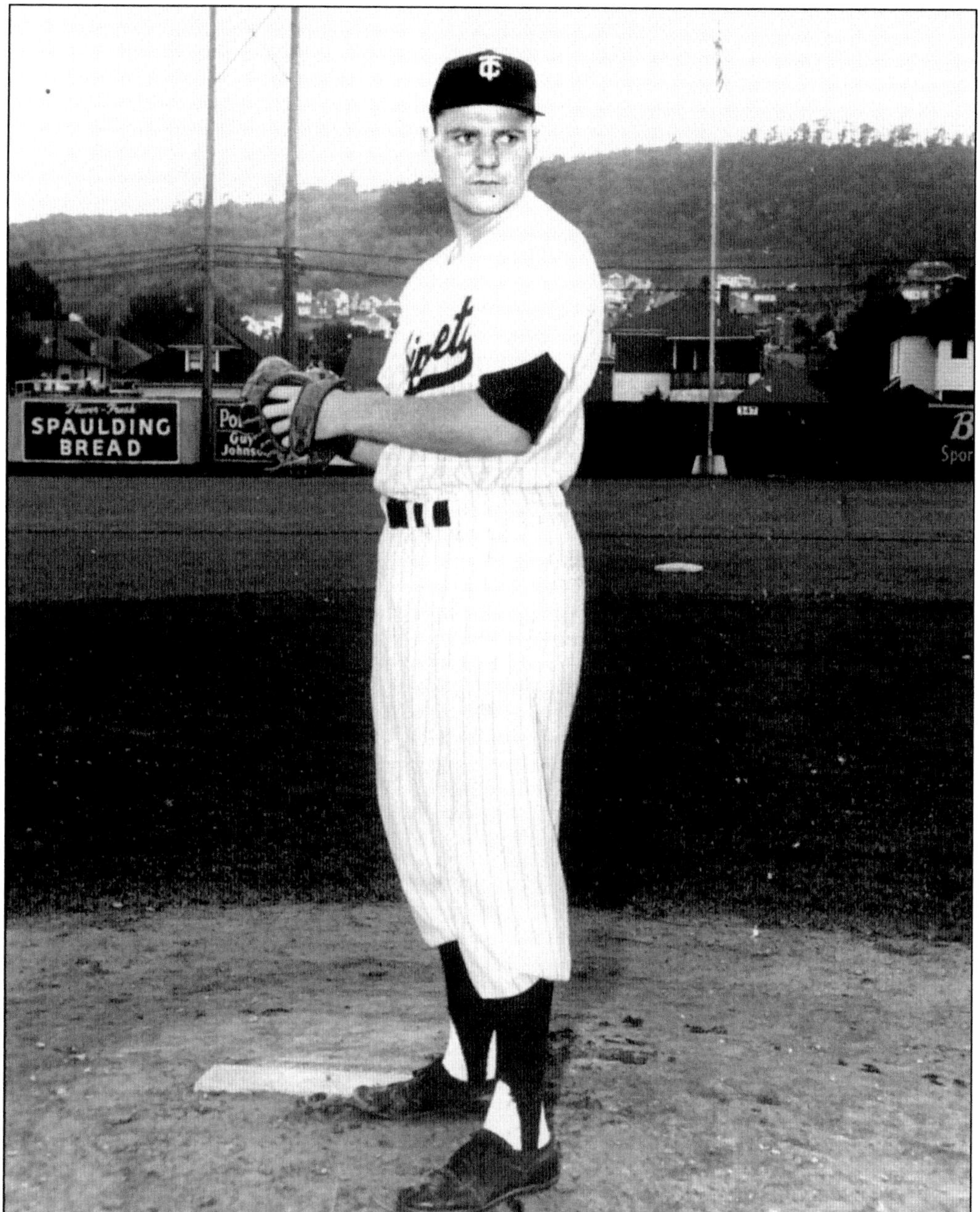

Before joining the Triplets in 1932, Bill Dietrich threw a no-hitter for Harrisburg on June 6, 1931. Six years later, almost to the day, on June 1, 1937, he pitched a no-hitter in the major leagues against the St. Louis Browns. This one earned him a place in the National Baseball Hall of Fame in Cooperstown, New York. Twenty years later, in 1957, another Bill Dietrich (shown here) was on the Triplets pitching staff. He did not record a no-hitter.

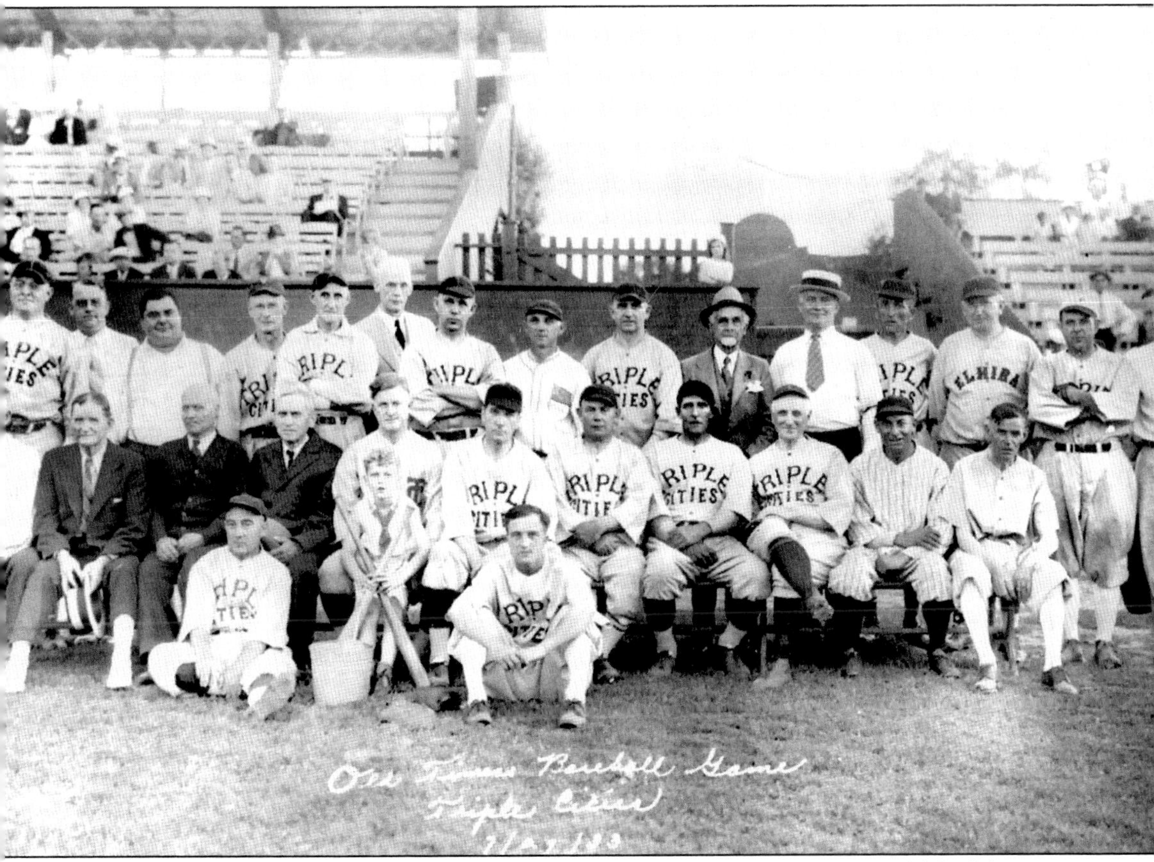

On July 27, 1933, the Triplets brought back as many former players as they could find for an old-timers' game. This gathering at the Johnson Field features a boater worn by the gentleman in the back row (fifth from the right) and another being held in the first row (second from the left). Note the naval blouse, so popular at the time, on the youngster holding the bats.

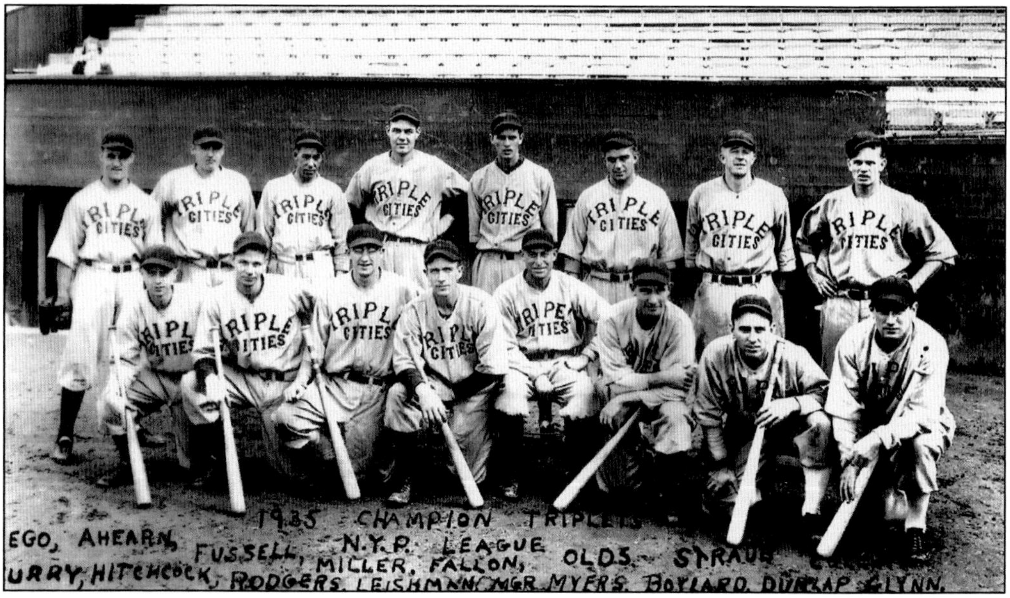

In 1935, the Triplets finished fourth in an eight-team race but won the playoffs to gain their second championship in the club's history. It was also their second championship in three years. John Glynn (front row, right) led the team in hits, doubles, triples, and runs batted in. He also led the league in total bases with 264. Despite that great season, Glynn never made it to the major leagues.

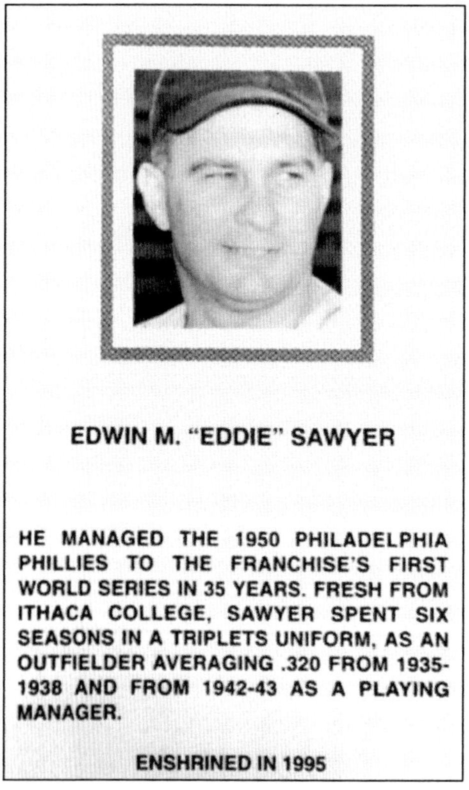

Eddie Sawyer was a major-league manager who never played in the majors. Nevertheless, Eddie was an excellent outfielder for the Triplets (1935–1938), who hit .325, .313, .345, and .299 over those four seasons. In 1942, he was named manager of the Triplets and finished only four games out of first place. The Phillies noticed and made him their manager at the end of 1948. In 1995, he was inducted into the Binghamton Baseball Shrine.

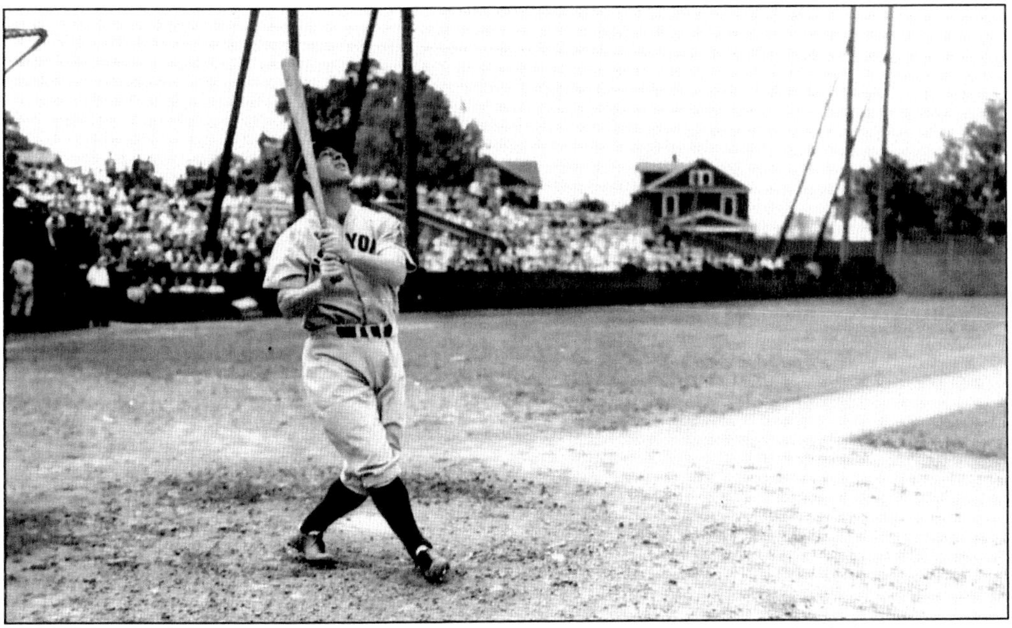

The Yankees and their great stars came to Johnson City for their annual exhibition game in 1938. It turned out to be a poignant one when fans later learned that it was to be Lou Gehrig's last full season. The "Iron Horse" (shown here) played in only eight games in 1939, before retiring due to the effects of what became known as Lou Gehrig's disease.

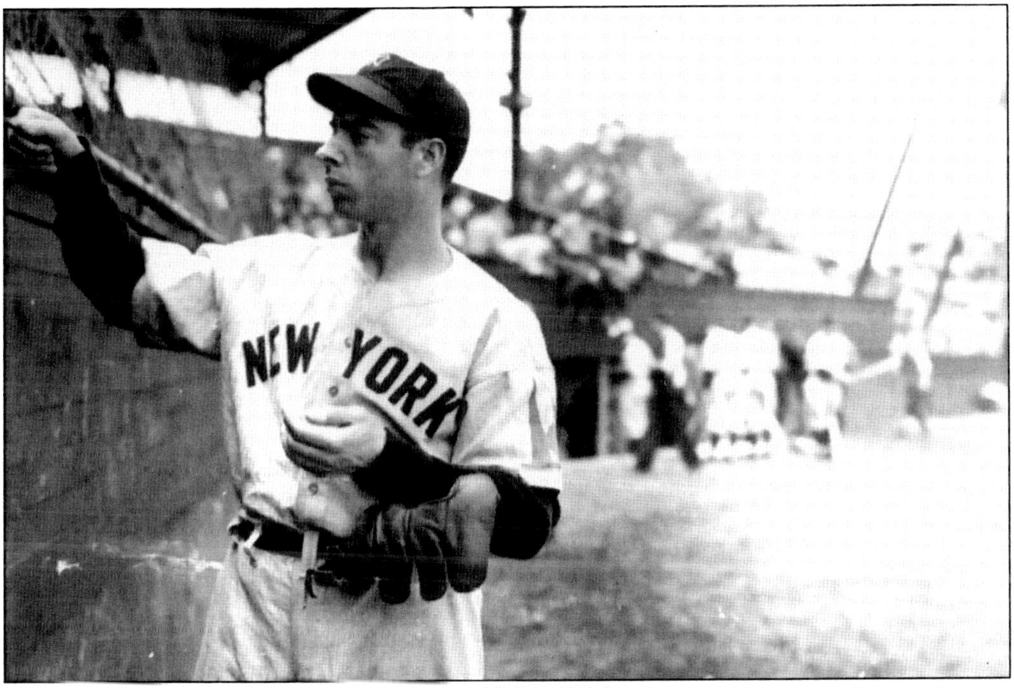

In that same exhibition game, a 23-year-old Joe DiMaggio returns a pen after signing an autograph for a lucky fan. The Yankee Clipper hit a home run in that game and basically spent the day surrounded by adoring Triple Cities admirers. If that autograph is still around after 65 years, it should be quite valuable.

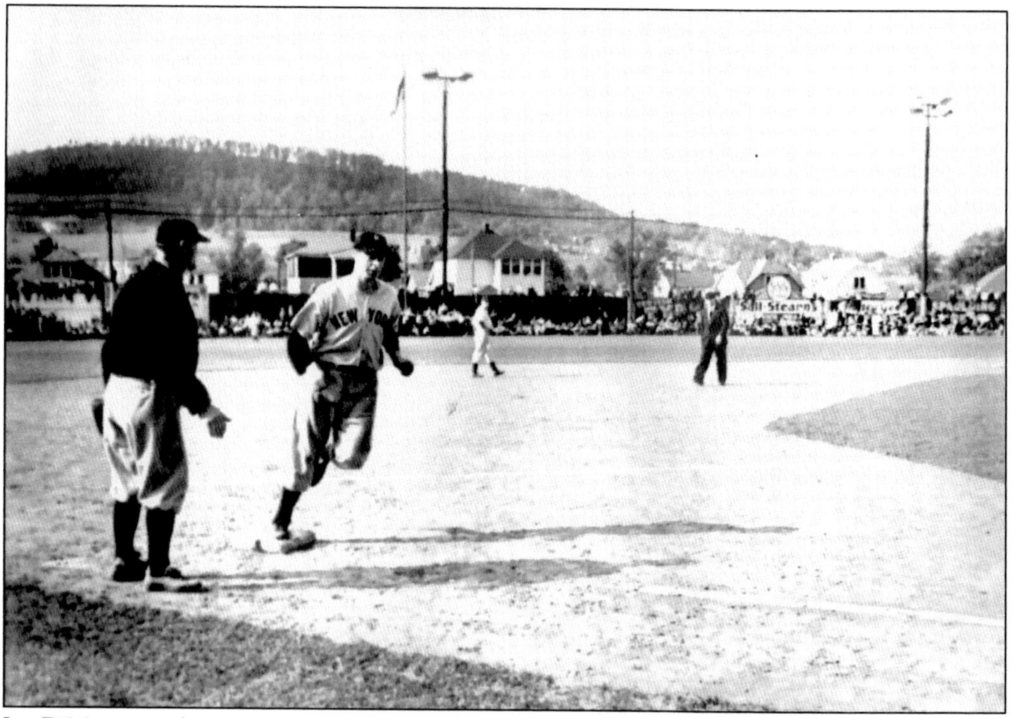

Joe DiMaggio is shown above rounding the bases after hitting a home run in the 1938 exhibition game against the Triplets. In the photograph below, the previously mentioned adoring fans swarm around their idol. DiMaggio led that year's world champions with 32 homers.

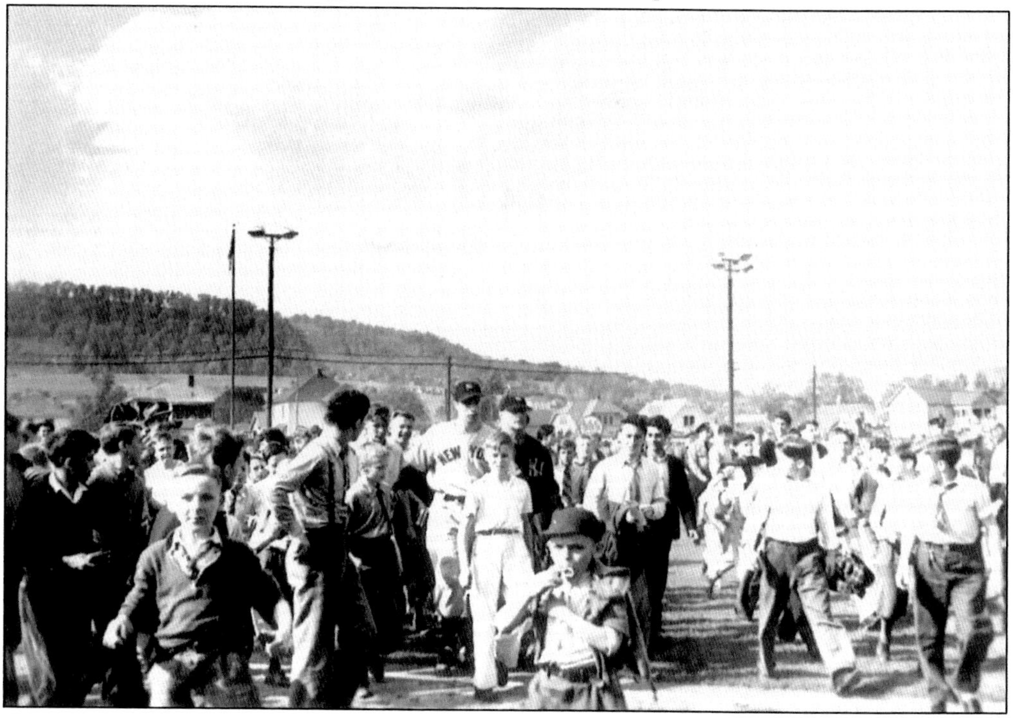

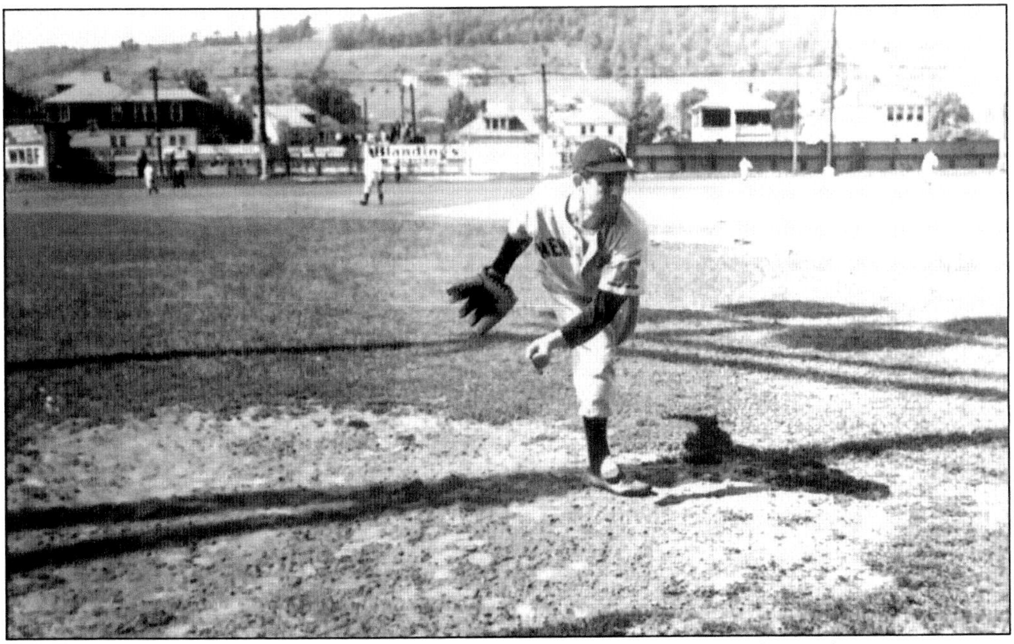

Lefty Gomez was inducted into the Baseball Hall of Fame in 1972. Shown here warming up before the exhibition game with the Triplets in 1938, Lefty was 29 at the time and would win 18 games for the world champions that year. He returned to the area as manager of the Triplets in 1946 and 1947.

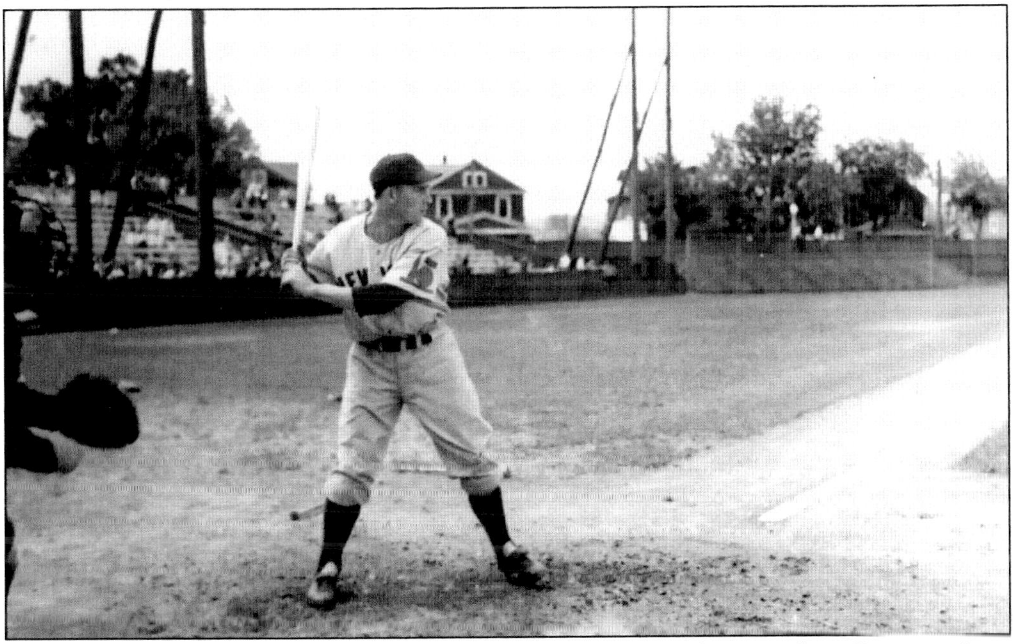

Joe (Flash) Gordon was a premier second baseman for the Yankees until 1947, minus three years of military service. In 1938, Gordon (shown here) was a rookie, getting his first look at Johnson Field. Gordon adjusted quickly to the big leagues, slugging 25 home runs that first year. To top that off, his homer and bases-loaded single was all that the Yankees needed to win Game 3 of that year's World Series.

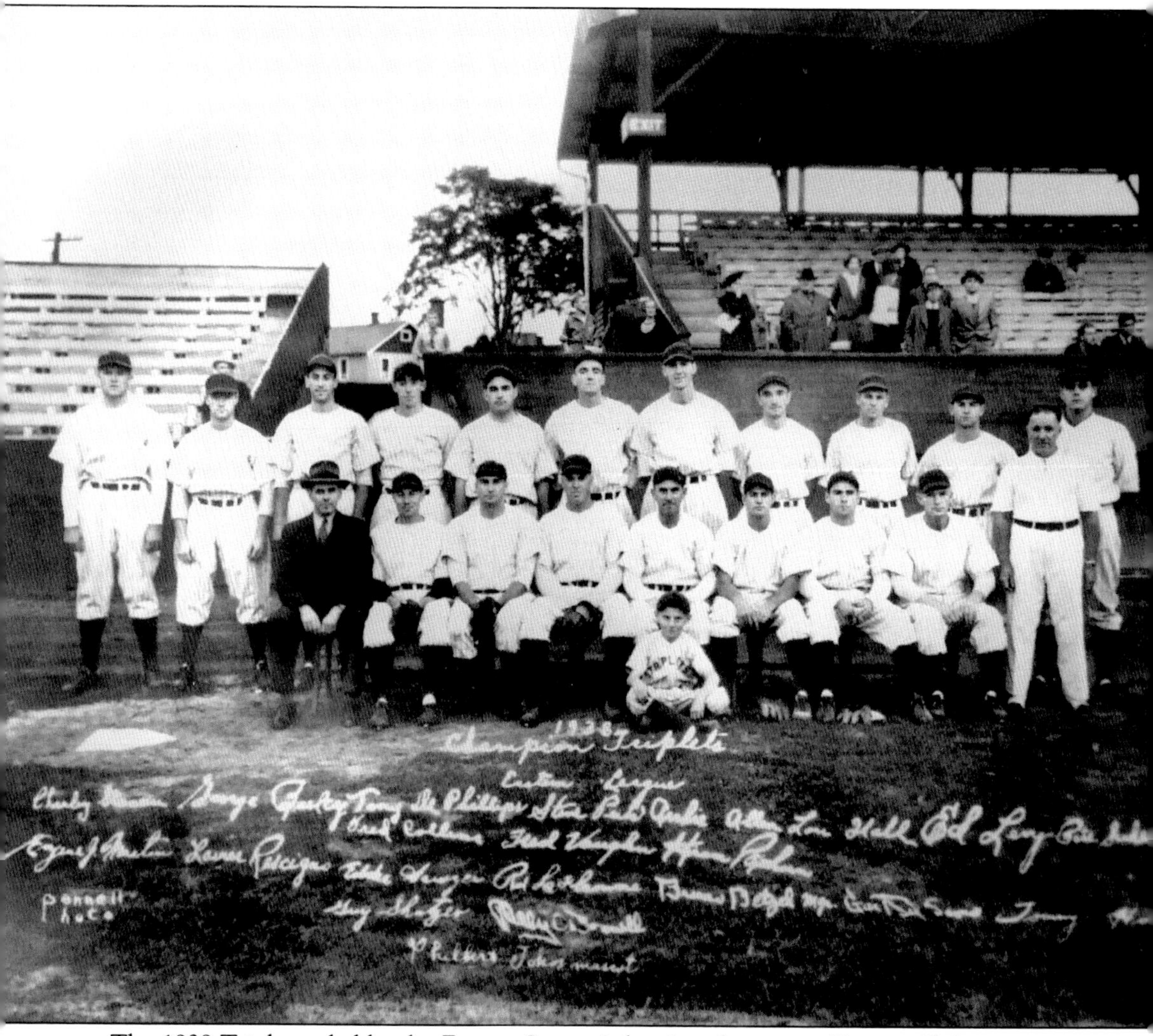

The 1938 Triplets—led by the Eastern League's batting champion, Tommy Holmes—were in first place at the end of the regular season. However, they lost in the league championship series to the third-place Elmira Pioneers. Elmira had finished 13 1/2 games behind Binghamton. Ironically, Triplets manager Bruno Betzel had won the league championship the previous year with the Elmira club.

Three

The Special 1940 Triplets

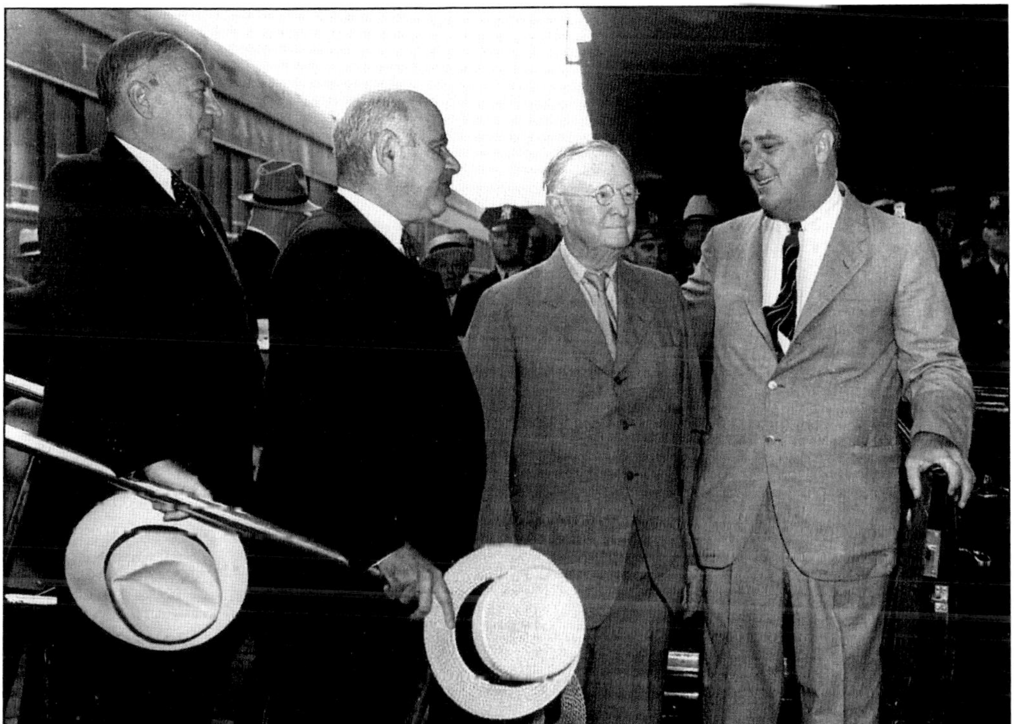

Pres. Franklin Roosevelt's visit to the Triple Cities in 1940 was historic. Roosevelt is shown with his arm around George F. Johnson while Amb. Averill Harriman (far left) and Gov. Herbert Lehman look on.

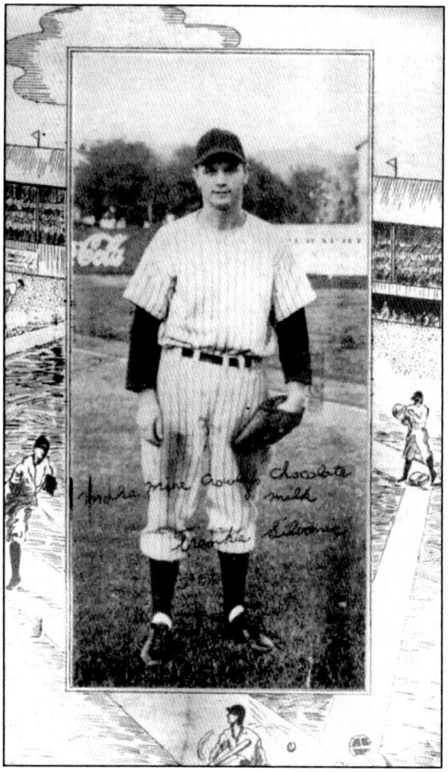

Johnson City native Frankie Silvanic never made it to the major leagues, but the young outfielder shown here definitely had charisma. Despite a .234 batting average in 120 games for the Triplets in 1940, he not only got himself promoted to Triple A but also had a Louisville Slugger bat named after him. Note his inscription for the Crowley card of 1940: "Make mine Crowley's chocolate milk."

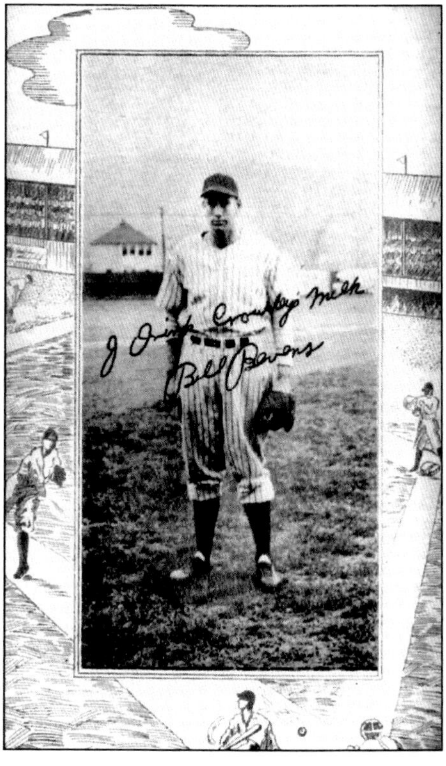

Bill Bevens was a workhorse for the Triplets in 1940. He appeared in the most games (34), pitched the most innings (202), and finished the season with a 14-12 record. Bevens was with the Yankees from 1944 to 1947 but will always be remembered for almost pitching the first no-hitter in World Series history. With two outs in the ninth inning of the third game of the 1947 World Series, the Dodgers' Cookie Lavagetto doubled home the winning runs.

Jimmy Adlam was the Triplets' new second baseman in 1940. While he hit only .207 in his first year, Adlam proved to be the perfect pivot man on the double play for the club. With Pete Suder as the only .300 hitter on the team (.301), defense and pitching were the keys to the Triplets' league championship. Adlam was the second baseman for two more years, before World War II service ended his baseball career.

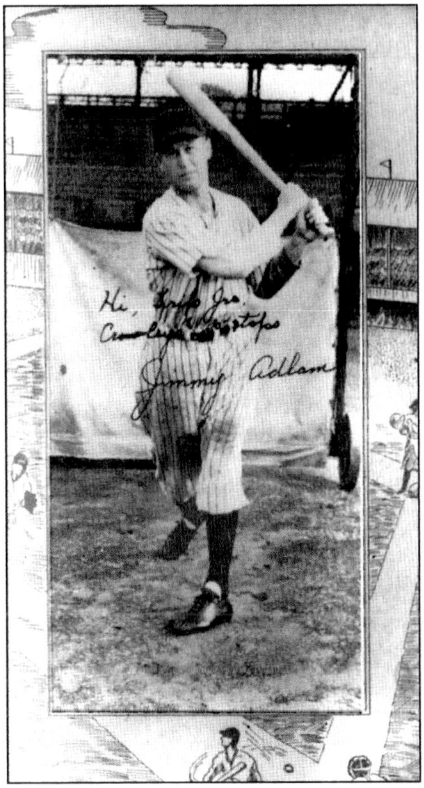

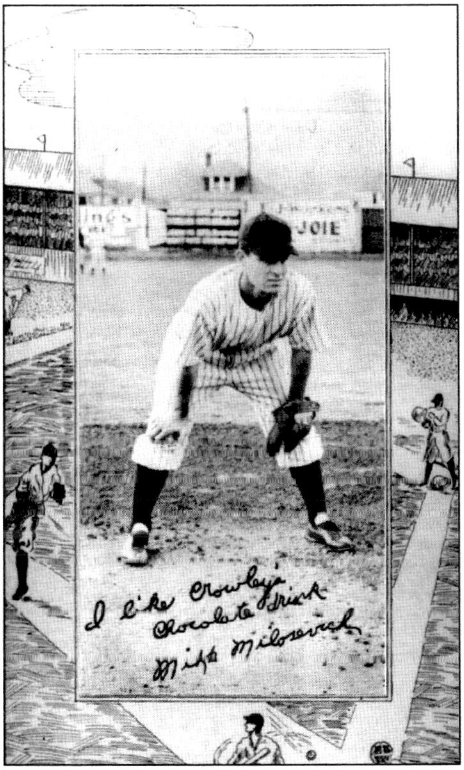

Mike Milosevich was the Triplets' shortstop from 1939 to 1941. His best year was 1939, when he hit .272 in 73 games, alternating with Russ Bergmann. Milosevich slumped to .250 as the regular shortstop in 1940. However, he proved to be a capable leadoff man for the club by leading the league in bases on balls with 93.

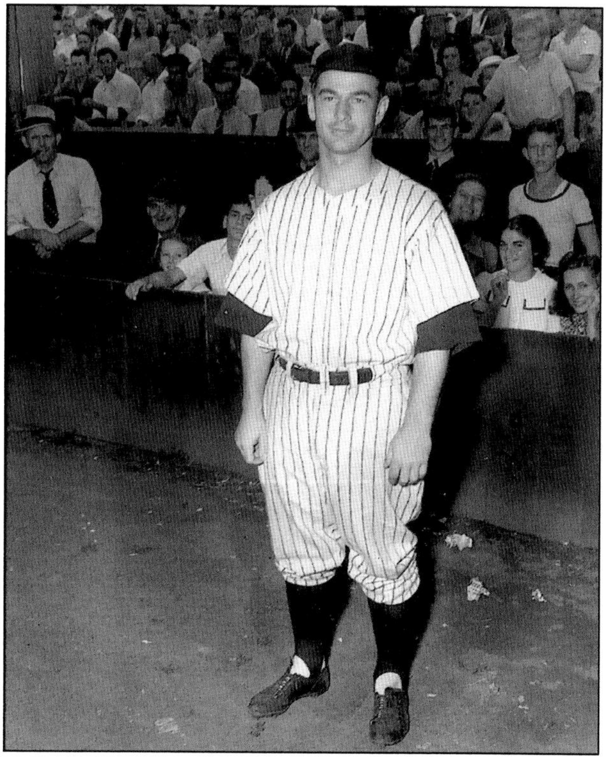

Russ Bergmann joined the Triplets in 1939. He shared shortstop duties with Mike Milosevich and hit a respectable .273 in 51 games. The team's decision to give Milosevich the job in 1940 made Bergmann a utility infielder for the eventual league champions. The new role did not suit him. He hit only .200 in 1940 and was not re-signed for 1941.

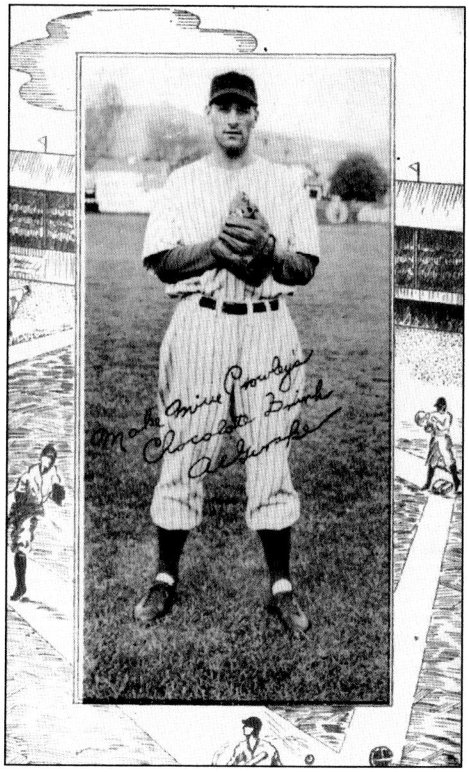

Al Gurske was another Triplets workhorse in 1939. He appeared in 35 games, finishing with a 9-10 record. In 1940, sharing playing time on a much improved Triplets pitching staff, Gurske threw for only 88 innings. His record was 5-4 for that championship club.

Jack Graham had a great year with the Triplets in 1940. He led the league with 20 home runs and the club in runs scored (83), triples (8), and even stolen bases (15). Unfortunately, his major-league career ended quickly, after trials with the Dodgers, Giants, and St. Louis Browns, when he could muster only a .231 batting average over two full seasons, although he blasted 38 home runs.

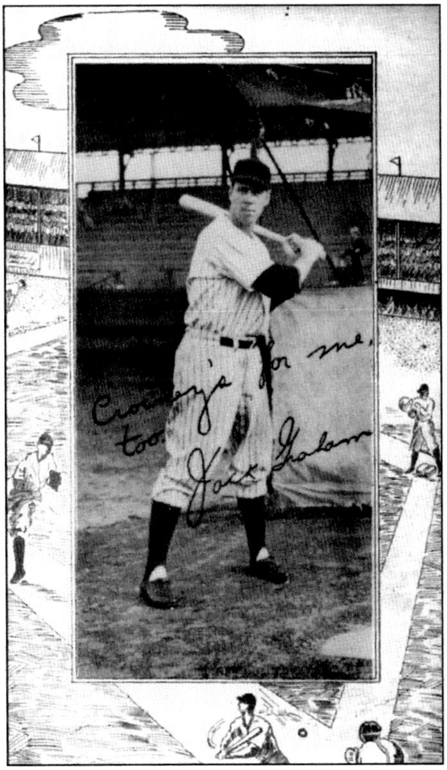

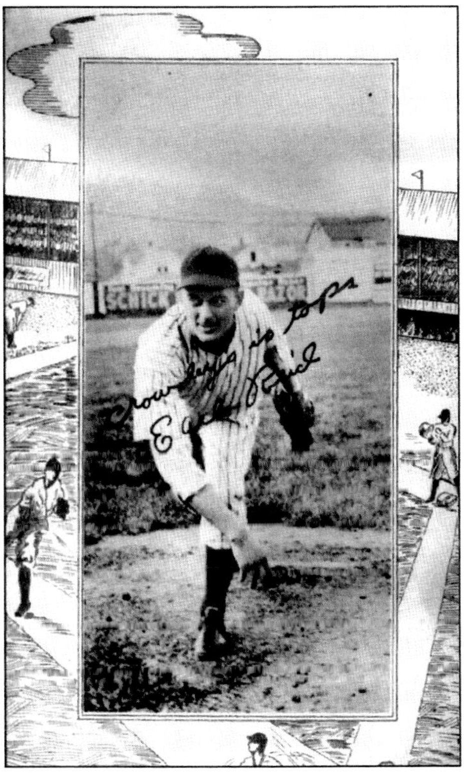

Earl Reid was an example of how World War II destroyed good prospects' chances of making it to the majors. He won 13 games for the Triplets in both 1939 and 1940. Reid led the club with 18 complete games in 1939 and 19 in 1940, when he also had the best staff ERA (2.89) and a league best of five shutouts. By war's end, now age 33, he won one game for the Boston Braves and was done.

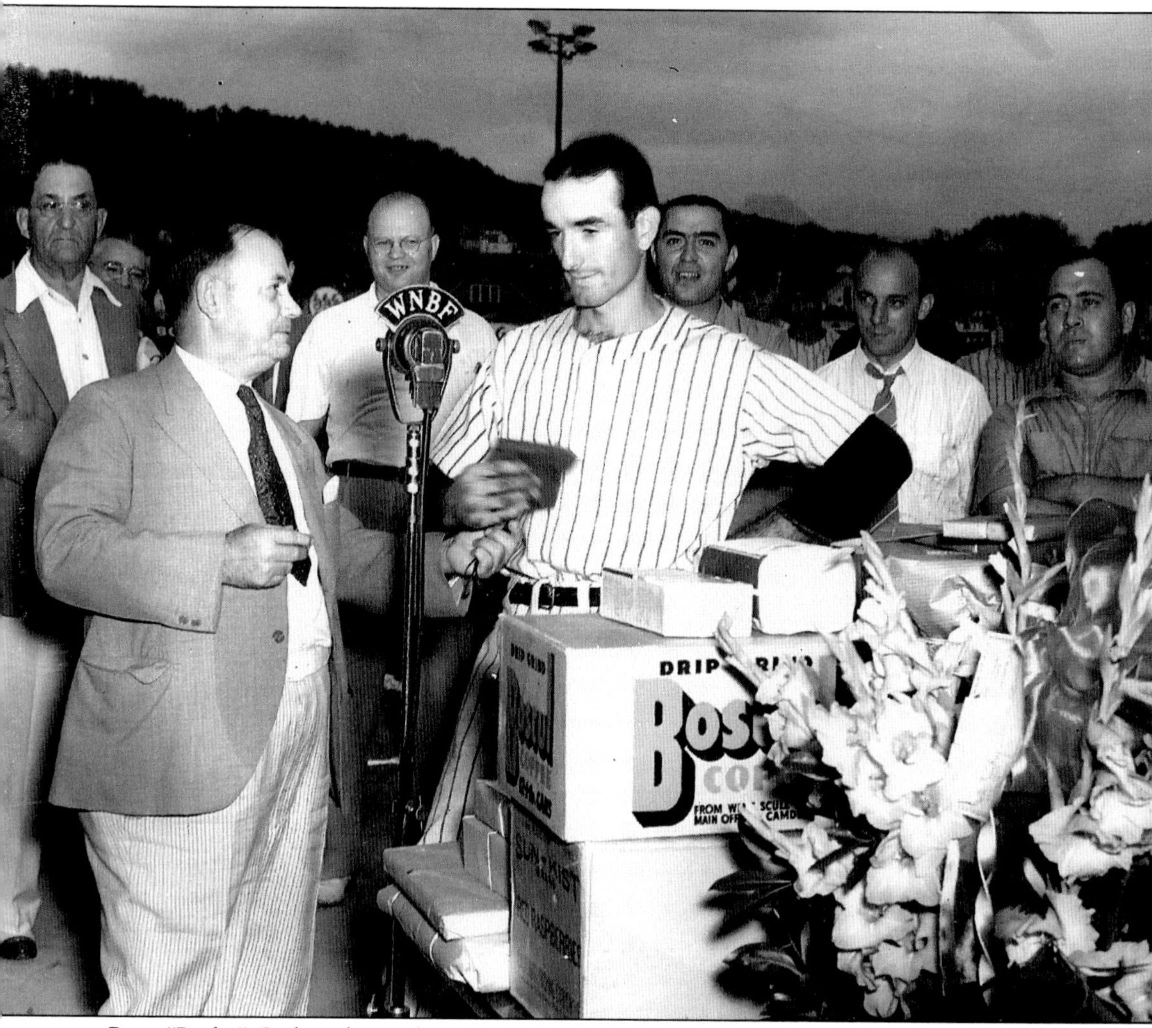

Pete "Pecky" Suder, shown here receiving gifts as player of the month for the Triplets in 1940, was brought into professional ball by fellow Serbian Joe Beggs. (Beggs later pitched for the Yankees and the Reds.) Known for his physical strength and defensive skills as a second baseman, Suder was signed by Connie Mack for his Athletics in 1940. A productive 15-year major-league career followed and led in 2003 to a place in the Binghamton Baseball Shrine.

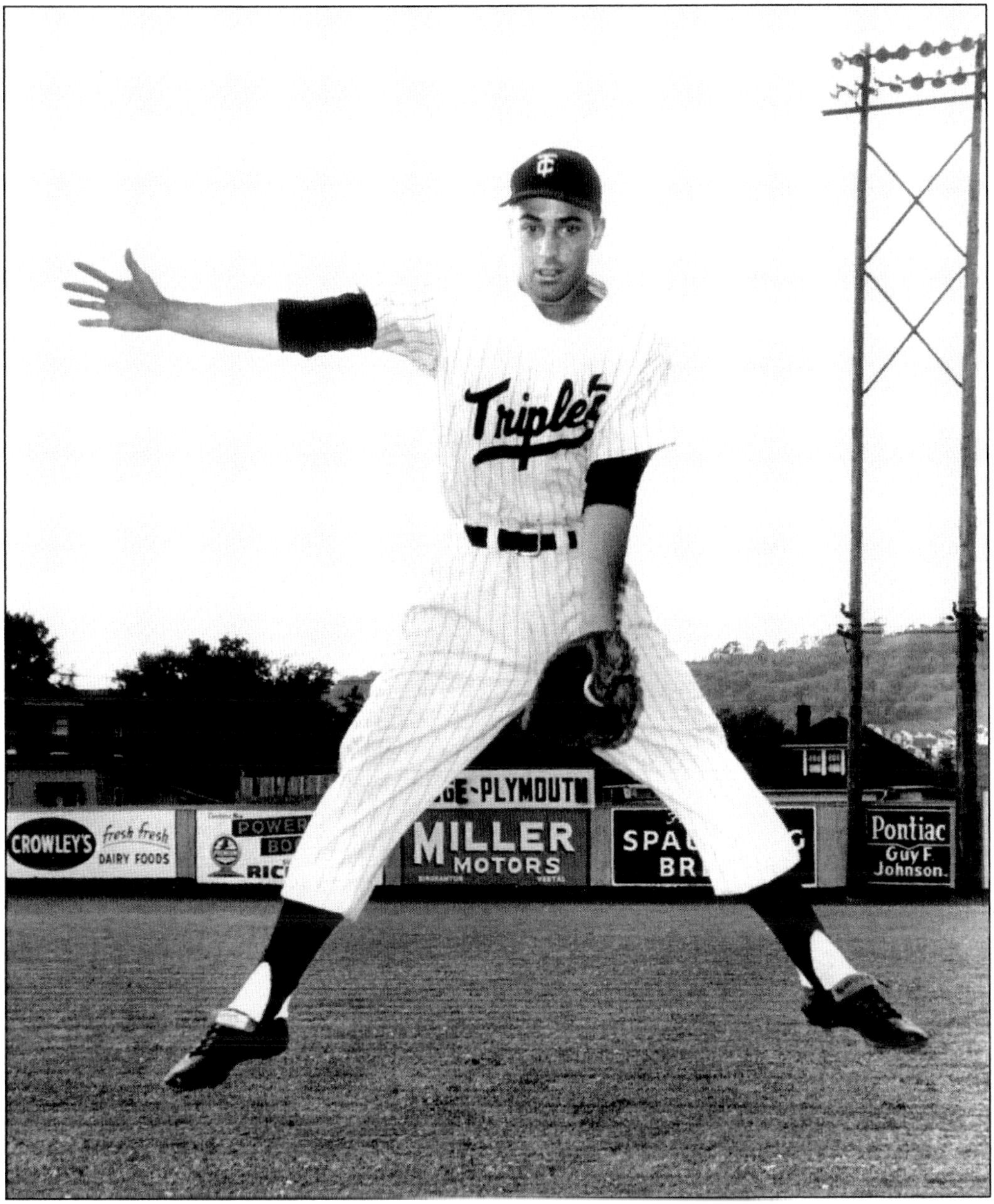

The 18-year-old phenom who replaced Pete Suder on the Athletics was Clete Boyer. However, Boyer was not yet ready, and after two dismal major-league seasons, he was with the Triplets in 1957. Fortunately, it was with a pennant-winning club. Boyer would later amaze fans with his glove work at third base for the New York Yankees in the early 1960s.

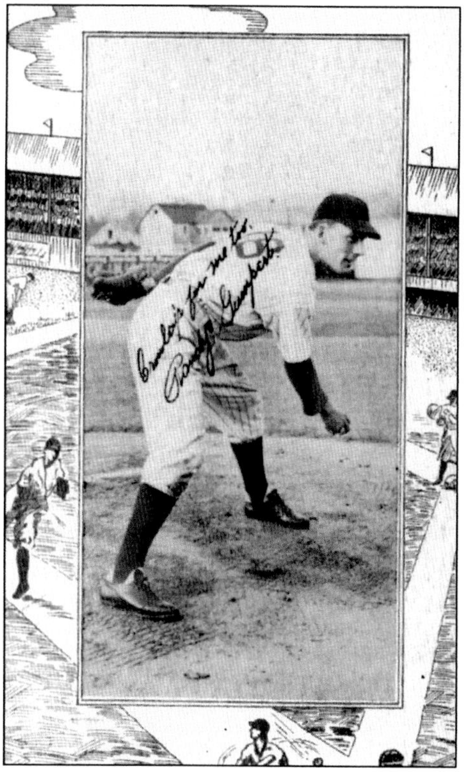

By 1939, Randy Gumpert had already spent three unsuccessful years pitching for Connie Mack's Athletics (1936–1938). He had been only 18 when he joined the Mackmen. In 1940, as a Triplet, he was ready. He led the staff with 15 wins, and despite losing three years to military service, Gumpert later spent seven years in the majors. He was 4-1 with the world champion Yankees in 1947.

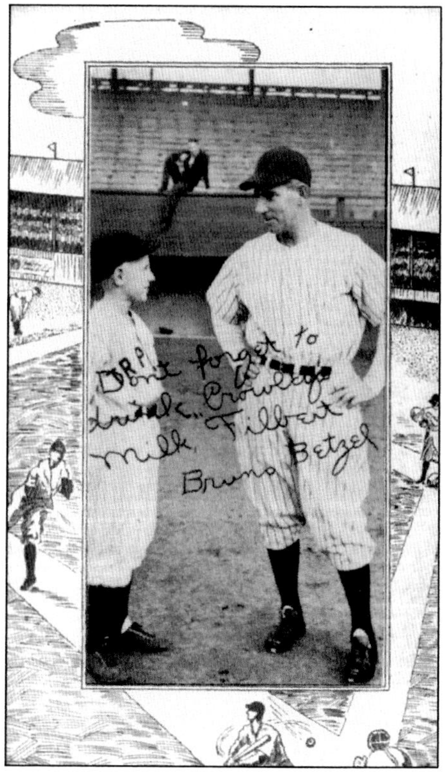

Christian Frederick Albert John Henry David Betzel, despite all of his given names forever known as Bruno, led the 1940 Triplets to the league championship. The Chattanooga, Ohio, native had spent five years with the Cardinals (1914–1918) as an infielder and part-time outfielder. Here, he gives some sage advice to his batboy "Filbert."

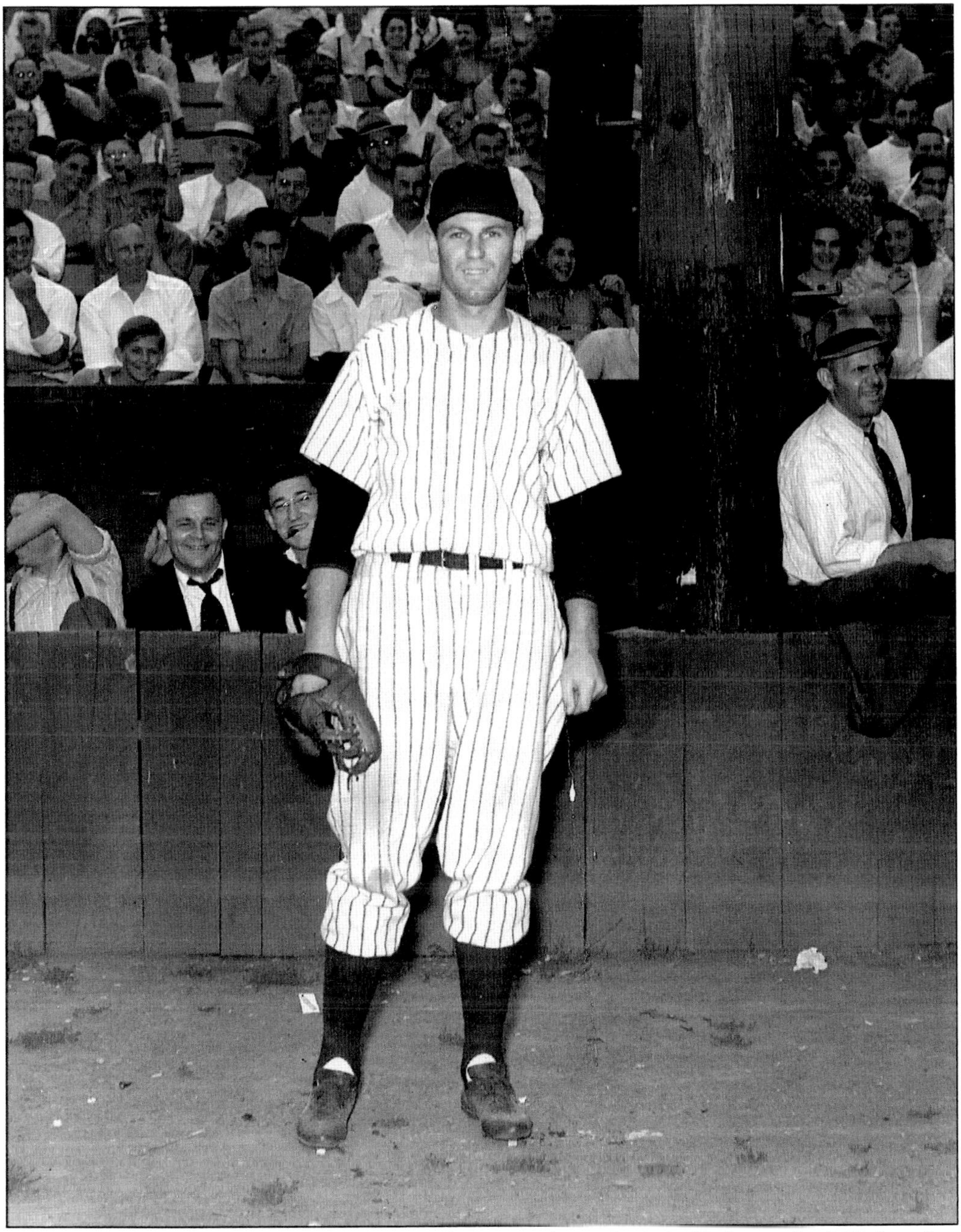

Outfielder Fred Collins played for the Triplets in 1939 and 1940. He hit only .267 that first year and dropped to .238 in 1940. A speedy leadoff man, he led the Eastern League in 1939 in times at-bat with 561. More impressively, he led the Triplets in doubles (27) and tied with Jack Graham in triples (16). He also set a league record by striking out 117 times.

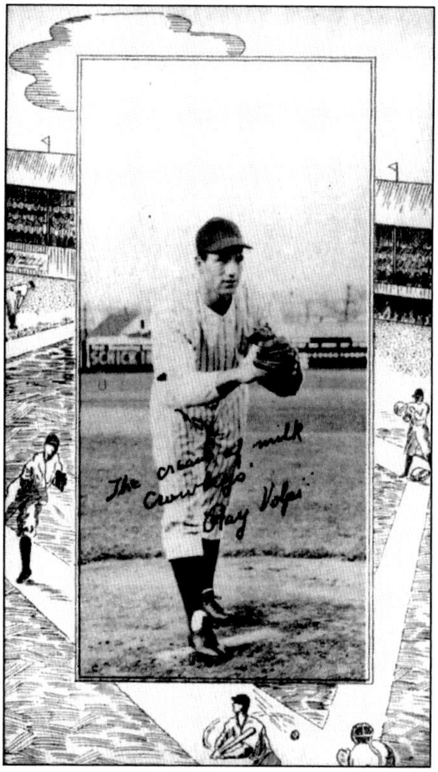

Ray Volpi had pitched 200 innings for the Triplets in 1939, while posting a 12-14 record. With Bevens, Reid and Gumpert being handed the ball for a total of 587 innings, Volpi was reduced to 112 innings in 1940. He produced a 9-7 mark.

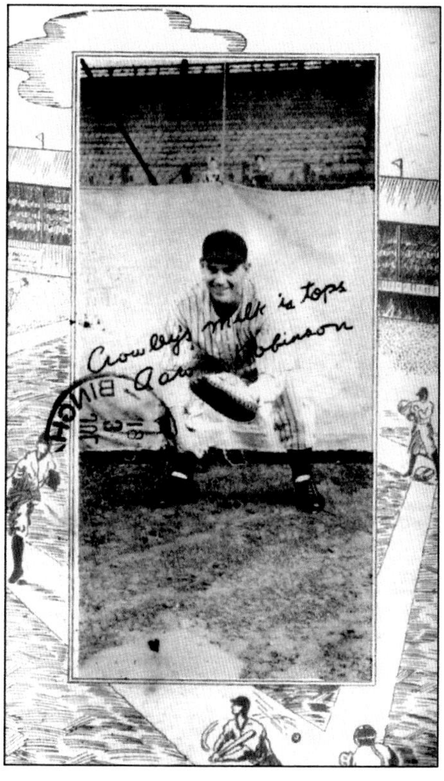

Due to military service, Aaron Robinson was already 30 when he reported to the Yankees in mid-1945. He became their regular catcher the following year and remained so through 1947. With Berra and Triandos available, however, Robinson found himself traded to the White Sox in 1948. As a Triplets catcher in 1940, he hit .280 in 63 games.

Four

From Glory to Goodbye

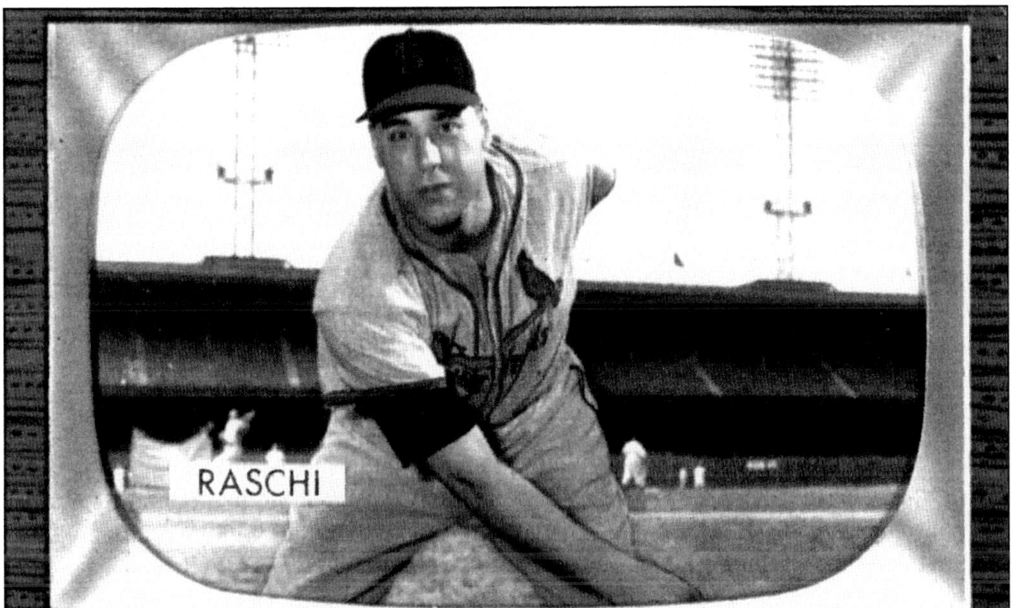

The Triplets finished last in 1946, and their top pitcher had a record of only 10-10. He went up to the Yankees that year and stayed until 1953. Known as the "Springfield Rifle," since he hailed from West Springfield, Massachusetts, Vic Raschi had a 10-year major-league career in which he won 132 games while losing only 66. That record included three consecutive years (1949–1951) of 20 or more wins.

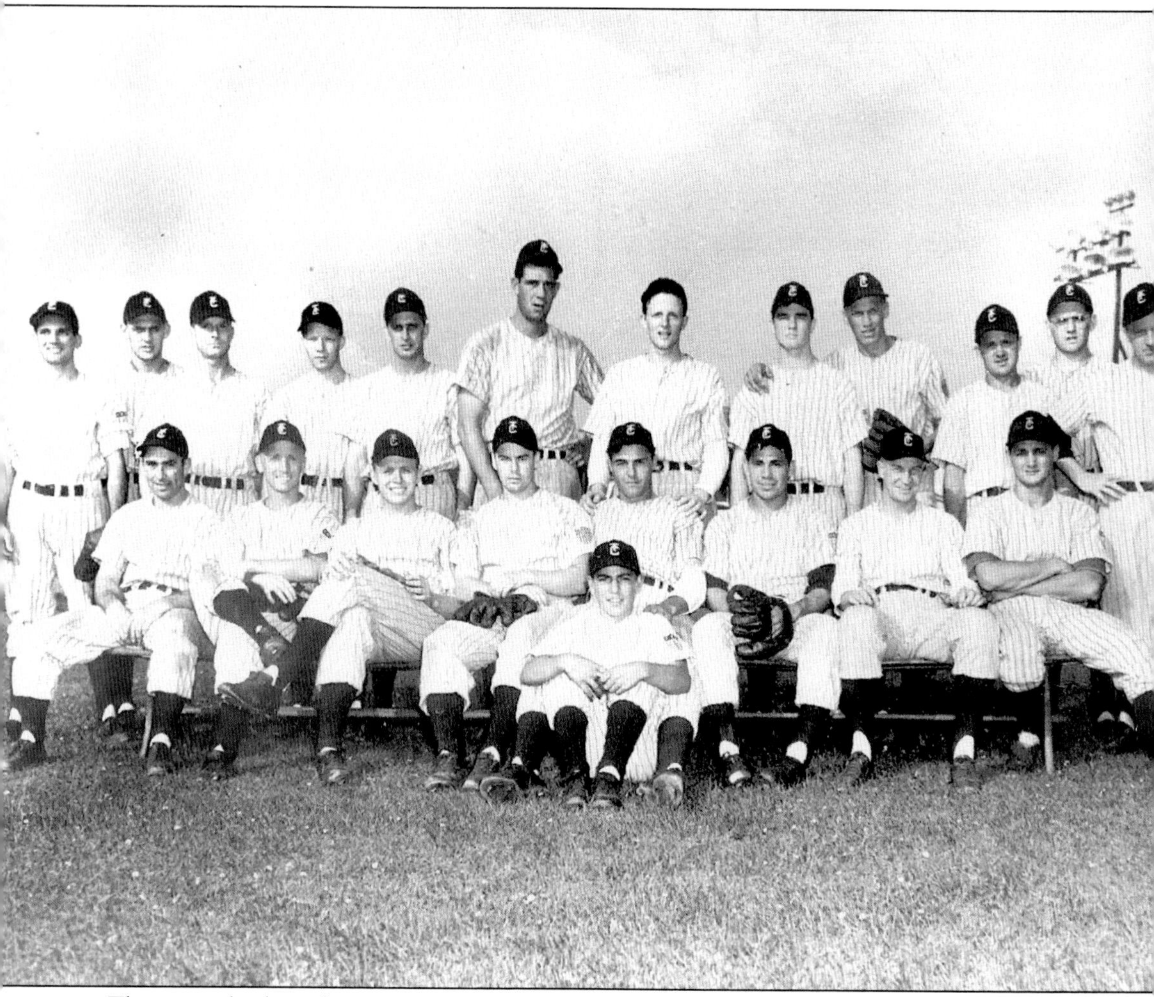

These are the last-place 1946 Triplets, who finished 45½ games behind first-place Scranton. Bringing in Lefty Gomez to replace manager Garland Braxton brought no relief. Leo Righetti, the father of future Yankees pitching star Dave Righetti, was an infielder for this club. Chris McKenna had the team's best batting average (.322), but Gerry Coleman led in virtually every other hitting category. Another future Yankee, Vic Raschi, led the pitching staff with 160 strikeouts and 15 complete games.

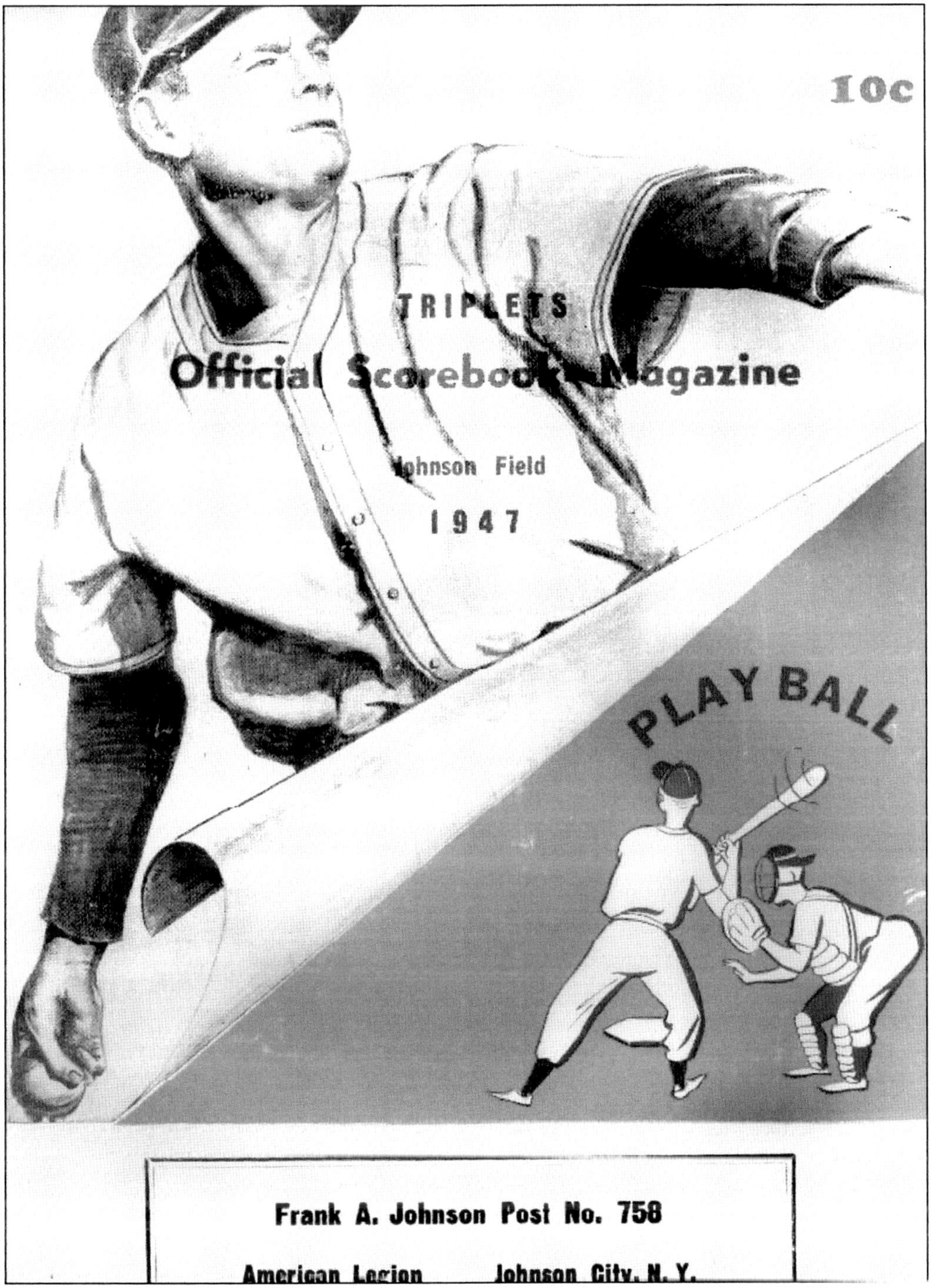

Pictured here is an "Official Scorebook Magazine" for a Triplets game in 1947. Note the sponsor: "Frank A. Johnson Post No. 758, American Legion, Johnson City, N.Y." The original Triple Cities club of 1923 was unique in all of organized baseball for being owned by three American Legion posts. In addition to Post 758, Binghamton Post 80 and Endicott-Union Post 82 shared ownership of the team.

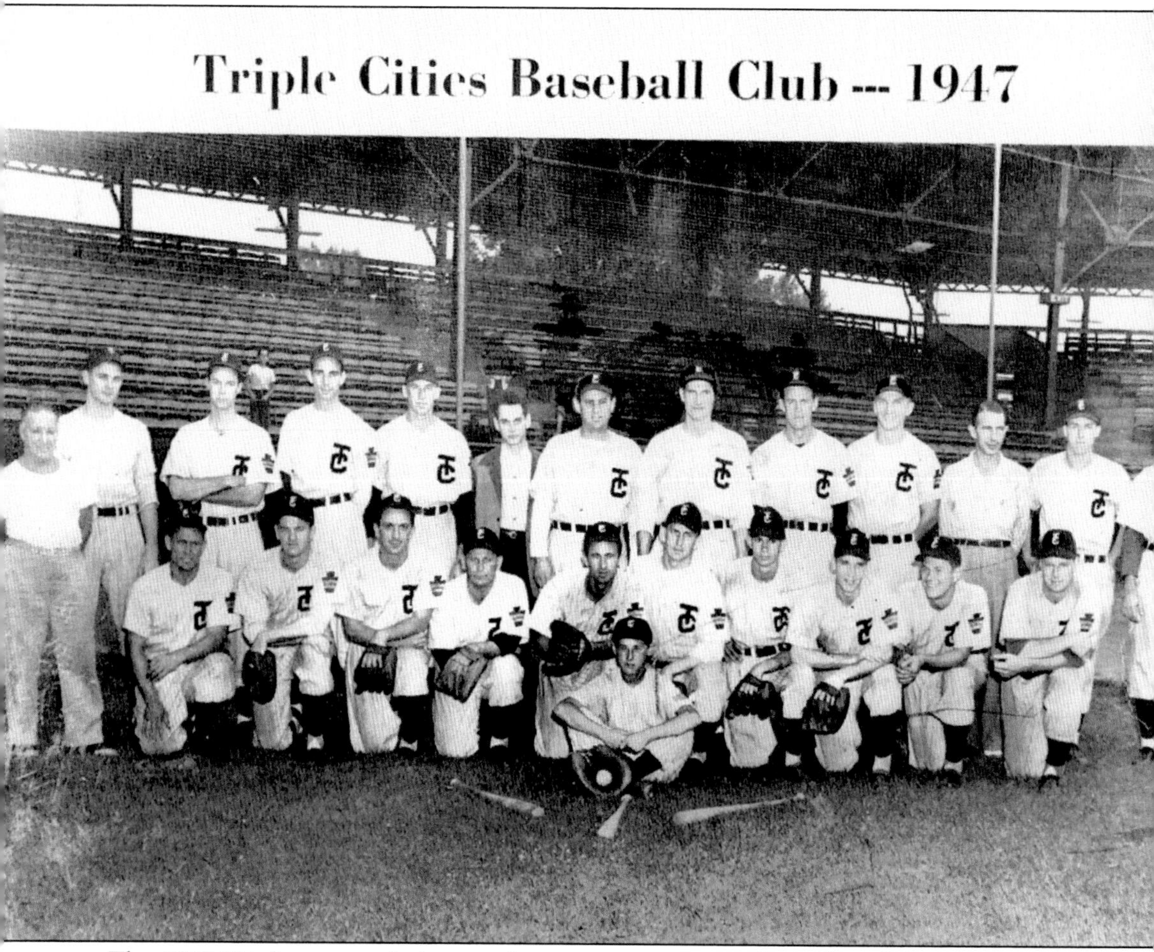

The 1947 Triplets spent their second consecutive year in the cellar of the Eastern League. Their skipper, Lefty Gomez, came from an entirely different tradition. His 13 years with the Yankees (1930–1942) had him participating in seven pennants and six world championships. Johnson City native Doc Farrell (seen earlier as a batboy for the 1915 Bingos) was a teammate of Gomez's in 1932–1933. (Courtesy of the National Baseball Hall of Fame Library, Cooperstown, New York.)

Jim Greengrass, from Addison, New York, had two great years with the Triplets before joining the Cincinnati Reds in 1952. In 1948, he led the Triplets in base hits (125), total bases (183), doubles (21), triples (8), and stolen bases (15). The following year, he was first in RBIs (60) and tied for the most doubles with 19. In 1954, he hit 27 homers for Cincinnati. Only teammate Ted Kluzsewski, who led the league, hit more for the Reds.

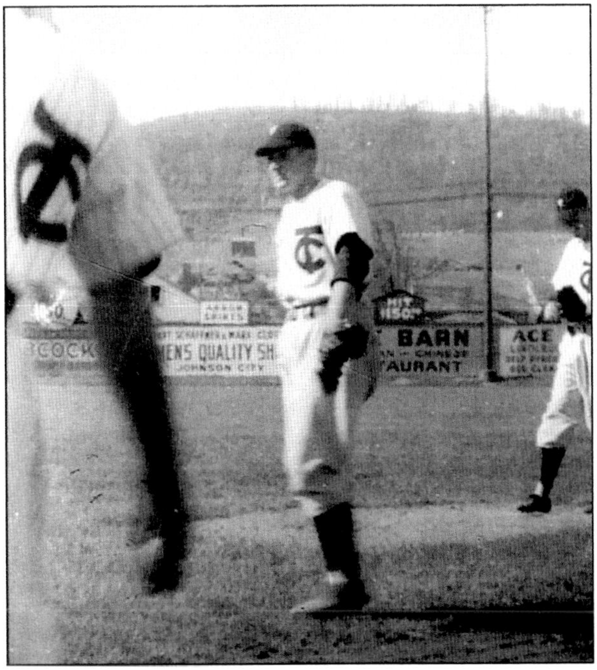

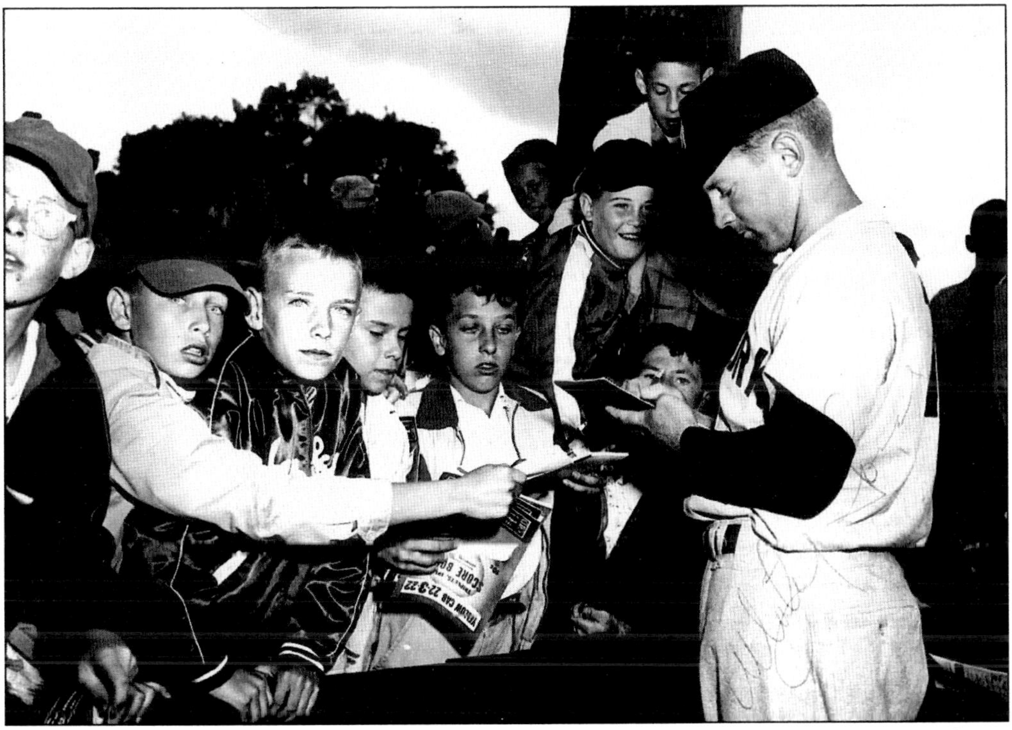

In 1949, 20-year-old Whitey Ford tied a previous Triplet record, which was set by Kent Stirlings, by producing a winning percentage of .762. He was 16-5 for the year. The very next year, he was a sensational 9-1 with the Yankees and never looked back. Despite two years of military service, the "Chairman of the Board" won 236 games, while losing only 106 in his Hall of Fame career.

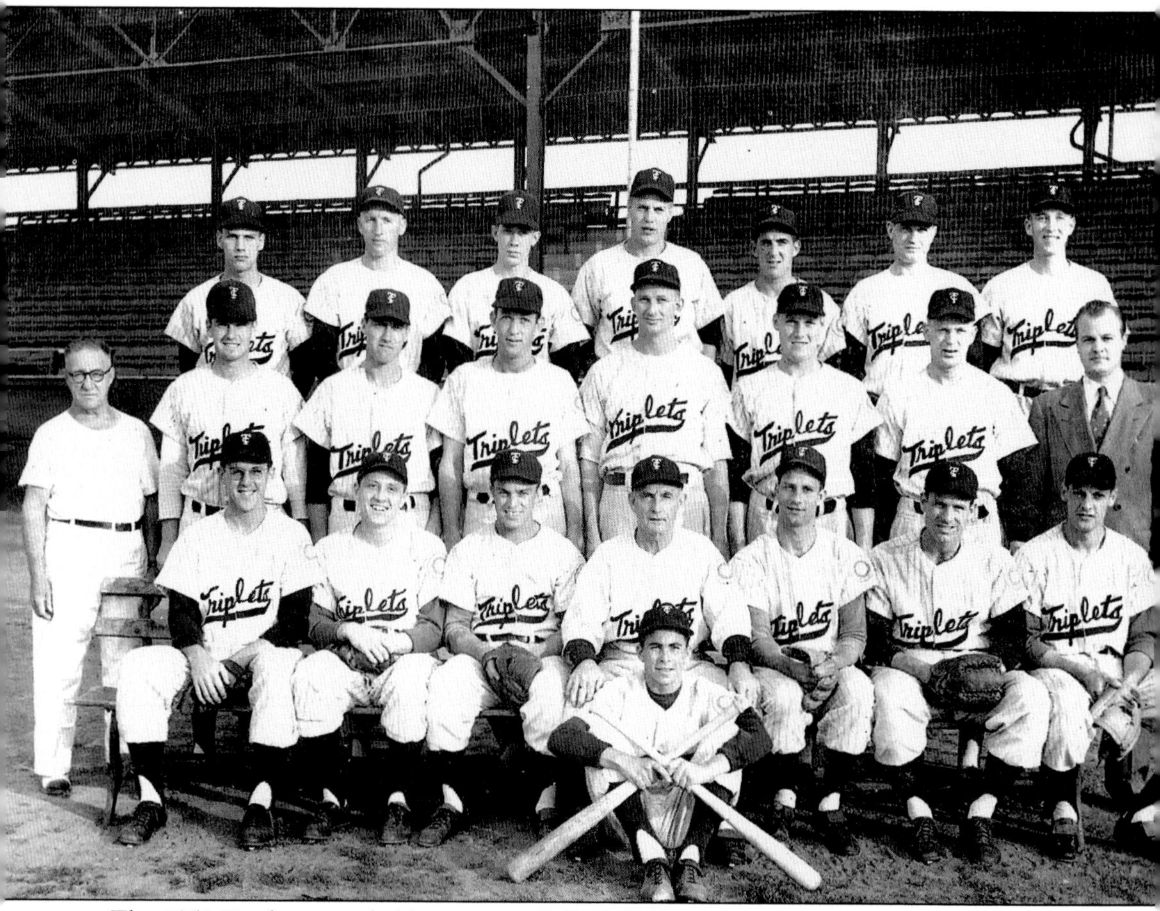

The 1951 Triplets were led by manager Bill Skiff (front row, center). After a season with the second-place Pirates of the National League in 1921, Skiff returned to the majors with the pennant-winning Yankees of 1926. A catcher during his playing days, Skiff provided valuable coaching for youngsters, such as pitcher Bob Grim (front row, third from right), who later became a valuable Yankees hurler.

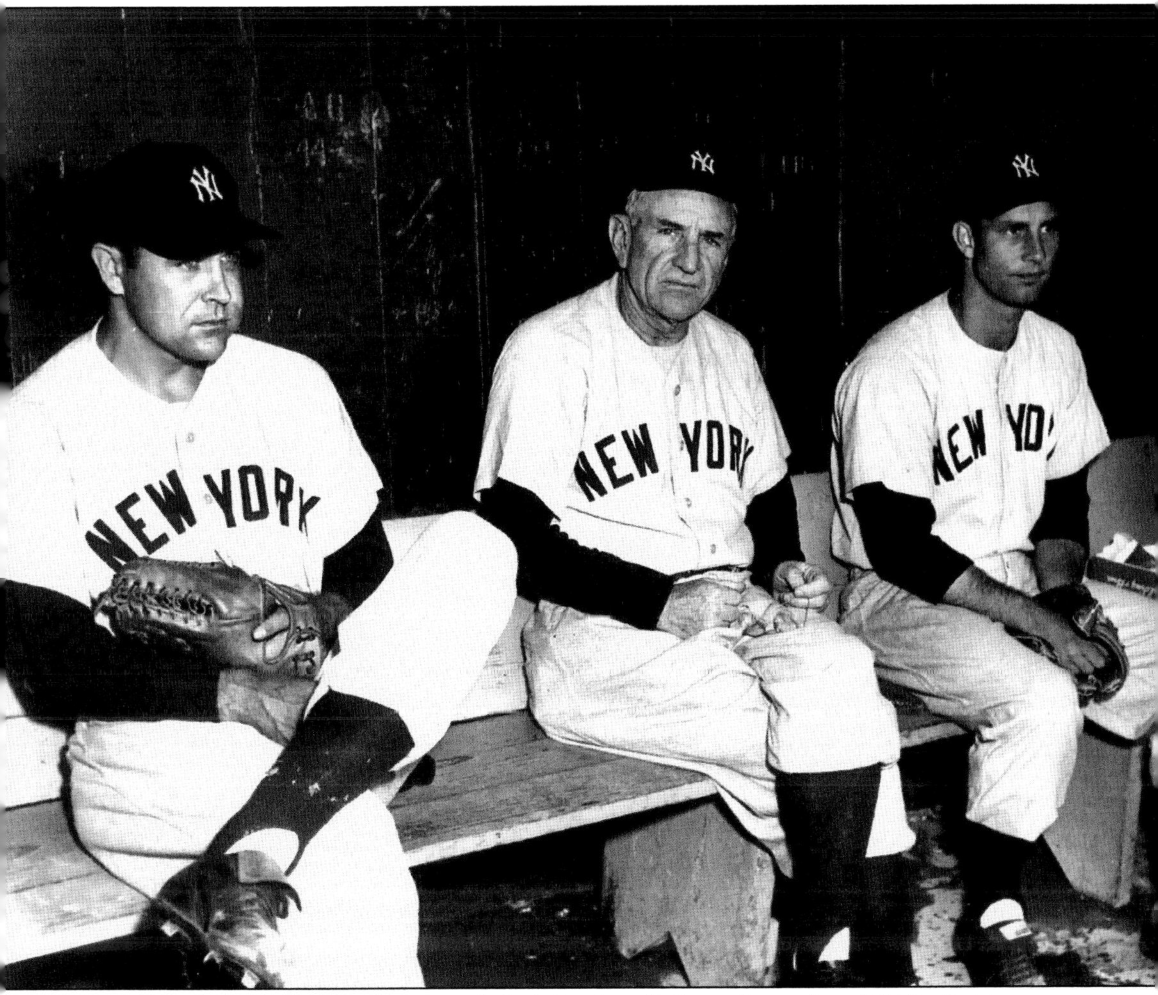

That same Bob Grim (right), shown with "Ol' Perfessor" Casey Stengel and Eddie Robinson, was a rookie with the New York Yankees in 1952. During the previous year, with the Triplets, he had led the staff with a 16-5 record and in strikeouts with 108. Three years later, he was a 20-game winner for the Yankees. That proved to be the highlight of his nine-year career in the major leagues.

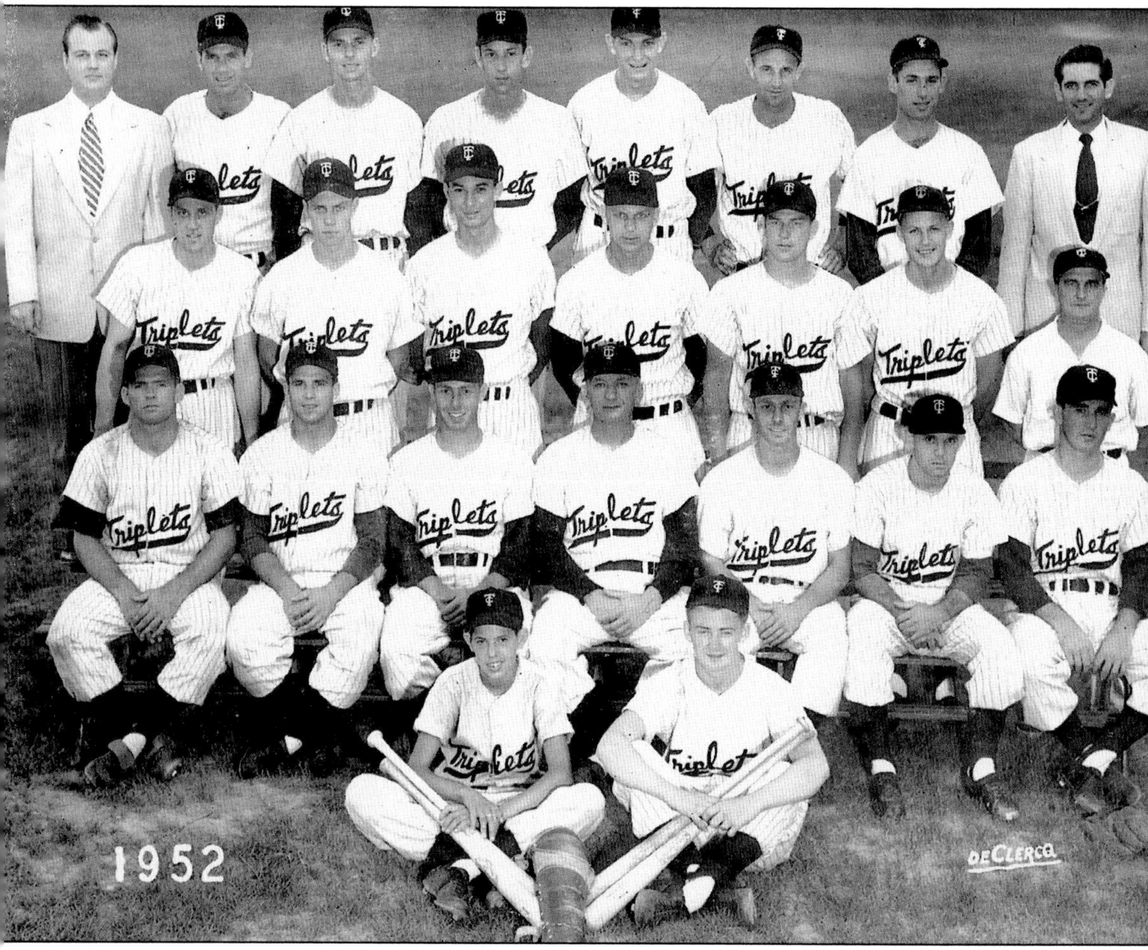

After a sixth-place finish the previous year, the 1952 Triplets had a new manager, Jimmy Gleeson. He proved to be the right choice. The team finished second to the Albany Senators during the regular season and then won in the playoffs to take the championship for the first time since 1944. A one-hitter by Al Cicotte in Game 4 of the playoffs was a highlight.

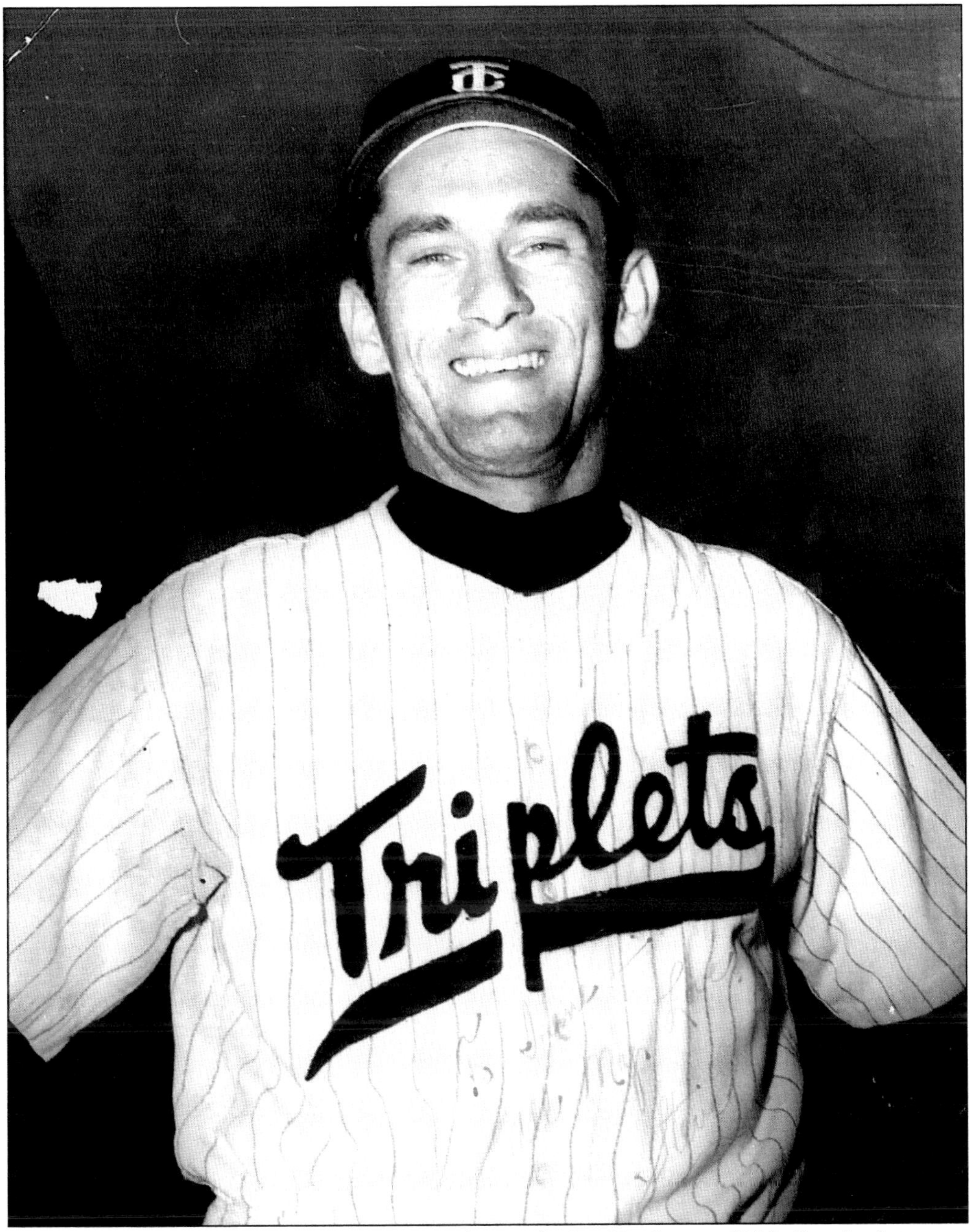

Steve (Lefty) Kraly had a season to remember with the Triplets in 1953. Besides being on the Eastern League's playoff winners, he led that circuit with an ERA of 2.08 and posted an incredible 19-2 record. That was quite an accomplishment, since the team boasted only two .300 hitters. He also led the club with 139 strikeouts and seven shutouts. No Triplets or B-Mets hurler has ever matched that number of shutouts in a single season.

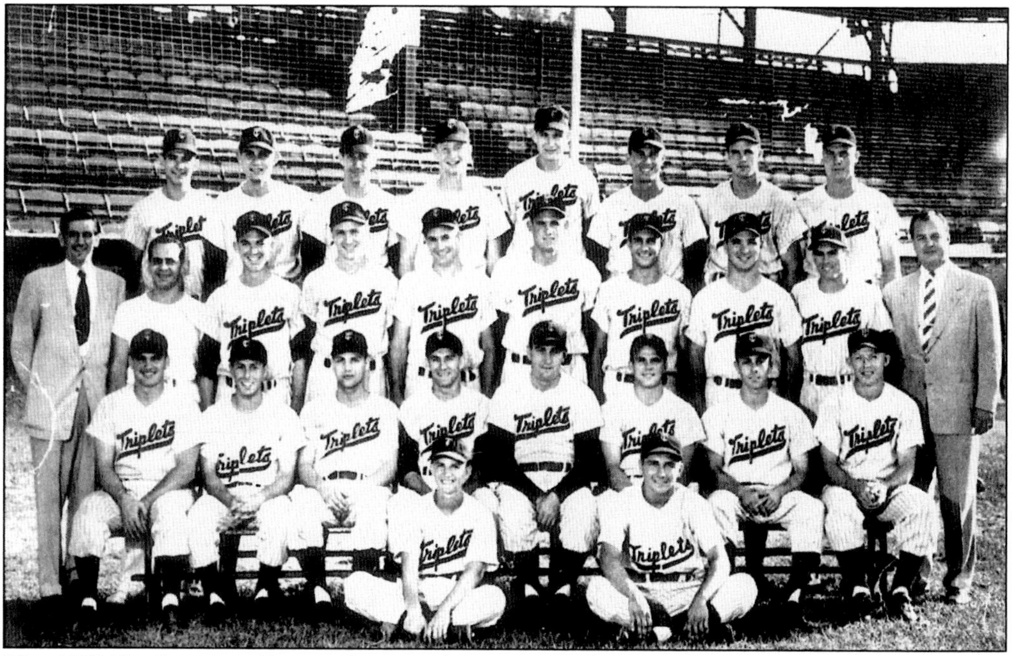

The 1953 Triplets were Eastern League champions under manager Phil Page. He had pitched for Detroit from 1928 to 1930. In his first year, as a 22-year-old southpaw, Page was 2-0; both were complete games. His major-league career ended in 1934, with manager Casey Stengel and a woeful Dodgers club that would not leave the second division for another five years. Page won his only start with the "Bums."

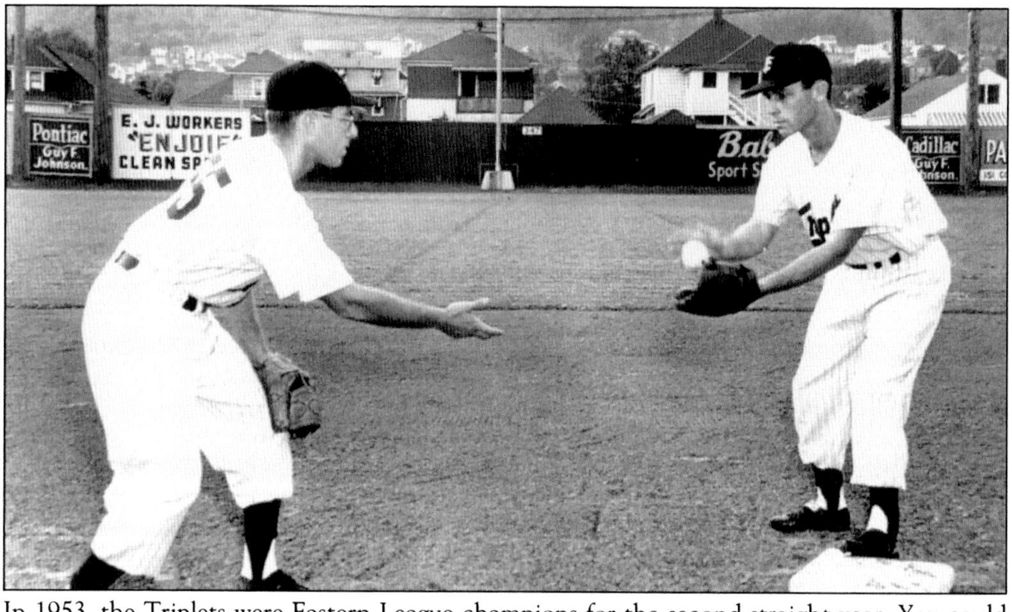

In 1953, the Triplets were Eastern League champions for the second straight year. You could point to Steve Kraly's brilliant 19-2 record or Wally Burnette's 21-10 mark as the keys. However, many old-timers might point out that the Triplets never won two consecutive titles without having the Charnofsky twins: Hal (left) at shortstop and Stan at second base. When their playing days were over, they became professors at California colleges.

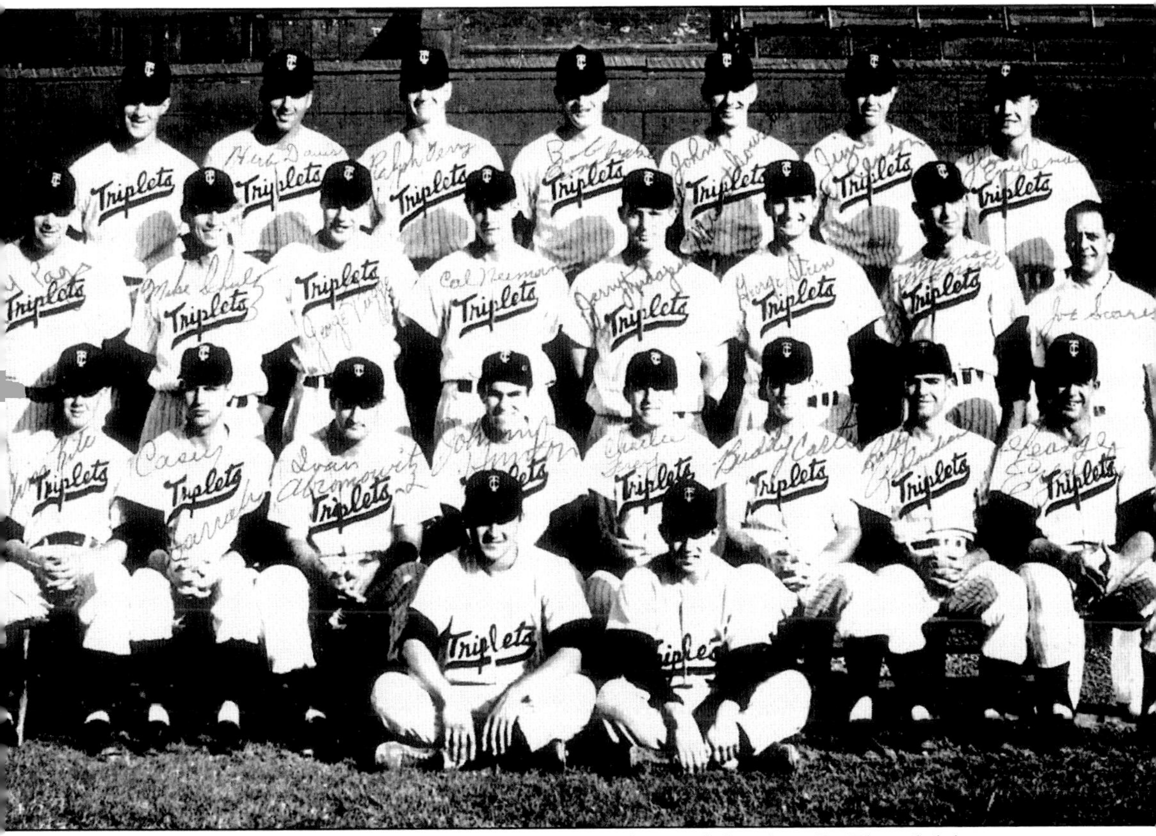

The 1954 Triplets broke even with a record of 70-70 and missed the playoffs. They did, however, have a couple of hot prospects. Bobby Richardson played every game at second base and led the team in batting average (.310), hits (171), runs scored (81), total bases (227), and doubles (29). It is little wonder that he was in pinstripes the following year. Teammate Ralph Terry, with an 11-9 record, had to wait until 1956 to begin his career with the Yankees.

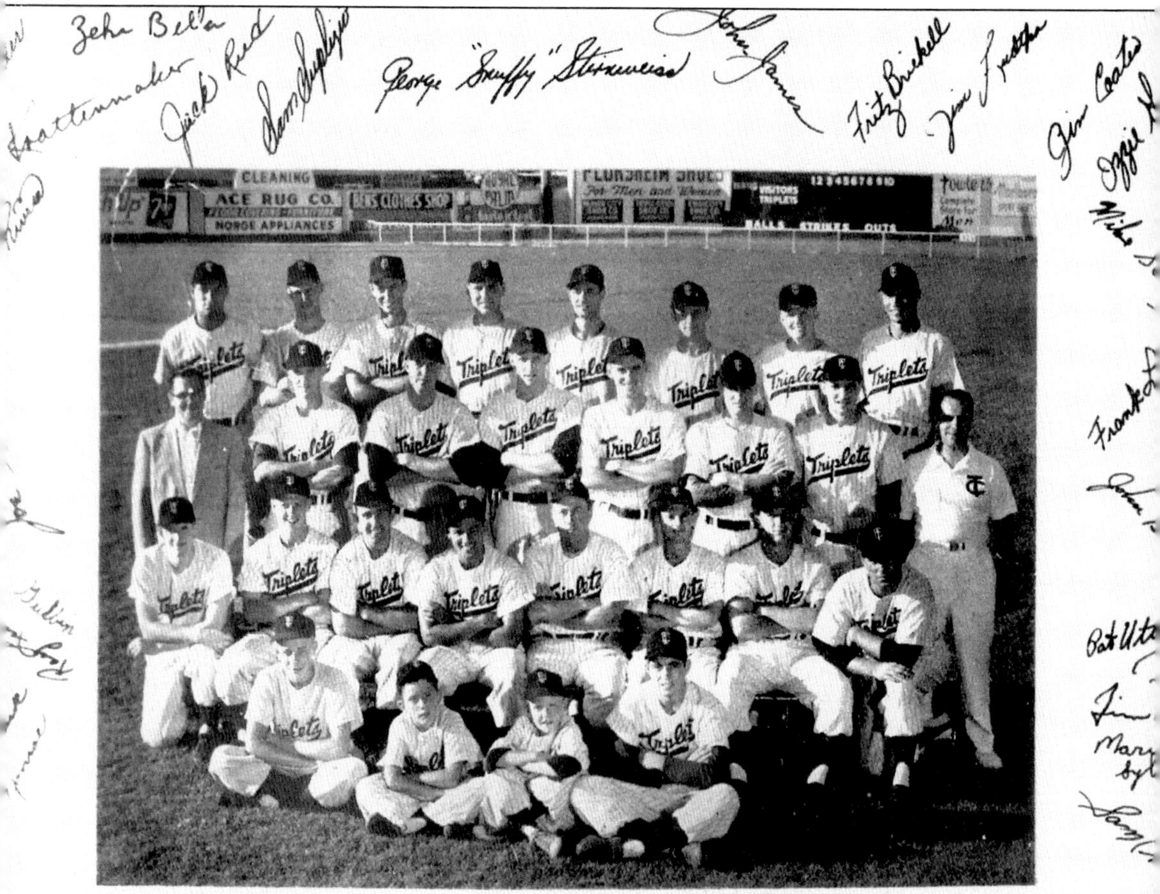

1955 TRIPLETS

First row—Richard Gulban, Pete Stirnweiss, Ed Stirnweiss, Mario Sylvester. Second row—Russ Snyder, Ray Lindquist, Zeke Bella, German (Chico) Rivera, George Stirnweiss, mgr.; Fritz Brickell, Jim Ludtka, Pat Utley. Third row—Herm Krattenmaker, business mgr.; Jack Reed, Frank Lucas, Jim Coates, John Jaciuk, Ozzie Grasso, John Blanchard, Joe Soares, trainer. Fourth row—Sam Chetta, Jim Post, Bob Meisner, Zack Monroe, Sam Suplizio, John James, Jim Lennon, Mike Schultz.

In 1955, the Triplets finished third to reach the playoffs, but it was Allentown's year to become league champions. Led by manager George "Snuffy" Stirnweiss—who had been the American League batting leader in 1945 with a .309 average (it was the last of the war years)—the Triplets featured the Eastern League batting champ John "Zeke" Bella, who had a .371 average. The club also benefited from John Blanchard's league-leading 34 home runs.

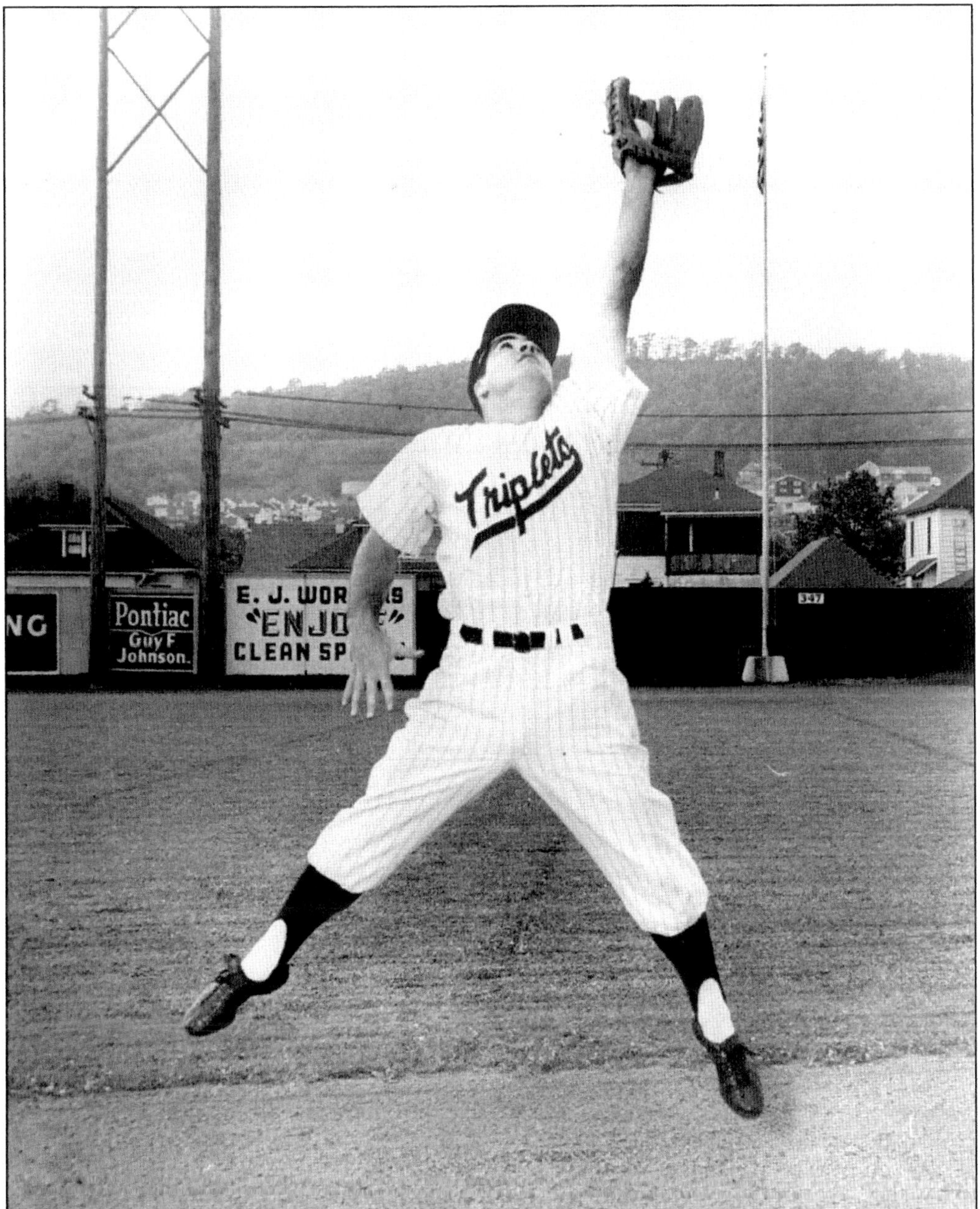

In 1957, the Triplets, under manager Steve Souchock, won the Eastern League pennant. A major factor in their success was the double-play combination of Clete Boyer at shortstop and Bob Deakin at second base. Deakin (shown here) outhit Boyer, .292 to .243, but it was Clete who went on to a 16-year major-league career.

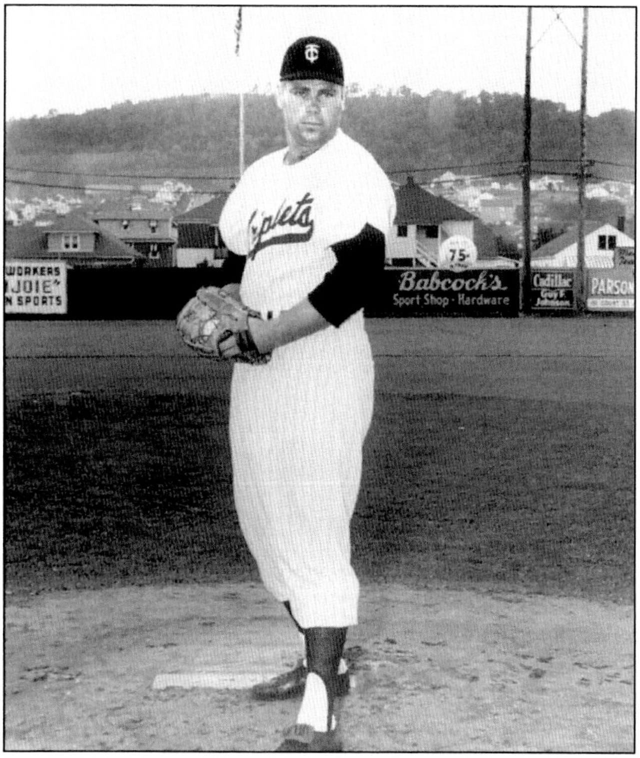

Thirteen was both a lucky and an unlucky number for two Triplets hurlers in 1955. Pat Utley (shown here) led the staff with a 13-6 record. He pitched the most innings (187) and gave up the most bases on balls (124). Jim Coates also won 13 games for Binghamton. He then began a 12-year major-league career the following season. Utley, on the other hand, never again won more than seven games for the Triplets.

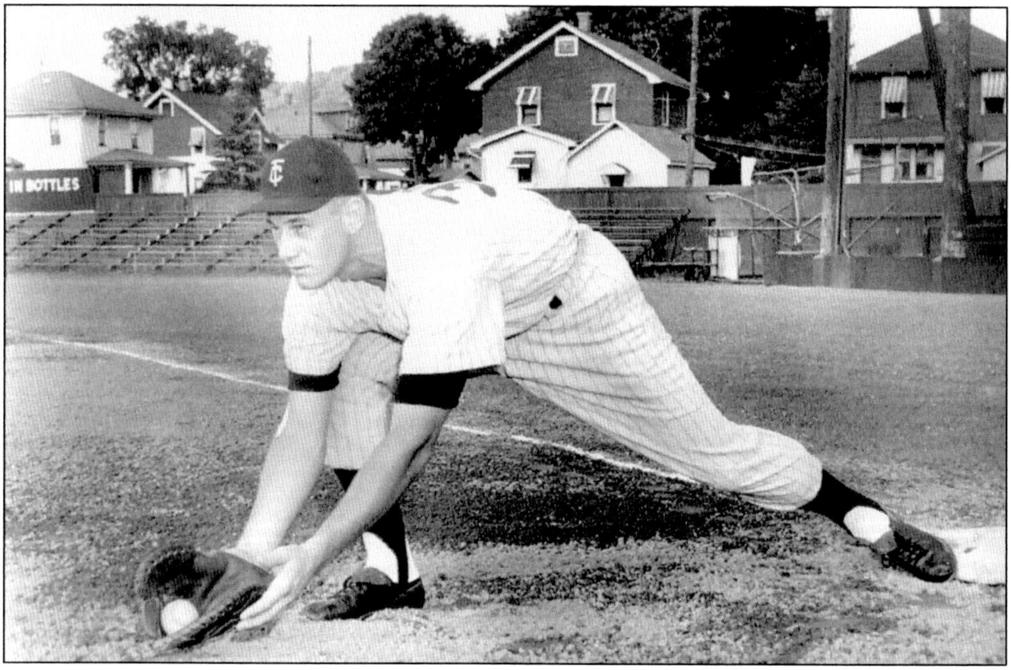

Frank Leja joined the Triplets in 1956 and became their regular first baseman in 1957. Despite a .244 batting average, he led that division-winning club in RBIs with 117 and tied Bob Deakins for the team lead in doubles with 25. In 1957, Deron Johnson dominated the hitting statistics for the Triplets, but Leja's bat clearly played a major role in its success.

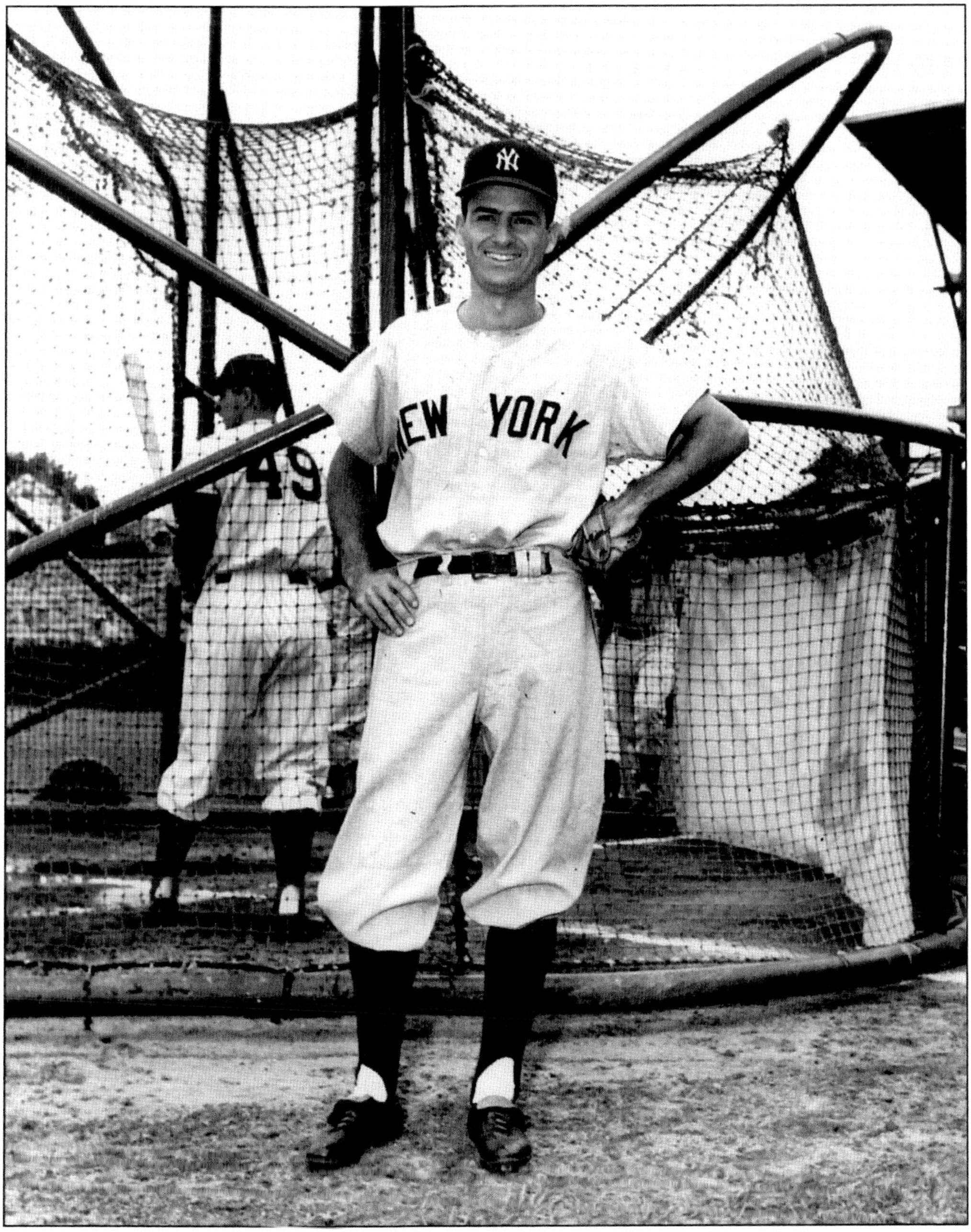

Gerry Coleman poses during an exhibition game with the Triplets. Coleman was with Binghamton in 1946 for 26 games. Three years later, he was at second base for the Yankees, turning double plays with future Hall of Famer Phil Rizzuto. He remained with the Yankees until 1957, when the presence of Bobby Richardson and Billy Martin rendered him expendable.

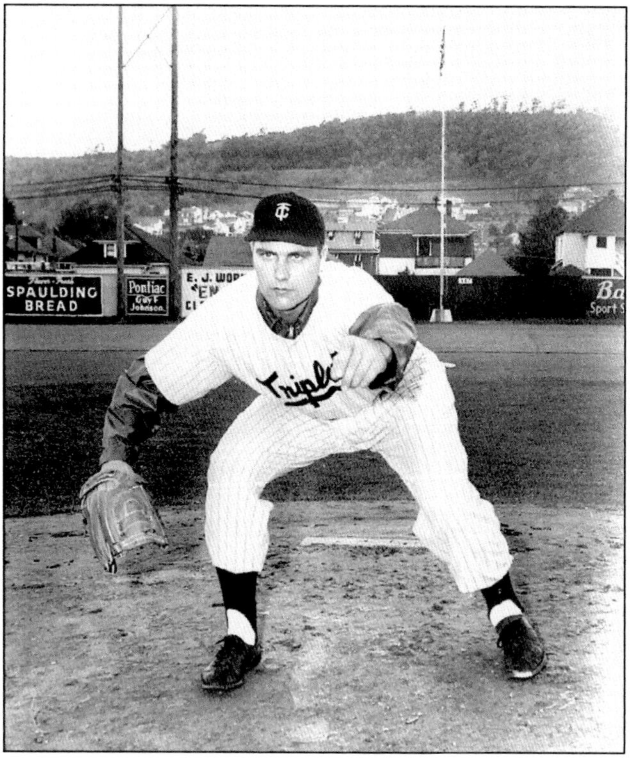

On that 1957 pennant winner were five hurlers with at least 10 wins. While Ed Dick was clearly the star of the staff with 18 victories, lefty John Davolio (shown here) chipped in with 10 wins in 100 fewer innings pitched. All of the pitchers got excellent hitting and fielding support: the Triplets led the league in home runs (100) and double plays turned (162).

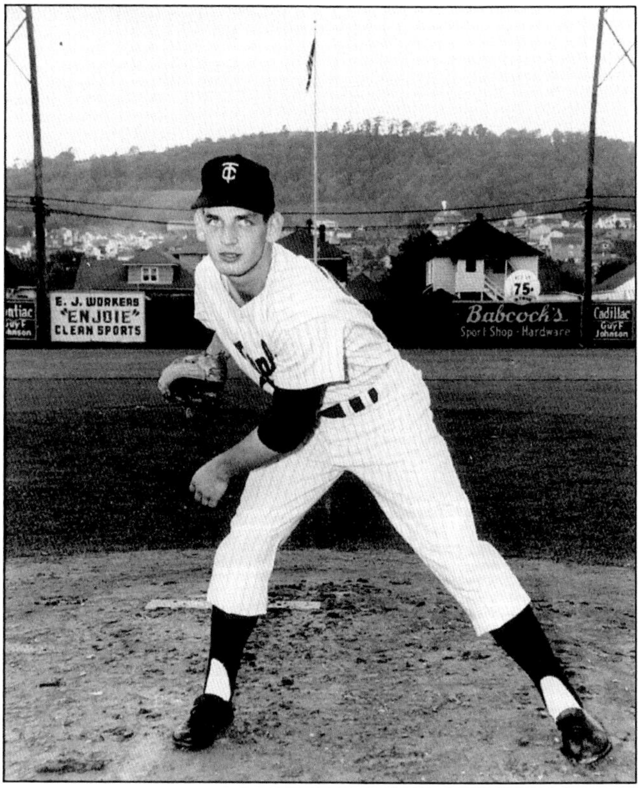

In 1957, Ed Dick led the Triplets pitching staff with a record of 18-9. Three years later, he pitched only 47 innings for the club and had a mediocre 1-4 record. His heroics in 1957 helped Binghamton to win the league championship. That season, he led the club in wins, innings pitched (237), complete games (21), and shutouts (5). His 204 strikeouts were tops for the entire league.

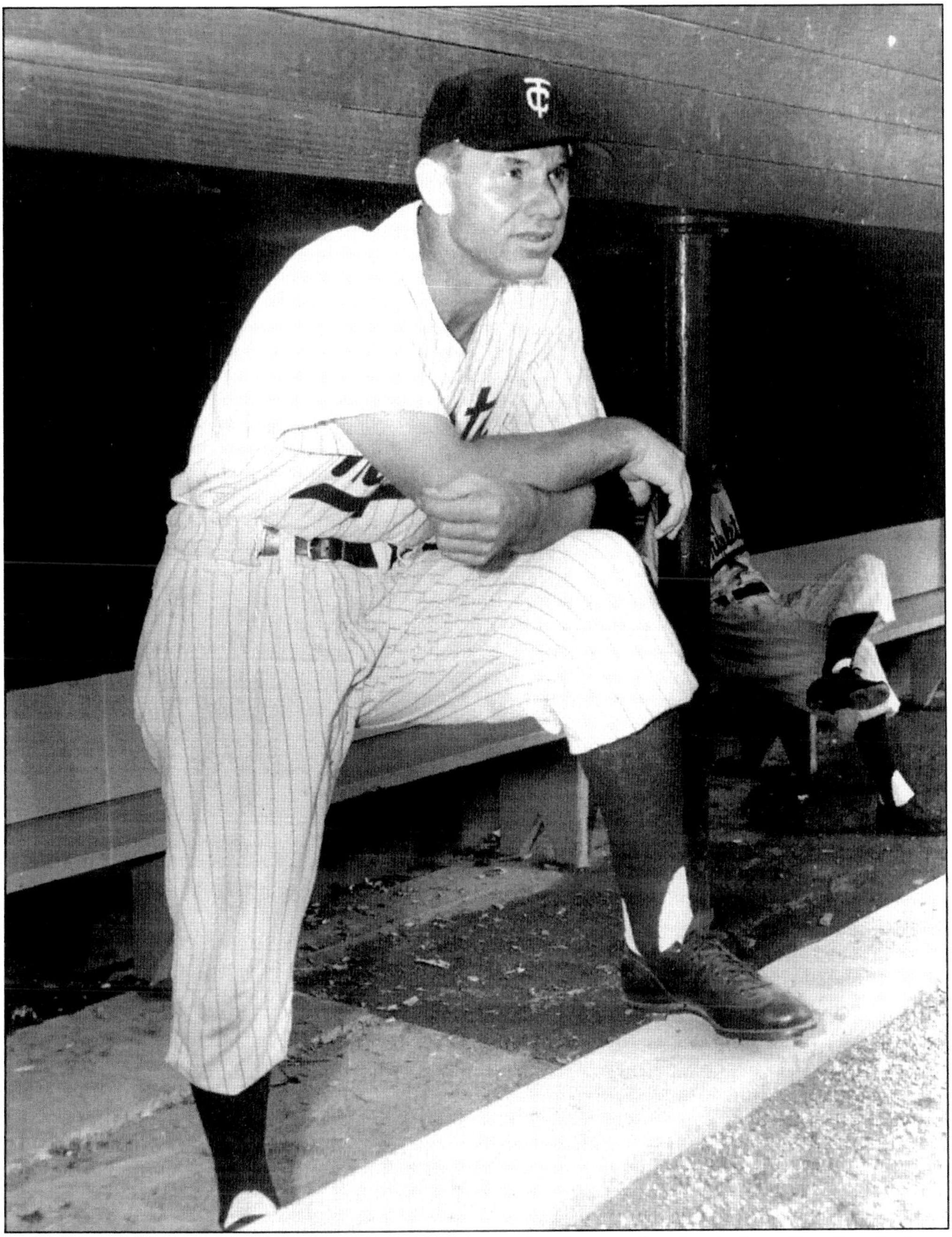

The 1957 Triplets won the Eastern League pennant but lost to the third-place Reading Indians in the playoffs. The slugging of Deron Johnson, who led the league in homers with 26, and the pitching of Ed Dick were key factors in the team's success. Manager Steve Souchock (shown here) turned it around the following year. His team finished third and went on to win the playoffs. It was sweet revenge for the former Yankees outfielder.

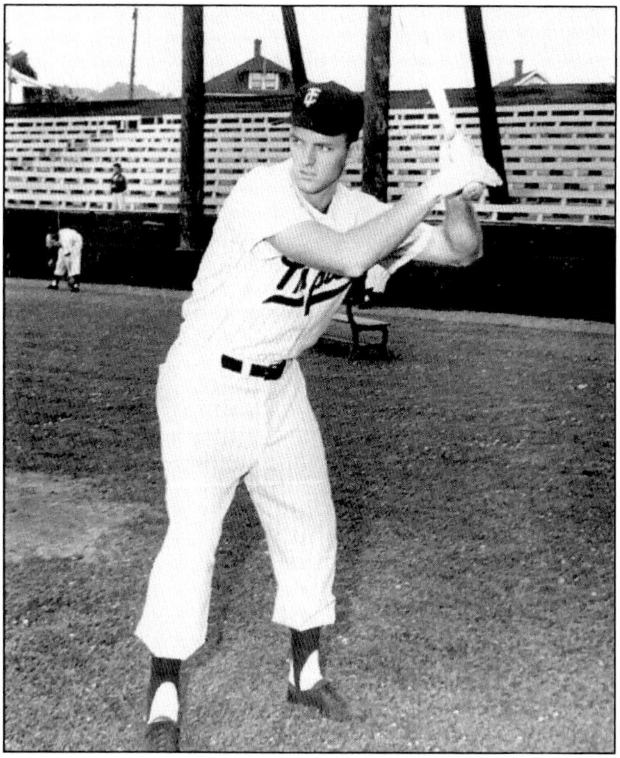

Leroy Thomas played first base for the Triplets in 1958 and led them with 17 home runs, 88 RBIs, and 216 total bases. In 1959, he was the club leader in home runs (25), hits (166), doubles (22), RBIs (122), and total bases (273). That led to a front row seat on the Yankees bench in 1961, watching Mantle and Maris struggle to reach Babe Ruth's home run record.

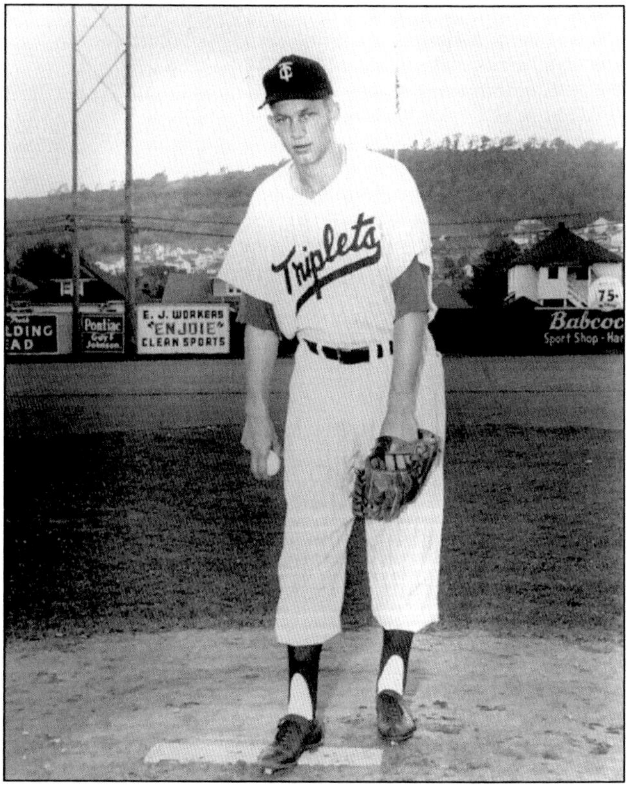

Despite an average 11-7 record with the Triplets, Bill Stafford impressed the Yankees brass by leading the Eastern League with a 2.25 ERA in 1958. By 1960, he was with the Yankees and remained there until 1966, when he was traded to Kansas City. During eight years in the major leagues, the youngster from Catskill, New York, won 43 games, including six shutouts.

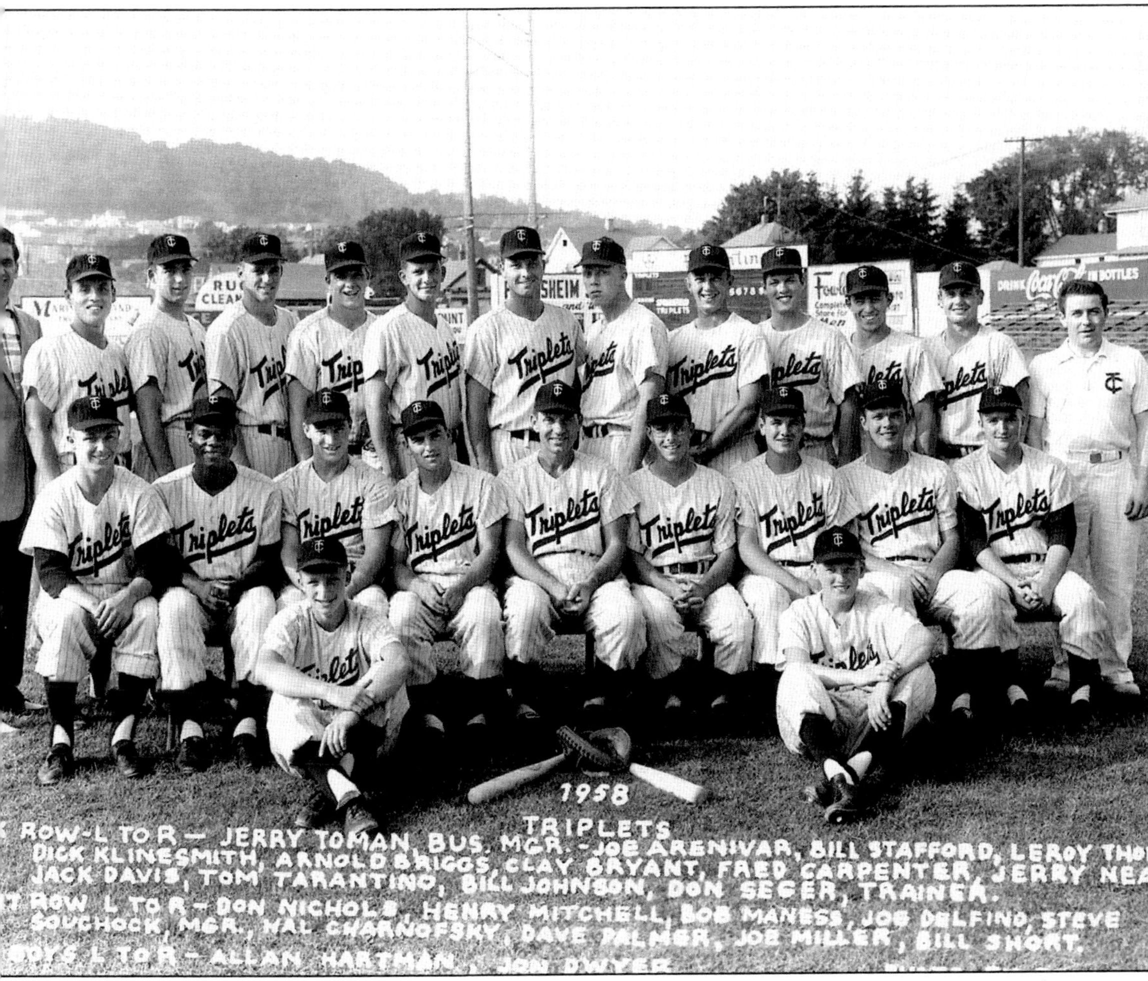

The Triplets were Eastern League champions in 1958. A major reason was the combination of Bill Stafford's league-leading 2.25 ERA and the club's timely hitting. Joe Arenivar (back row, left, next to business manager Jerry Toman) led the club with a .293 batting average. He also tied Henry Mitchell for the club lead in hits with 137. Leroy Thomas, who accumulated 216 total bases, was the only one of those three batting stars to make it to the major leagues.

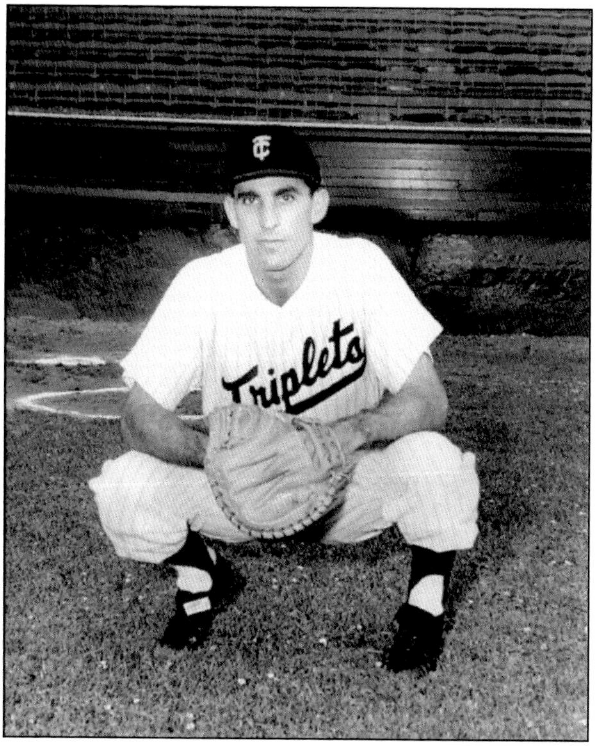

Lamar North was the catcher for the Triplets in 1957 and 1959. With Charlie Silvera as his manager in 1959, North got priceless help from the longtime backup to Yogi Berra. That took care of defense; unfortunately, North's problem was offense. His batting average in 1959 was already down from a respectable .260 in 1957 to .247. Since the Yankees had Berra, with Elston Howard and John Blanchard as backups, North was clearly expendable.

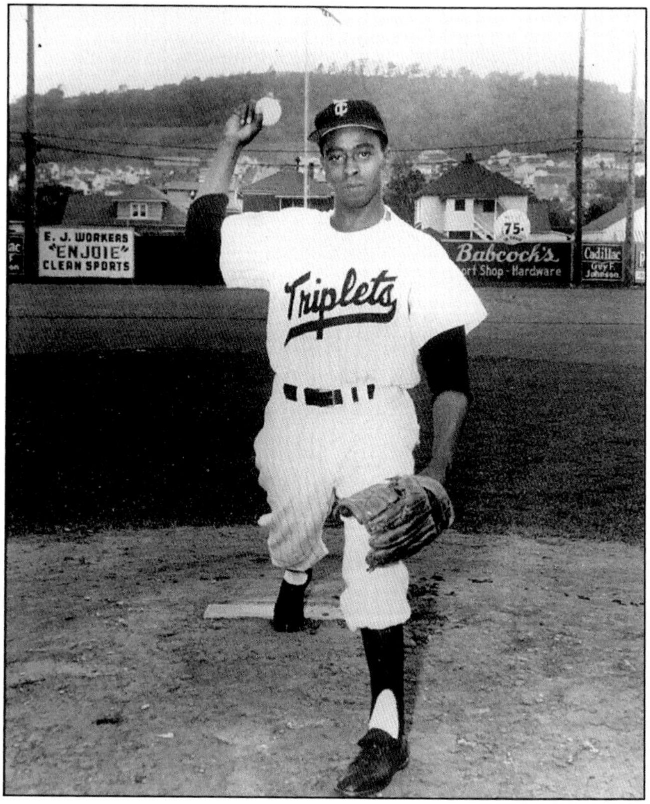

Leonardo (Len) Ferguson pitched for the Triplets from 1959 to 1961. His 3.35 ERA in 1959 led the club. He also tied for complete games (13) and shutouts (2). Sadly, after winning 11 games in 1959, he won only six in the next two years combined. Despite being a hard thrower who struck out 365 batters in three years, he never made it to the big show.

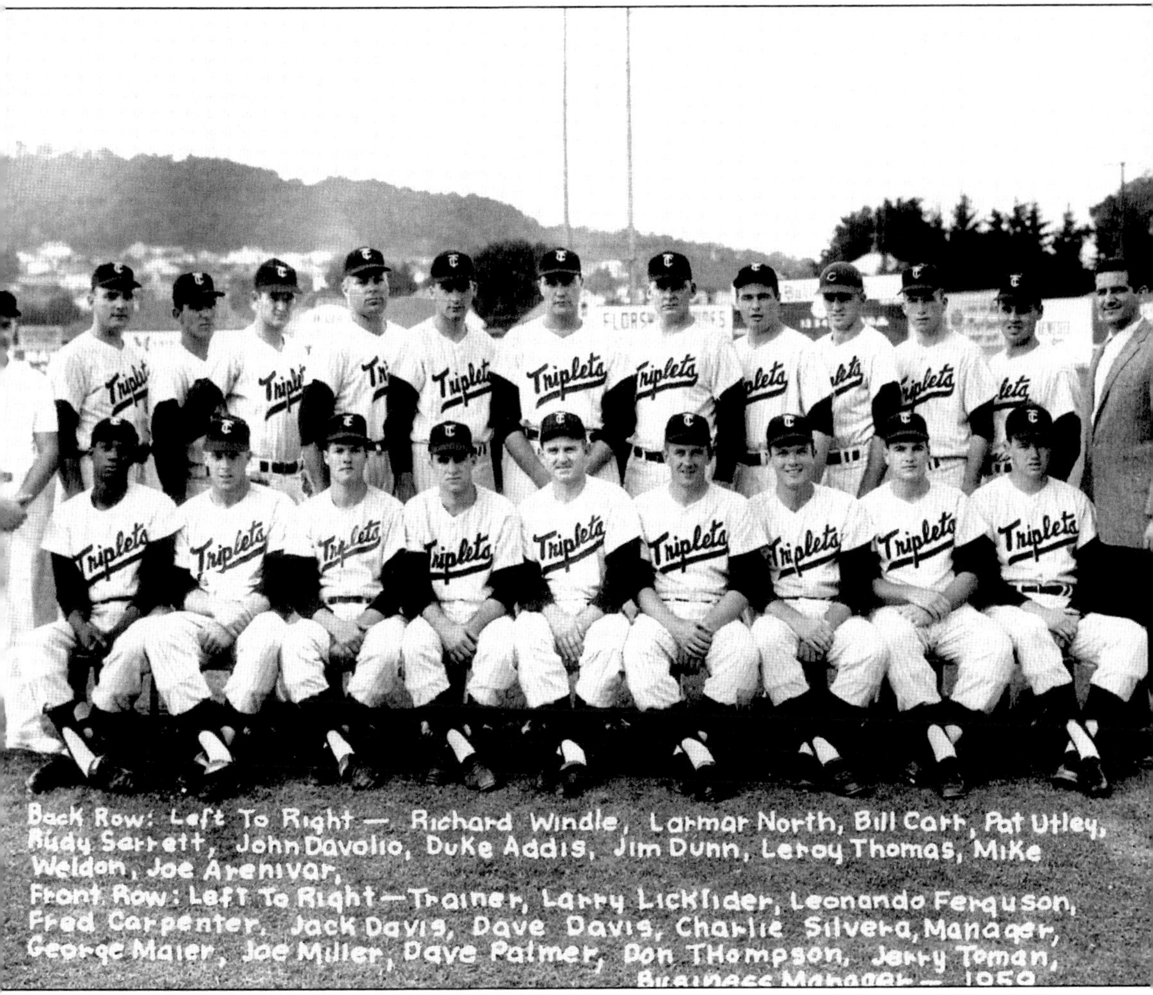

In 1959, the Triplets manager was Charlie Silvera (front row, center). Nicknamed "Swede," the San Francisco native had spent nine years with the Yankees, mostly as a valuable backup to Yogi Berra. By 1955, the Yankees catcher of the future, Elston Howard, had arrived. Still, from 1949 to 1956, Silvera had shared in the glory of a club that won seven pennants and six world championships.

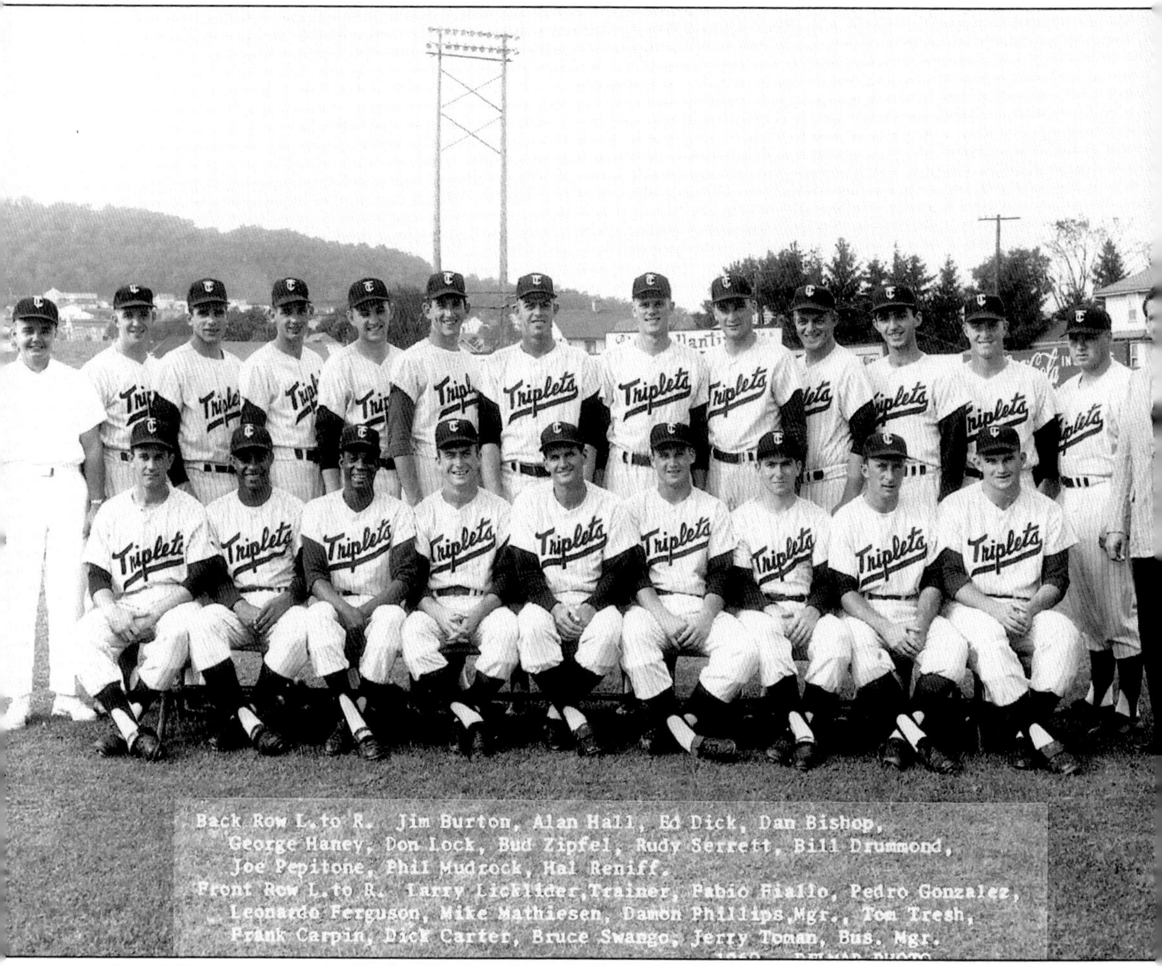

In 1960, a year in which the Yankees' hopes for a world championship would be shattered by Bill Mazerowski's homer in the ninth inning of the seventh game, three future Yankees were starring for the Triplets. Joe Pepitone and Tom Tresh are better known, but that year Pedro Gonzalez won the Eastern League batting title with a .327 average. Another teammate, Don Lock, led the league with 35 homers and 117 RBIs. Despite these heroics, Williamsport and Springfield were co-champions of the Eastern League that year.

In addition to the great players and managers who wore Triplets uniforms, many future baseball legends honed their skills in the Eastern League. In 1962, six years before beginning his Hall of Fame career as manager of the Baltimore Orioles, Earl Weaver is shown entering the visitors' dugout at Johnson Field. Weaver won two championships with Elmira and had two second-place finishes from 1962 to 1965.

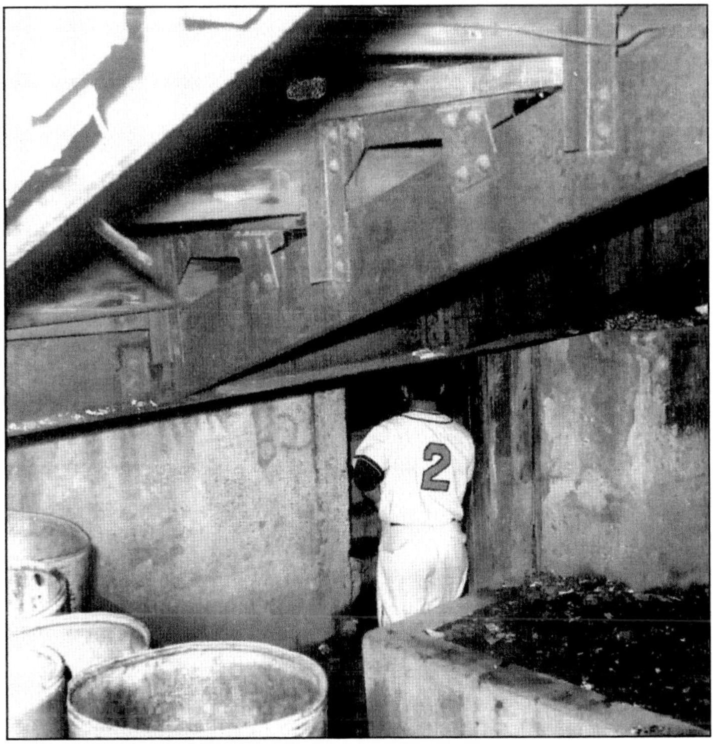

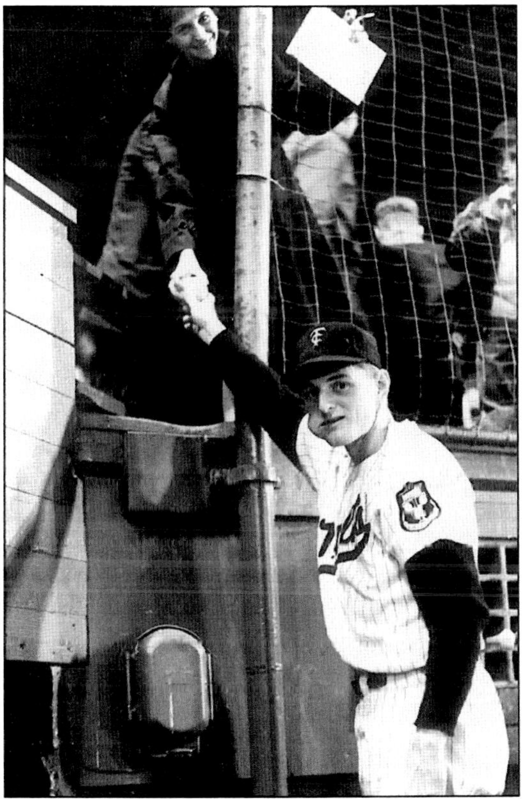

In 1962, the Triplets Ken Harrelson set two Eastern League records: home runs (38) and RBIs (138). The ball that he hit to set the RBI record is shown here being given for safekeeping to the wife of Triplets catcher Milo Fuller. Harrelson went on to hit 131 homers in the major leagues for Kansas City, Cleveland, and the Boston Red Sox.

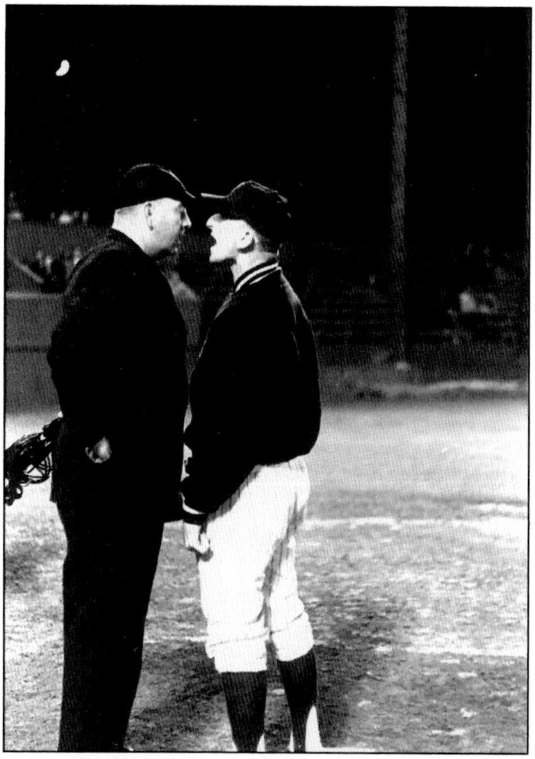

In 1963, the Triplets, who had finished last the previous year, moved up to fourth place under manager John McNamara, shown here discussing a call by umpire George Maloney. McNamara's club featured Ed Millerstrom, who led all pitchers with a 13-4 record and a fine 2.42 ERA. The Triplets, in their last year as an affiliate of the Kansas City Athletics, also boasted future major-league star Bert Campaneris, who was their only .300 hitter.

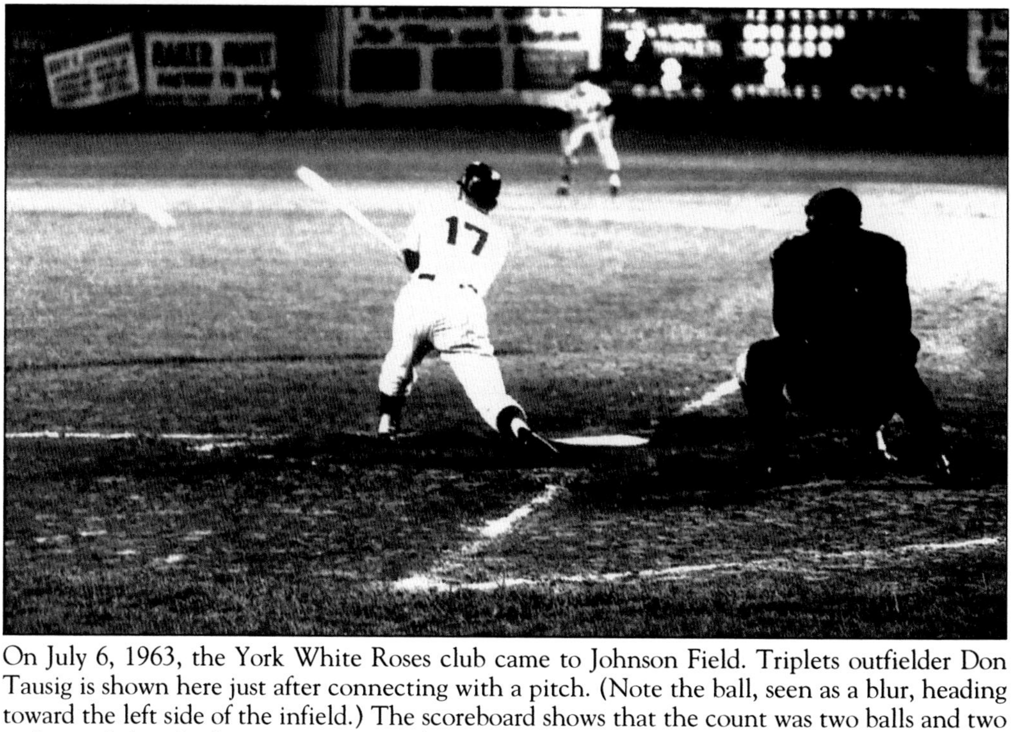

On July 6, 1963, the York White Roses club came to Johnson Field. Triplets outfielder Don Tausig is shown here just after connecting with a pitch. (Note the ball, seen as a blur, heading toward the left side of the infield.) The scoreboard shows that the count was two balls and two strikes and that the home team was trailing 2-1 in the bottom of the seventh inning when this moment was frozen in time.

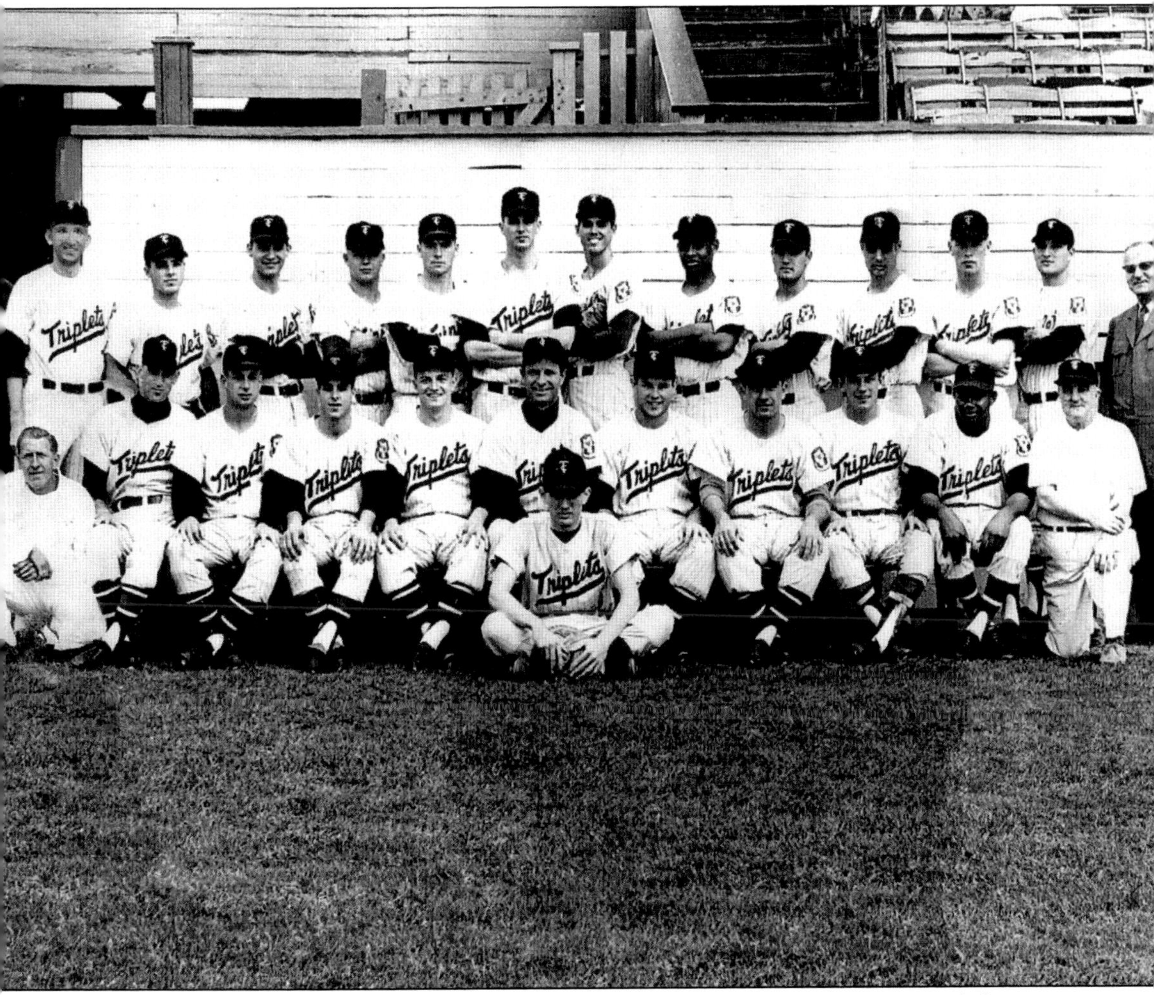

The Milwaukee Braves were associated with the Triplets for only one year, in 1964. With former major-league star Andy Pafko as manager, the team, now in the New York–Penn League, gained notoriety when outfielder Johnny May successfully pulled a "hidden ball" trick. That attracted so much attention that May was contacted by famed sportswriter and broadcaster Bill Stern to be on his show. On the field, Bill Etheridge led the club with a .365 batting average.

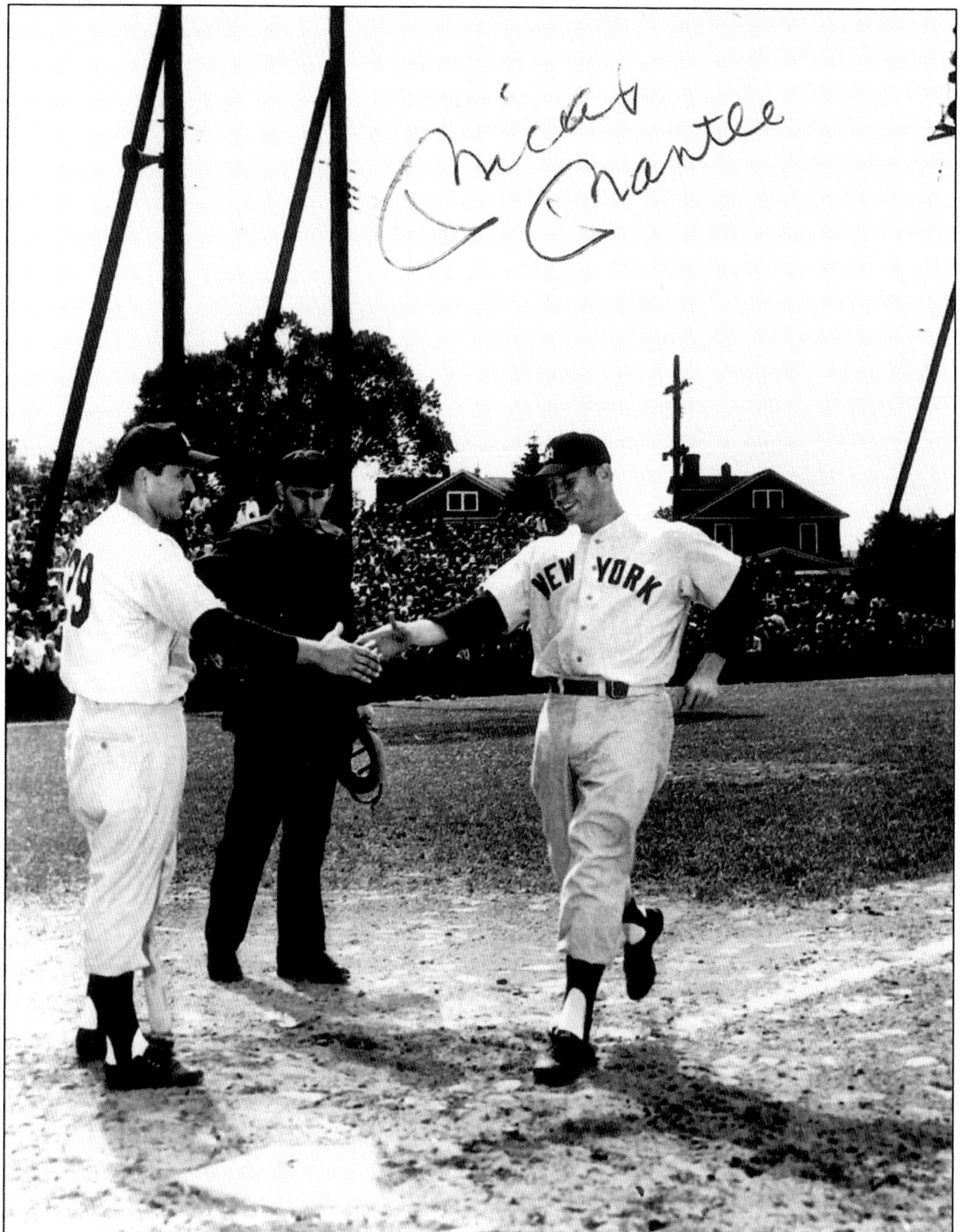

Exhibition games between the Triplets and the Yankees at Johnson Field gave local fans the opportunity to see the big stars in action. Here, Mickey Mantle rounds the bases after giving the folks a thrill by blasting one of his prodigious home runs. These meetings were always a major event to be anticipated and savored. This one was certainly no exception.

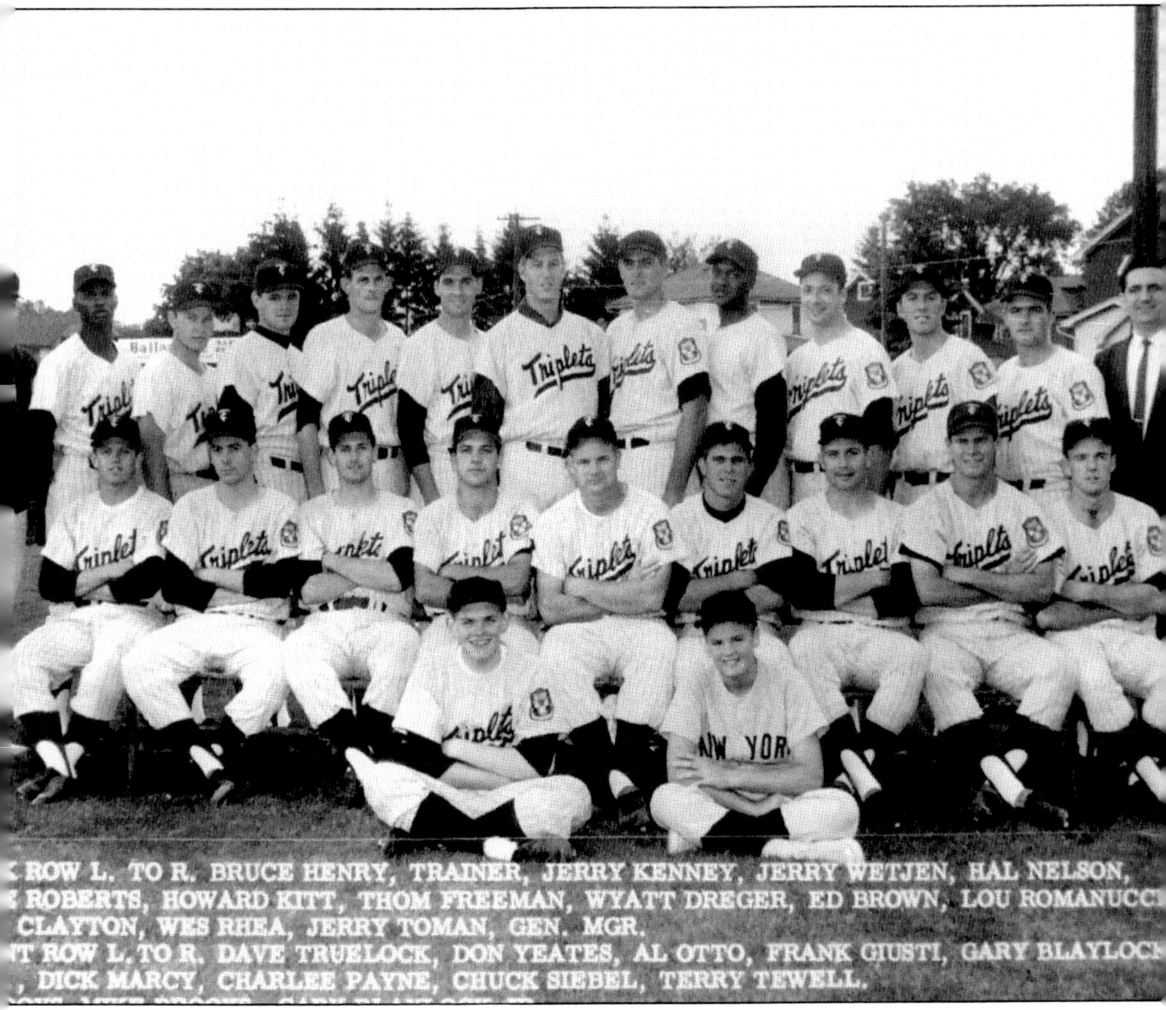

In 1965, the Triplets were back with the Yankees organization, although still in the New York–Penn League. Gary Blaylock managed the club, and Howard Kitt was their best hurler with a 12-4 mark. At the plate, Tom Shopay, later to spend eight years in the American League, led the team with a .321 mark. Right behind him was a bright, young prospect, Jerry Kenney, with a .312 mark. Kenney later spent five years with the Yankees as a utility infielder.

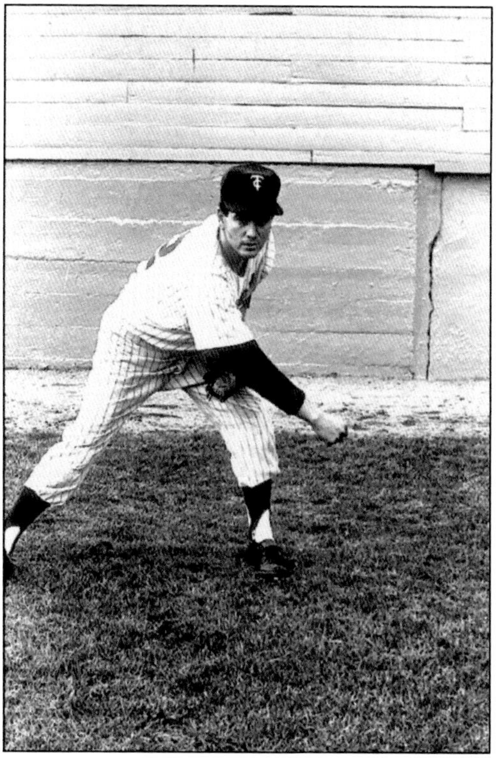

Don Yeates starred on the mound for the Triplets in 1965. He had a fine 8-1 record through 110 innings on a club whose biggest winner was Howard Kitt with 12 victories. The team was once again affiliated with the Yankees organization, after a year with the Milwaukee Braves. They were still in the New York–Penn League.

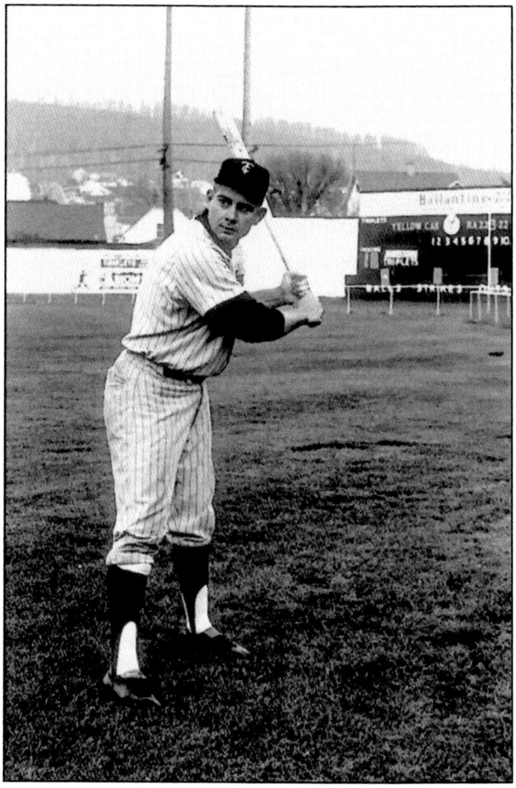

Charlie Payne was a left-handed-hitting outfielder for the Triplets in 1965. Limited to appearances in only 54 games, he still hit .280. His timing was unlucky, as management was taking a long look at Al Otto that year. Even Billy Clayton, who hit a weak .221, got into more games that year than did Payne. Successful careers sometimes hinge on more than just talent.

Statistics, such as batting averages, do not always define a player's value to their team. A case in point is Chuck Siebel (shown here) alternating at catcher with Frank Guisti in 1965. Neither one hit much. Siebel finished at .210, while Guisti hit .238. They made up for their weak hitting, however, by coaxing a young pitching staff into winning 81 games against 45 losses. The young pitchers surely knew their value.

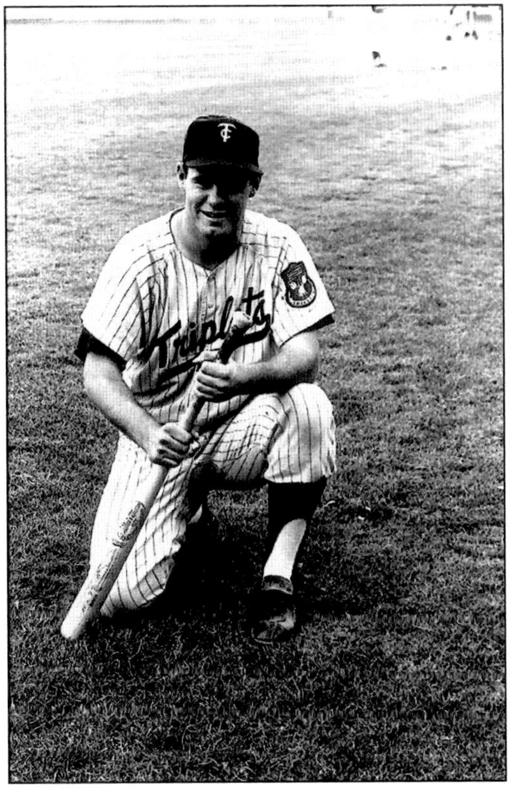

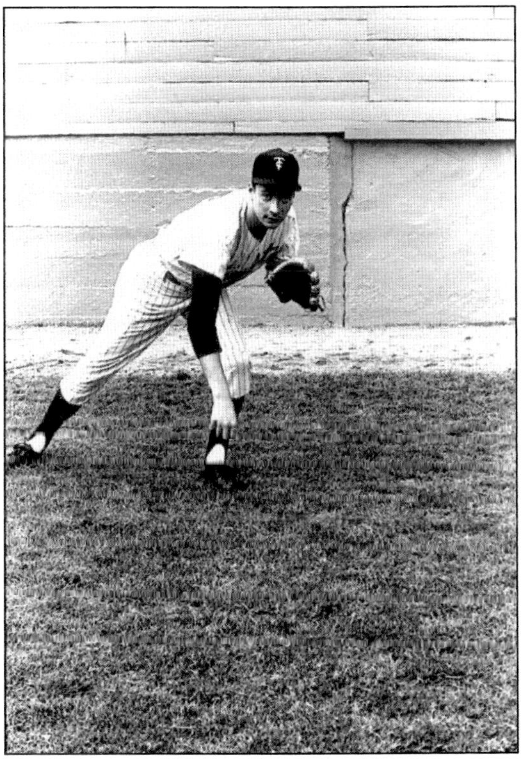

Lou Romanucci had a fine year as one of the pitching aces for the Triplets in 1965. His 9-3 record in 111 innings tied him with teammate Howard Kitt for best winning percentage on the club (.750). Romanucci led the staff with eight complete games, had the lowest ERA (2.53), and tied Ed Brown by hurling three shutouts. Unfortunately, he also led the team in bases on balls (82).

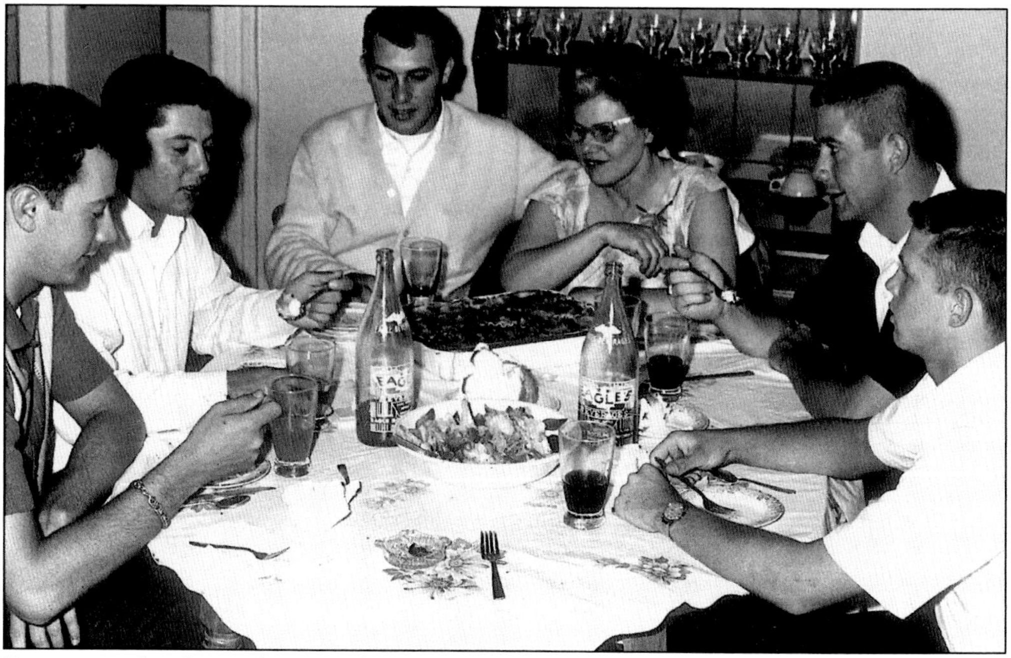

Youngsters who play in the minor leagues often miss their families desperately. One of the worst days for them has to be Mother's Day. Fortunately, there are kind members of the community, such as Mrs. Militello (shown above), who are willing to be surrogate moms. In this 1965 photograph, she shares the day with, from left to right, Lou Romanucci, Frank Giusti, Joe Mackey, Charlie Payne, and Dave Truelock. That evening of May 9, the rains came after three innings in their New York–Penn League game with Jamestown (below).

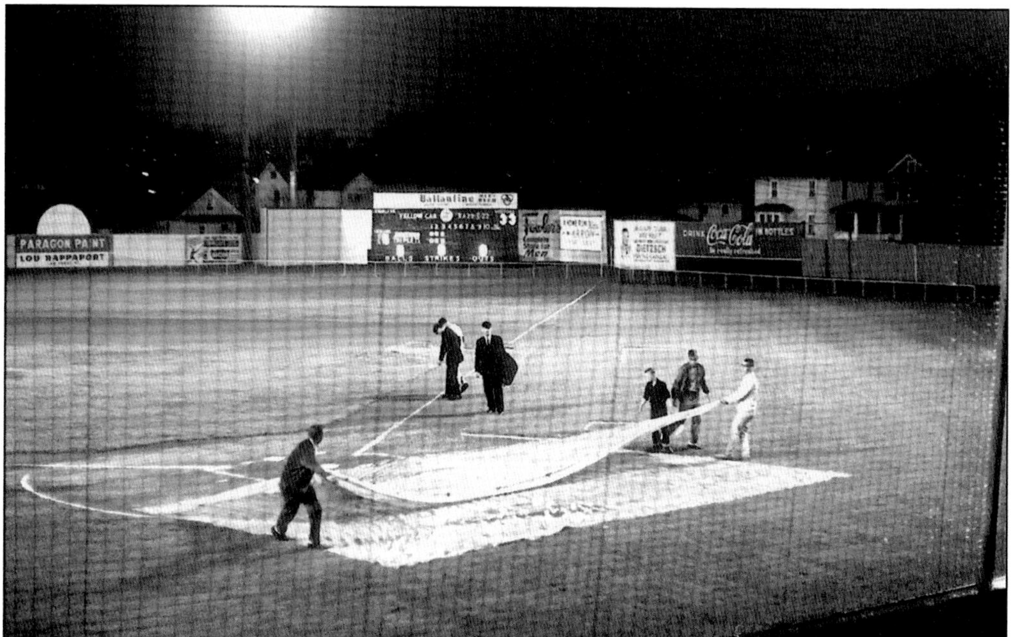

Al Otto was a power-hitting outfield prospect for the Triplets, but his inability to make contact with pitches on a regular basis proved to be his downfall. In 1965, he hit only .246 in 105 games, while managing to lead the club in strikeouts with 106. Things got worse in 1966, when he hit only .179 in 20 games.

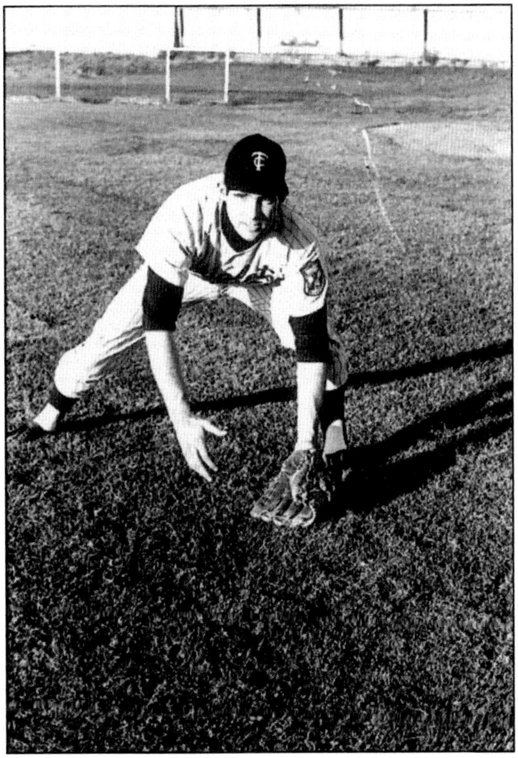

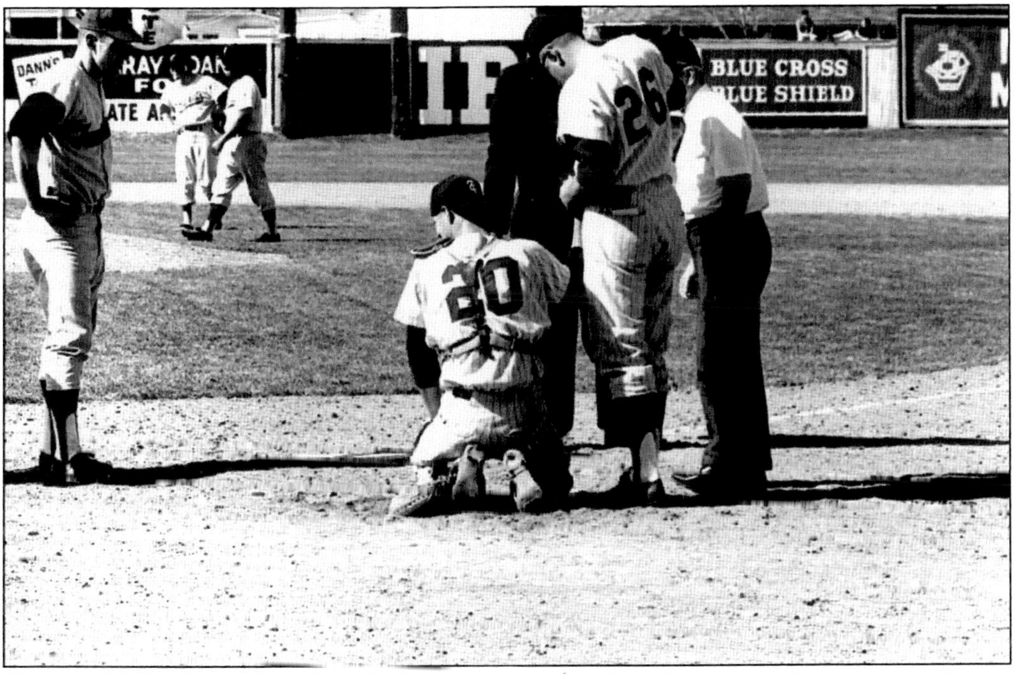

"The tools of ignorance" is often the expression used to describe a catcher's equipment. In any case, no one would dispute how difficult and dangerous the position is. In this 1966 photograph, manager Frank Verdi (No. 26) checks on the condition of his catcher, Jesse Plemons. The two umpires and the Triplets pitcher look on sympathetically.

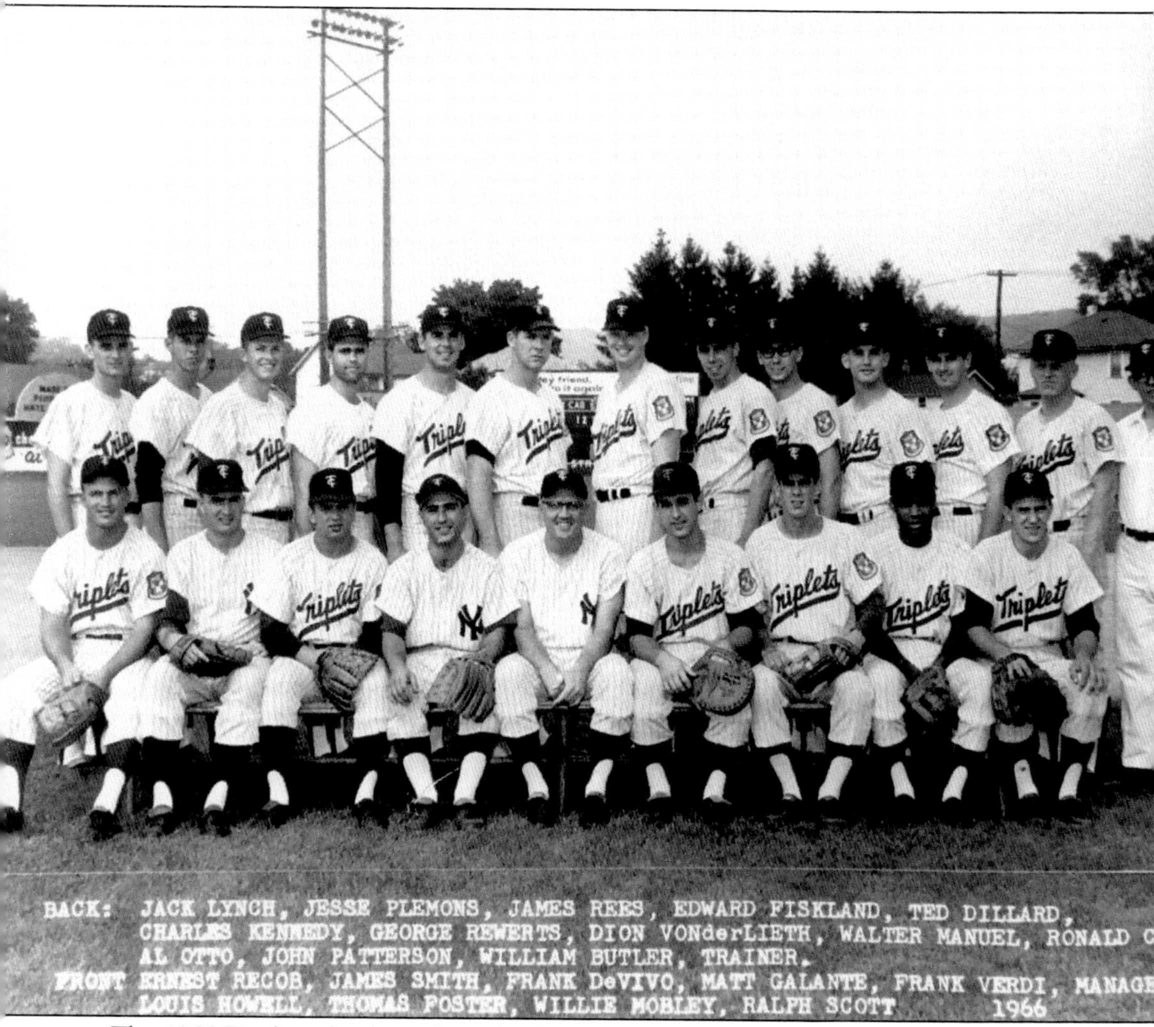

The 1966 Triplets, finishing their third year in the New York–Penn League due to lack of financing for Eastern League membership, had a new manager, Frank Verdi. The Brooklyn-born Verdi had spent one day of the 1953 season with the Yankees in the year that they beat his hometown Brooklyn Dodgers in the World Series for their fifth consecutive championship. Although Verdi had starred for the Triplets in 1952, he never got to bat for the Yankees.

Mickey Scott, shown here warming up in the Triplets bullpen, was their leading pitcher in 1966. His 15-5 record tied him for the Eastern League lead in wins with Jerry Hudgins of Pittsfield. He also led the club in innings pitched (170), strikeouts (190), complete games (12), and bases on balls (67). That record got him a promotion, but in 1968, he was back in Binghamton compiling an 8-6 record.

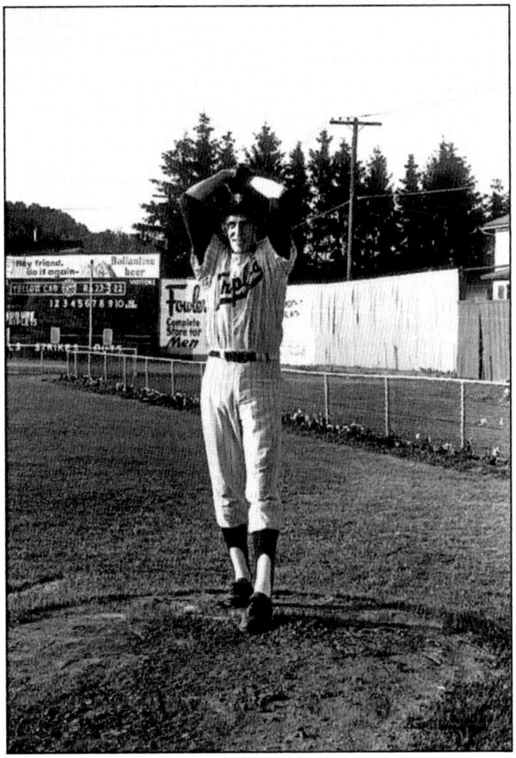

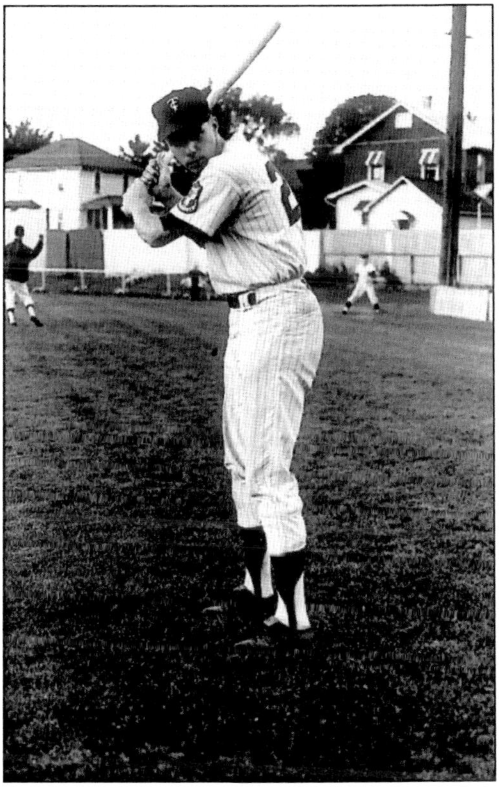

Shortstop is such a key defensive position that weak hitting can sometimes be overlooked. "Good field, no hit" is a term often applied to those with great gloves and weak bats. Unfortunately, Dion von der Lieth fit that description too well. In 1966, his one year with the Triplets, he hit only .201 in 99 games.

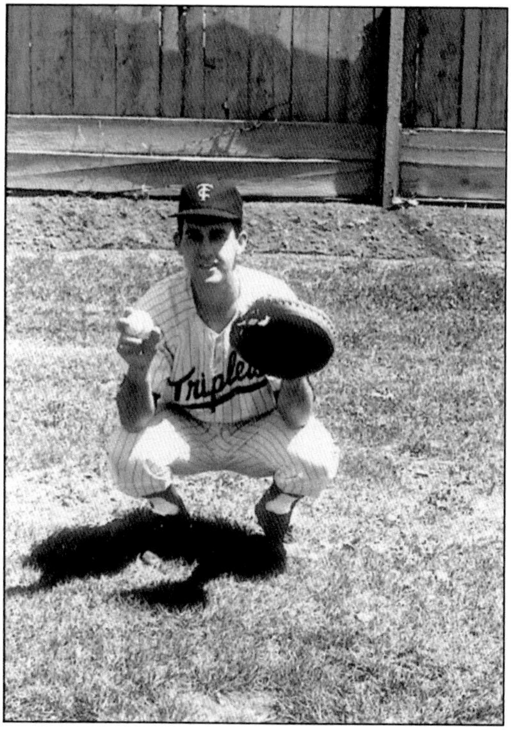

Lou Howell was the Triplets' catcher in 1966, the club's last year in the New York–Penn League. Howell caught 101 games and hit a respectable .274. He never equaled that when the Triplets returned to the Eastern League. He hit only .228 in 1967 and, with Thurman Munson on the scene in 1968, Howell appeared in only 19 games. His father, Dixie, played for the Dodgers, and his son, Mike, is currently with the Detroit organization.

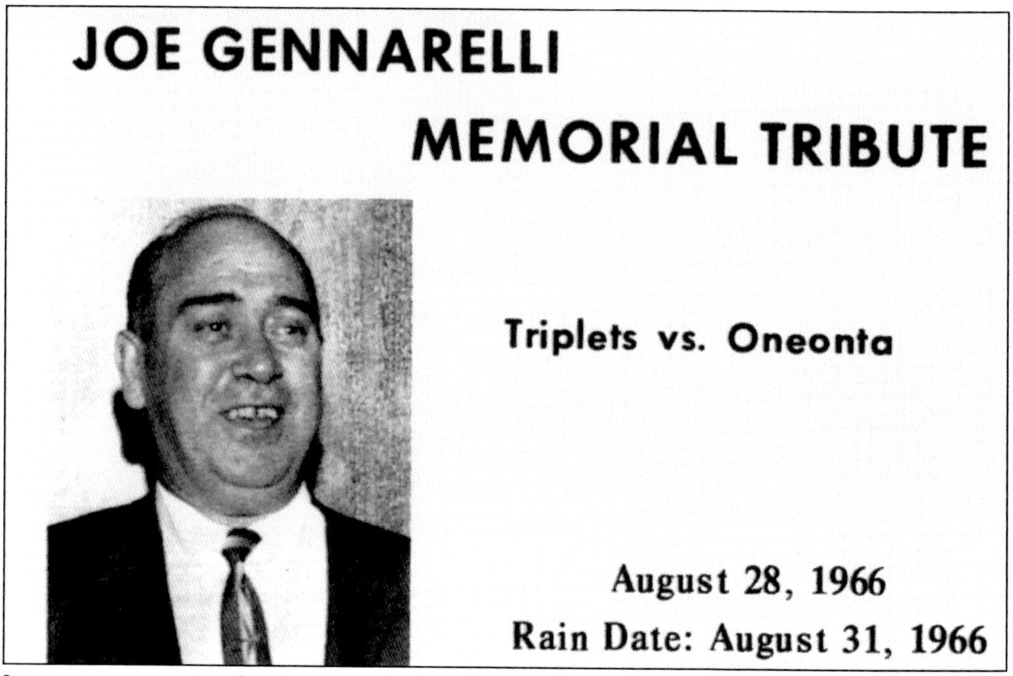

In every community that has a professional team, there always seems to be one person who stands out—one booster who does more to support the club and its players than anyone else. In the Triple Cities, that person was Joe "Ginger" Gennarelli. While he operated a florist business, his passion was the Triplets. Gennarelli would do anything to help the club. His death in 1966 was a great loss to everyone who knew him.

Archie Moore (shown here) played in 33 games for the Triplets in 1967, hitting only .228. Moore was one of six Triplets outfielders that year. Only one, Tom Martz, hit over .300 (.317), but he played in only 47 games. Yet, the team won a championship, which proves, once again, how far good pitching and tight defense can take a club.

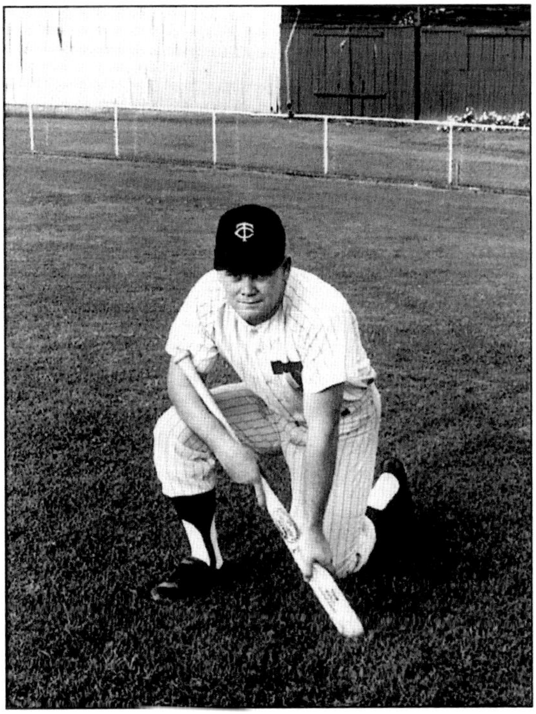

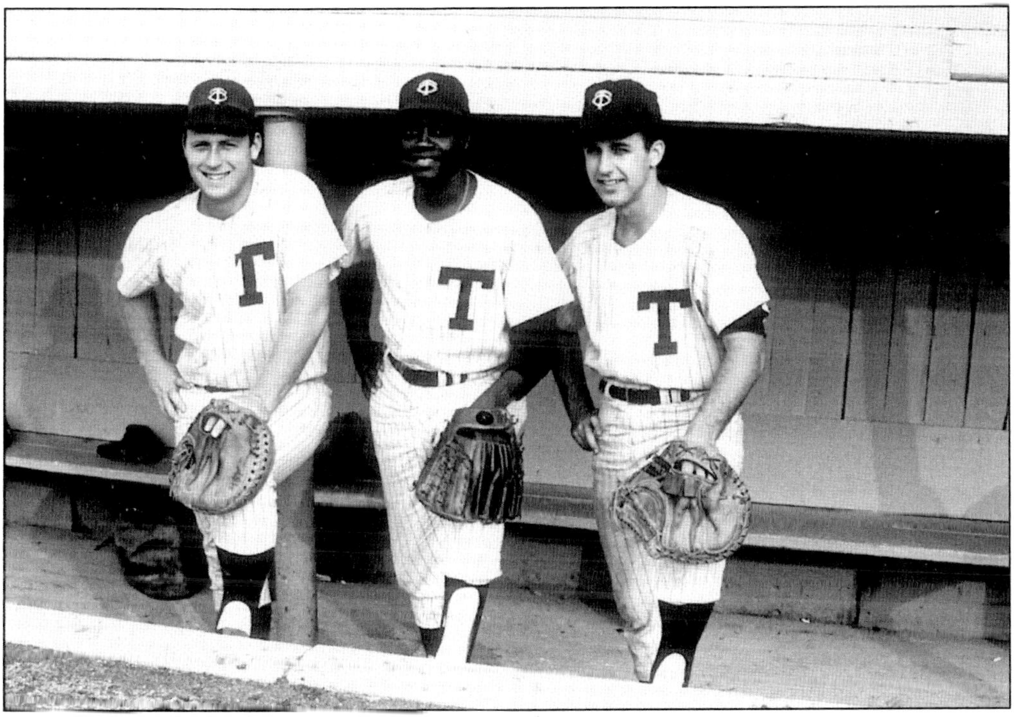

The pitching star for the 1967 club, Jim Horsford, is shown here flanked by his two catchers: Mike Ash (left) and Lou Howell (right). On a team that featured good pitching, Horsford stood out. He led the club in winning percentage with a 13-2 record and had the staff's lowest ERA (1.57). Gary Girouard also helped with a sparkling 14-6 performance.

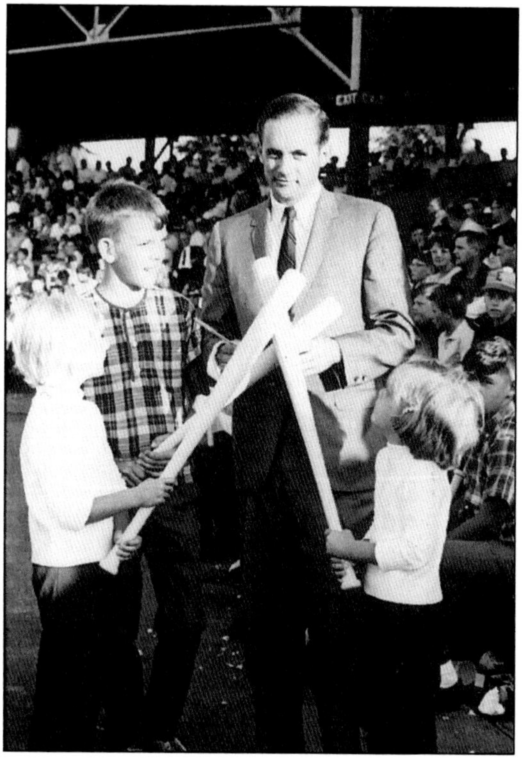

August 6, 1967, was Bat Day at Johnson Field, and a couple of starry-eyed fans are shown here getting Dick Howser's autograph on their lumber. Howser was in his first year with the Yankees, after six seasons with the Athletics and the Indians. Unfortunately, he had broken his wrist after 63 games with his new club and had to sit out the rest of the year. He later managed both the Yankees and Kansas City clubs.

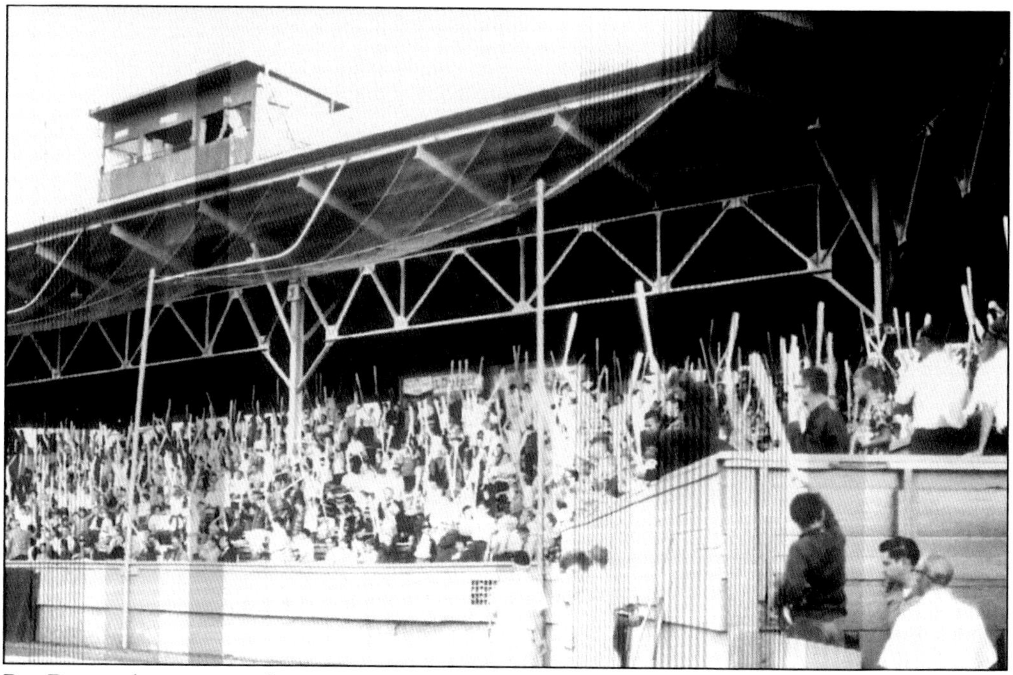

Bat Day is always a popular promotion, and this event, on August 6, 1967, was no exception. Binghamton's opponent was Pawtucket, but the bats were clearly the main attraction. Note the Triplets play-by-play announcer leaning out of his booth atop the bleachers, exhorting the crowd to raise their souvenirs high.

Another contributor to the Triplets' championship in 1967 was pitcher Bill Burbach. In his only year with the club, Burbach worked 145 innings and finished with a record of 10-9. Although he led the team with four shutouts, wildness was a problem. He led the staff with 86 bases on balls.

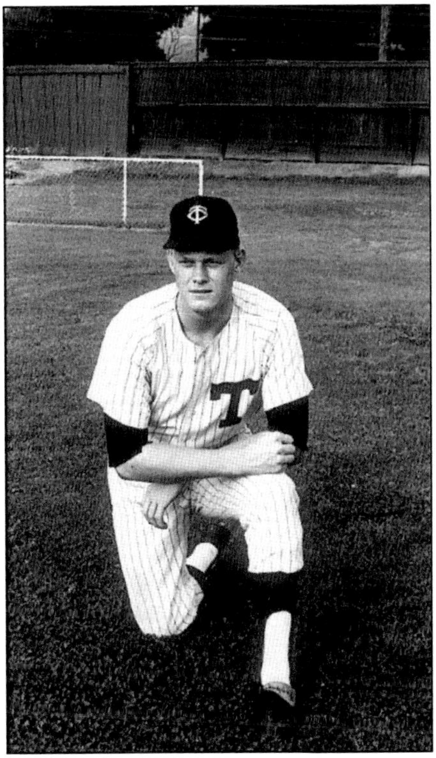

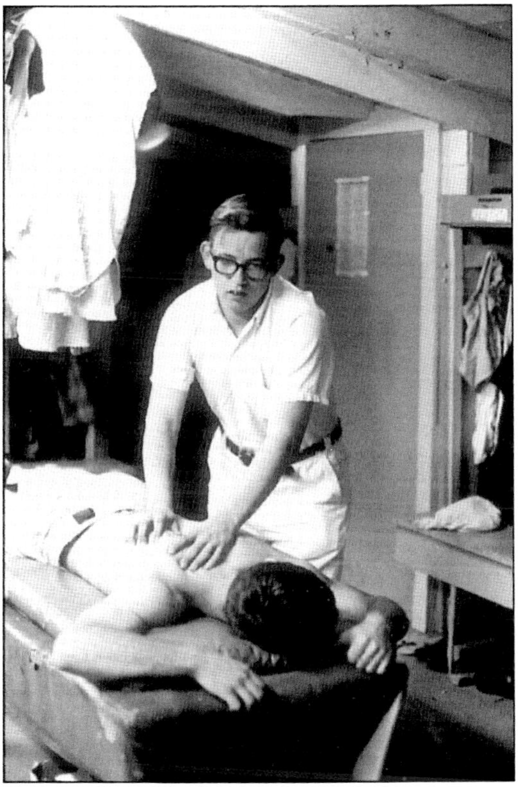

If anyone ever asked, many professional athletes might choose the team trainer as the club's most valuable member. Shown here is Triplets trainer William Butler at work. The trainer often puts in more hours than anyone on the club. Players come in early for treatment and stay after the game to have their aches and pains attended to. Pitchers are especially needy. After all, sore arms can end careers.

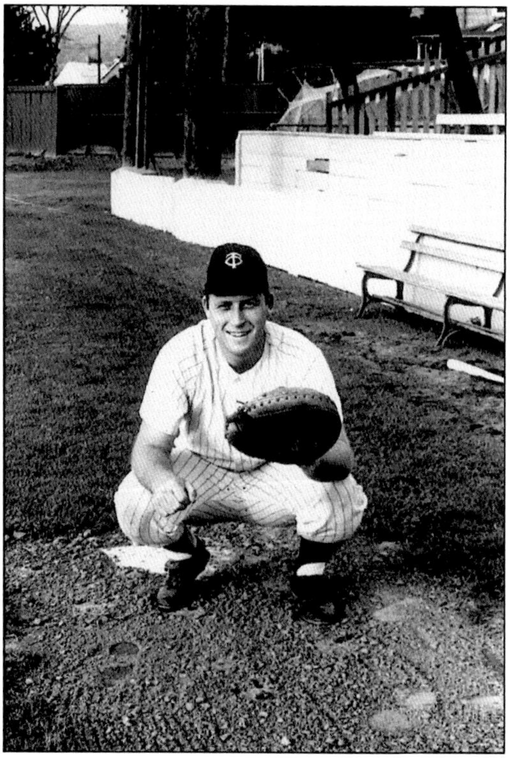

Mike Ash (shown here) caught 44 games for the Triplets in 1967. Lou Howell did the bulk of the catching but hit only .228. Clearly, there was a window of opportunity for Ash, but he could only muster a .191 batting average. At least he had the thrill of being on the Eastern League's championship club for that season.

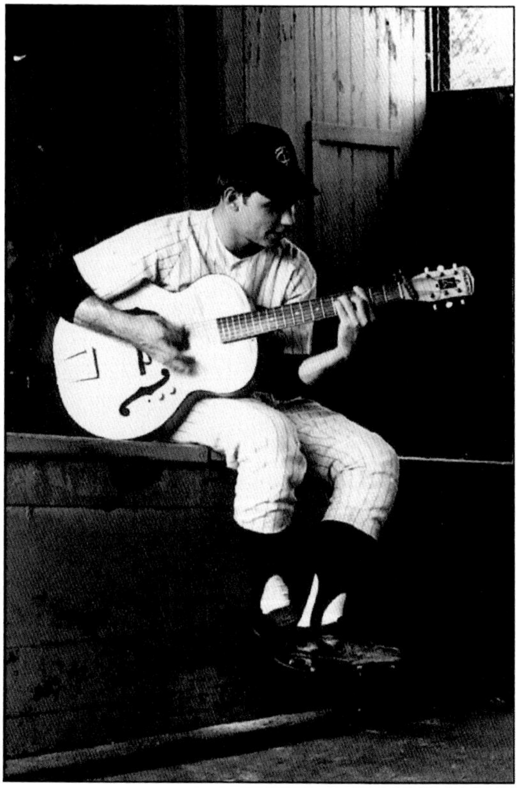

John Schroeppel, shown here with his guitar, made some pretty music on the mound for the 1967 Triplets. He led that championship club in strikeouts with 116 and did it again in 1968 with a total of 81 whiffs. Unfortunately, he also had losing records in both years. Even with the league's champions in 1967, he had only an 8-10 mark.

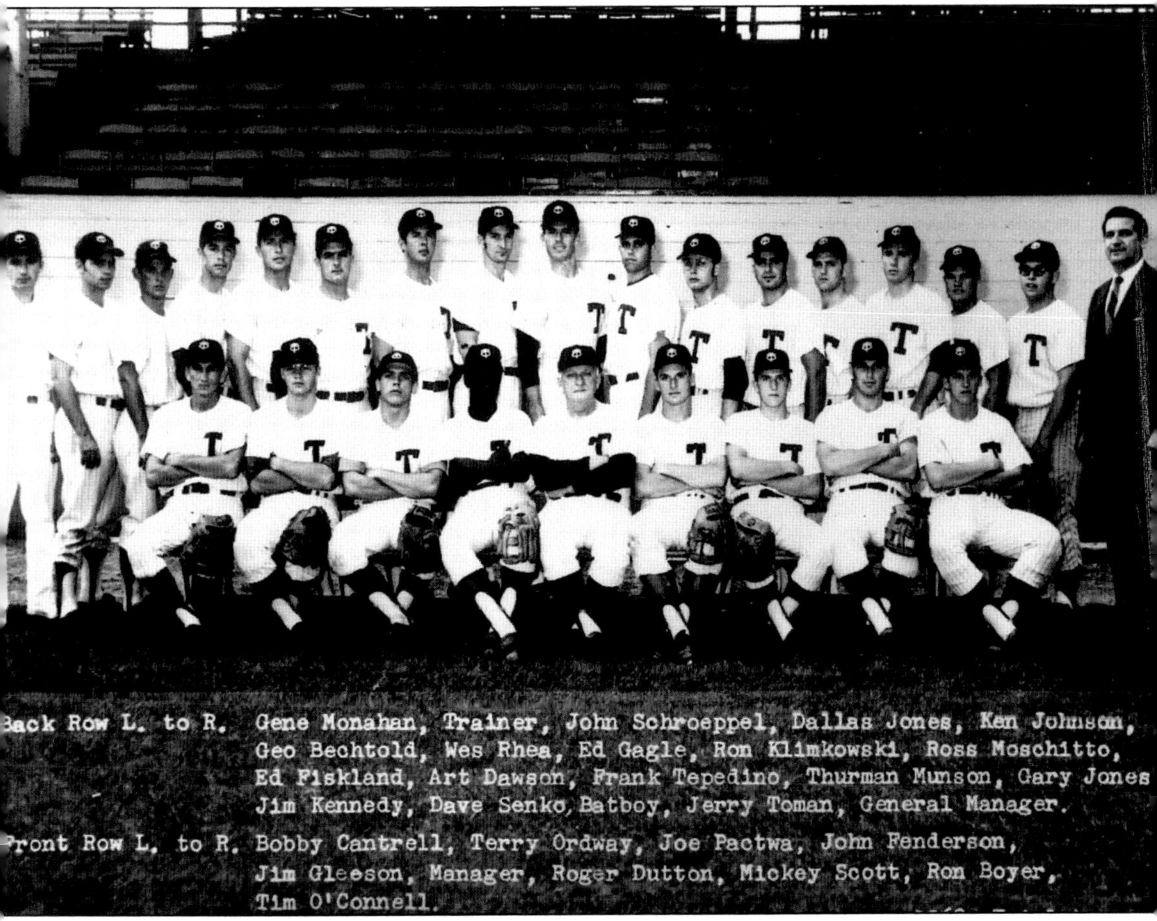

After winning a championship in 1967, the Triplets' final season at Johnson Field ended not with a bang but a whimper. They finished fourth in a six-team league. Thurman Munson, 21 years old, can be seen in the back row. He joined the Yankees the following year and remained there until his untimely death in 1979. There would be no professional baseball in the Triple Cities for the next 24 years.

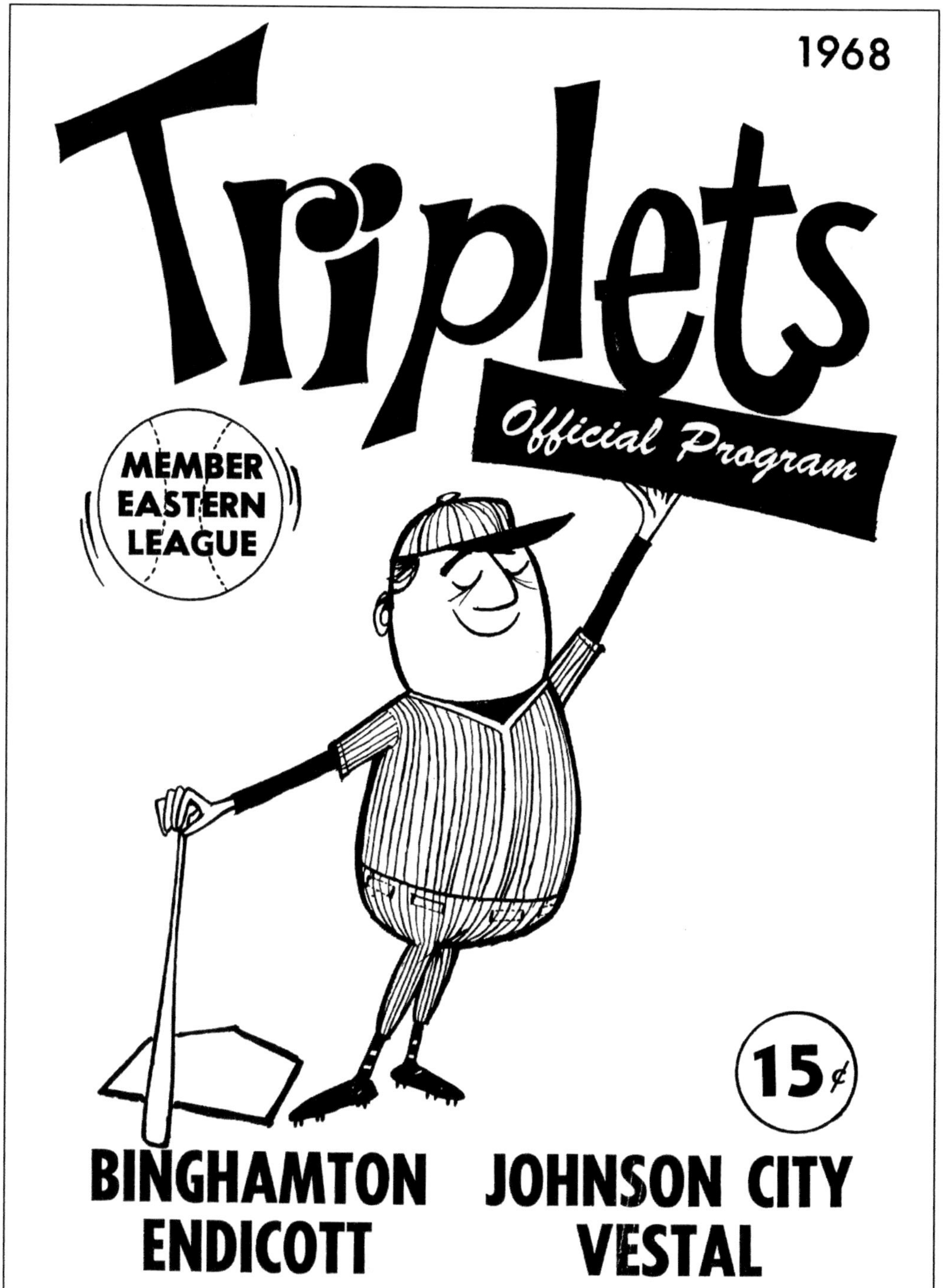

Pictured here is an official 1968 program for the Triplets. In its last year at Johnson Field, the team featured future star Thurman Munson at catcher. He led the club in batting with a .301. No one else came close. Only one pitcher, Gary Jones, won more than eight games. He was 11-5. The team struggled all year, and having three managers—Frank Verdi, Cloyd Boyer, and Jim Gleeson—did not help.

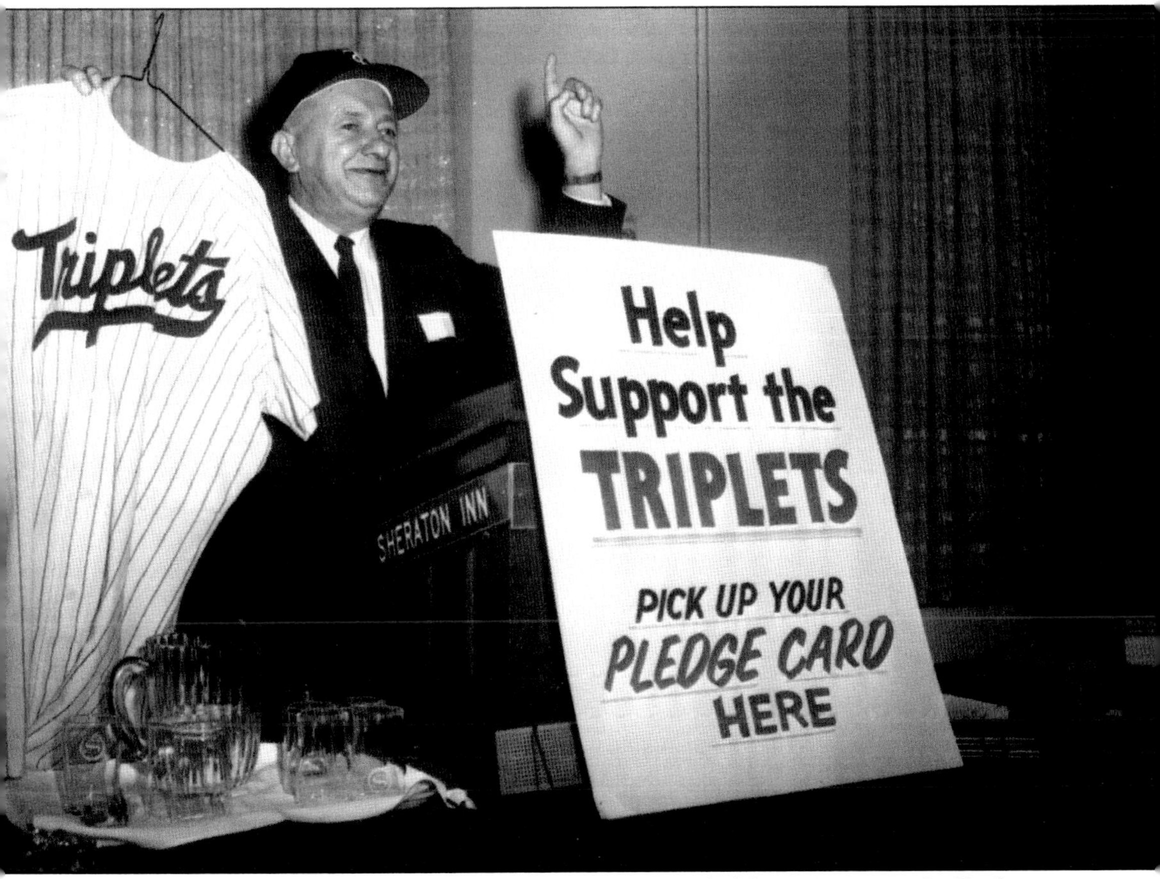

The 1960s were a tumultuous decade for the Triplets. At the end of the 1961 season, the Yankees, who had owned the franchise since 1932, dropped it and moved their players to Augusta, Georgia. The Triplets became a community stockholders operation. By 1964, funds were so low that the club moved to the New York–Penn League, and by 1968, it was over. Through it all, club president Lou Rappaport kept them together with fundraisers like this one.

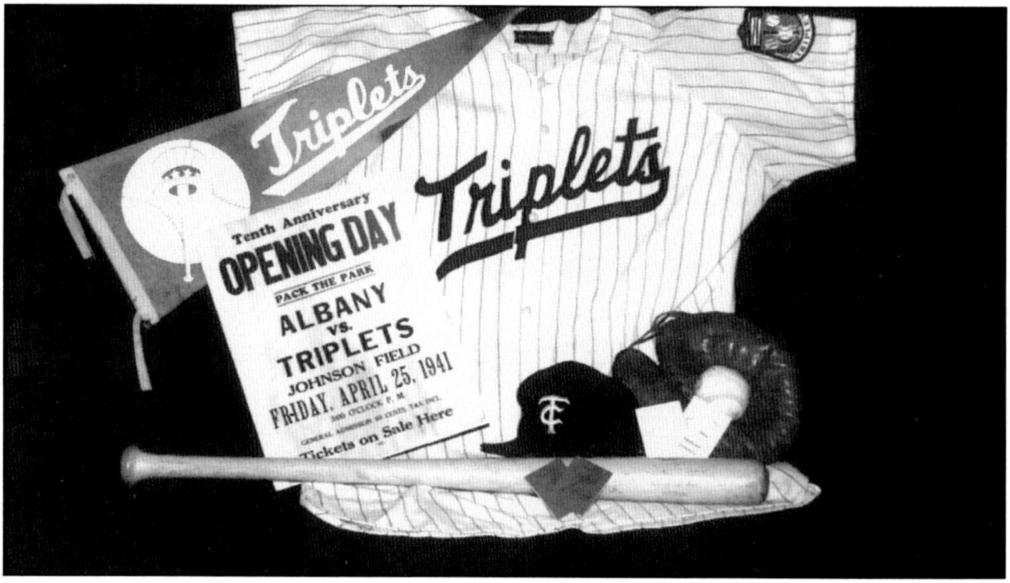

The "Tenth Anniversary Opening Day" sign that asks fans to "Pack the Park" for the game between Albany and the Triplets at Johnson Field, on Friday, April 25, 1941, highlights this collection of memorabilia. This group of autographed baseballs, bats gloves, caps, tickets, and a Triplets uniform were all individually acquired by co-author Mike McCann. Incidentally, neither team made the playoffs that year.

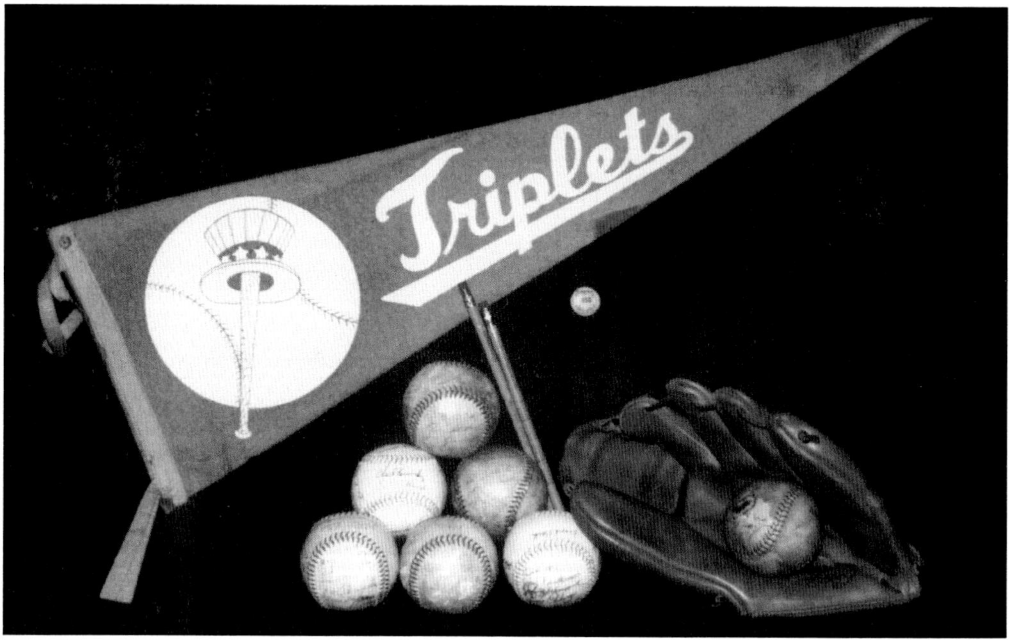

Five

A New Beginning in Binghamton

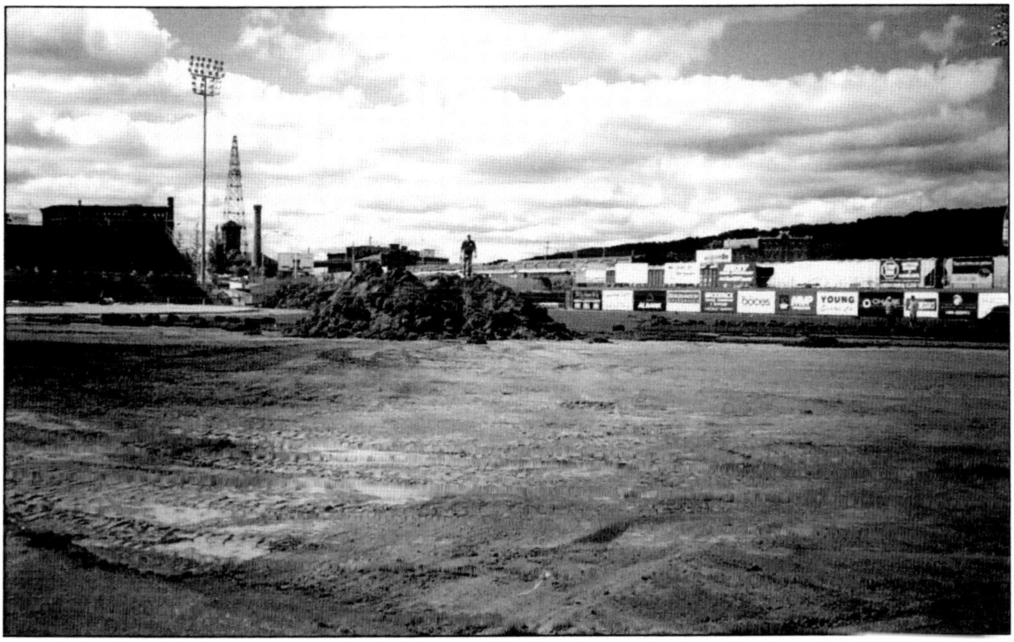

After the city of Binghamton spent $115,000 on demolition and clearance of the site at Henry and Fayette Streets, other problems were discovered. Nearly $100,000 more was required to deal with asbestos removal in old buildings on the Henry Street railroad property. Another $400,000 was spent on mostly unused architectural designs. The New York Mets saved the project by providing the $6 million needed to actually build the stadium.

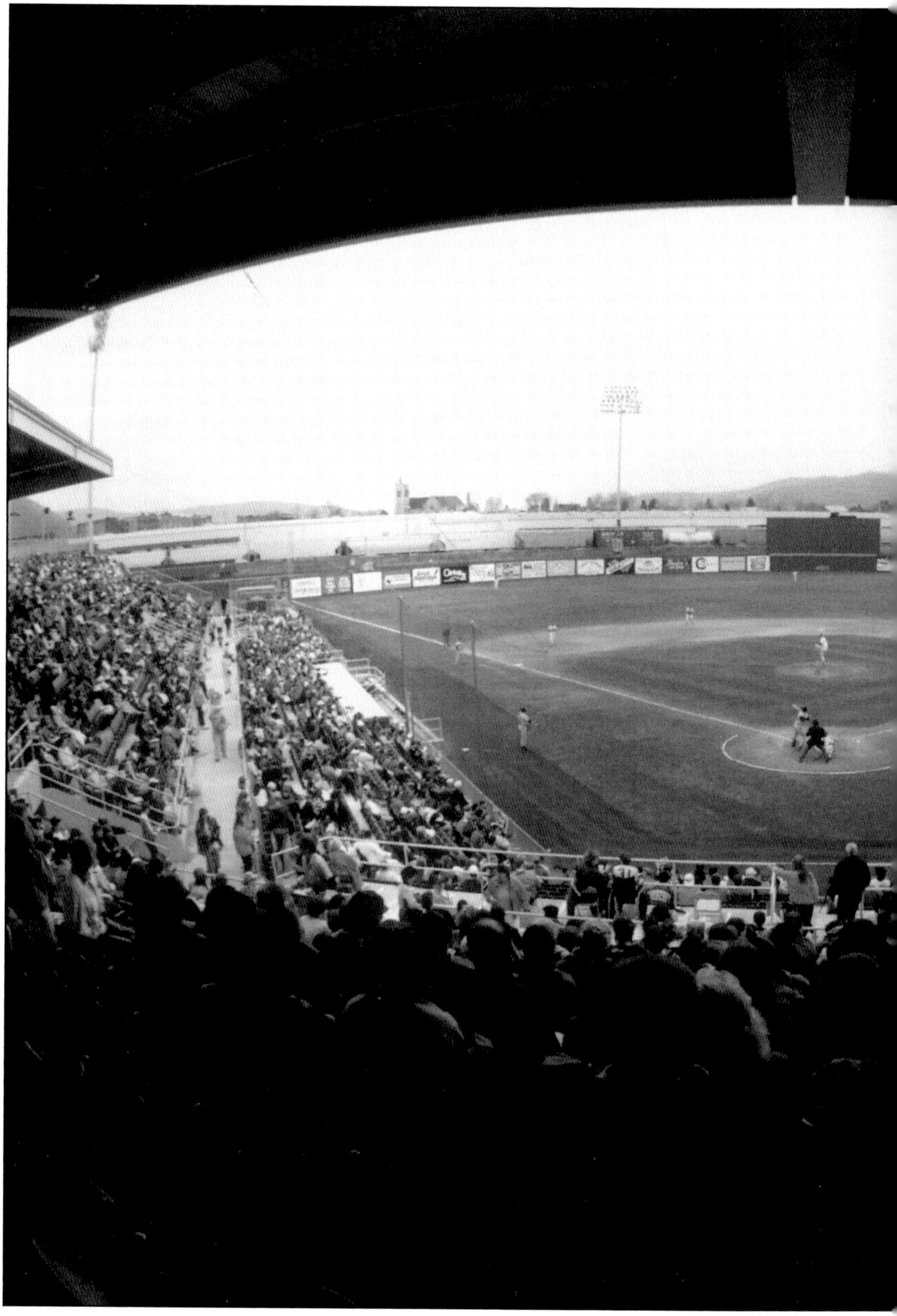

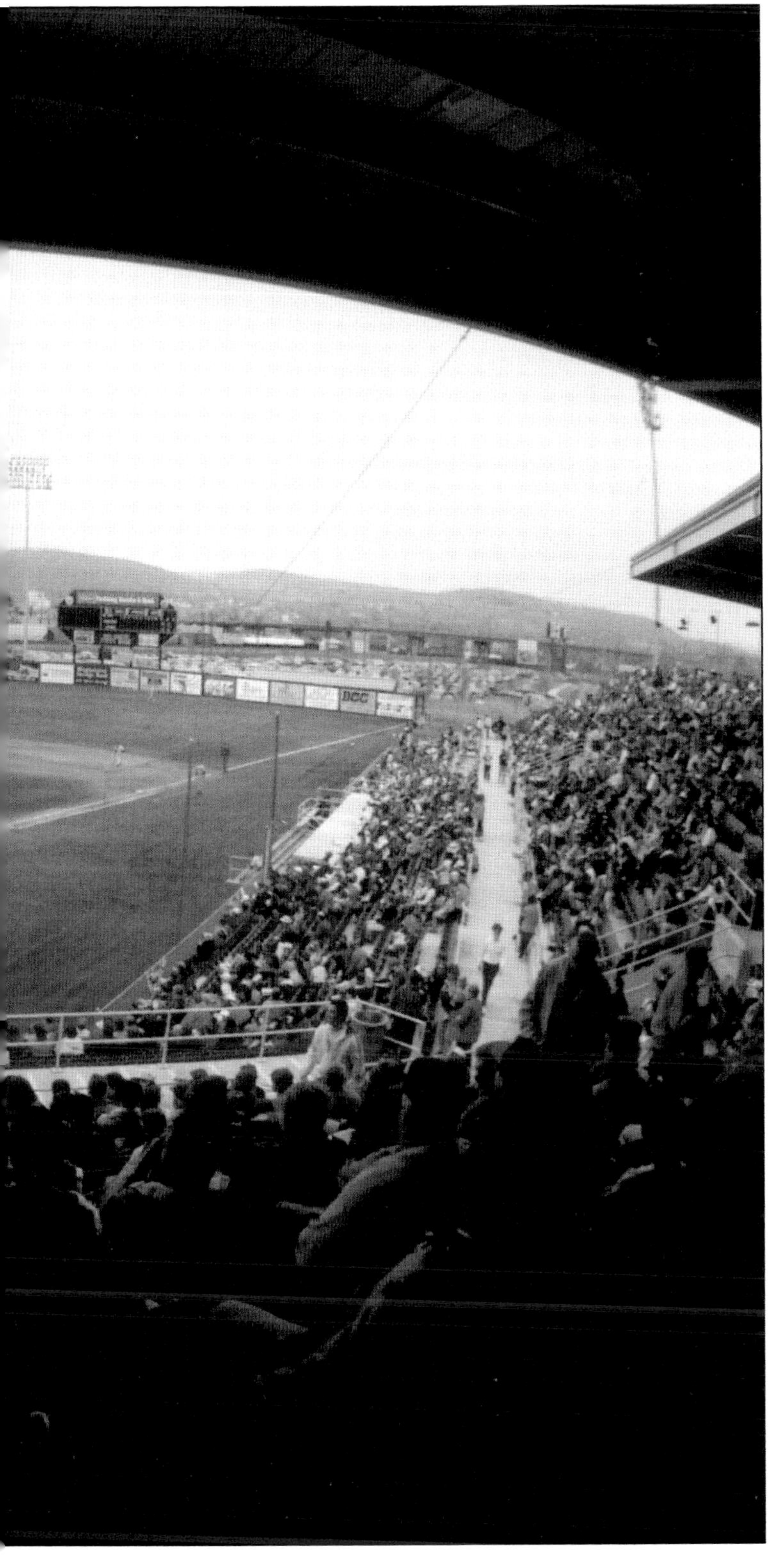

Minor-league baseball returned to the Triple Cities in 1992 as a brand-new stadium welcomed the Binghamton Mets. The beautifully laid out park, with excellent lighting for night games, was the culmination of years of work to raise the necessary funding and, in the end, a last-minute rescue by the New York Mets organization. (Note the train passing beyond the outfield fence.)

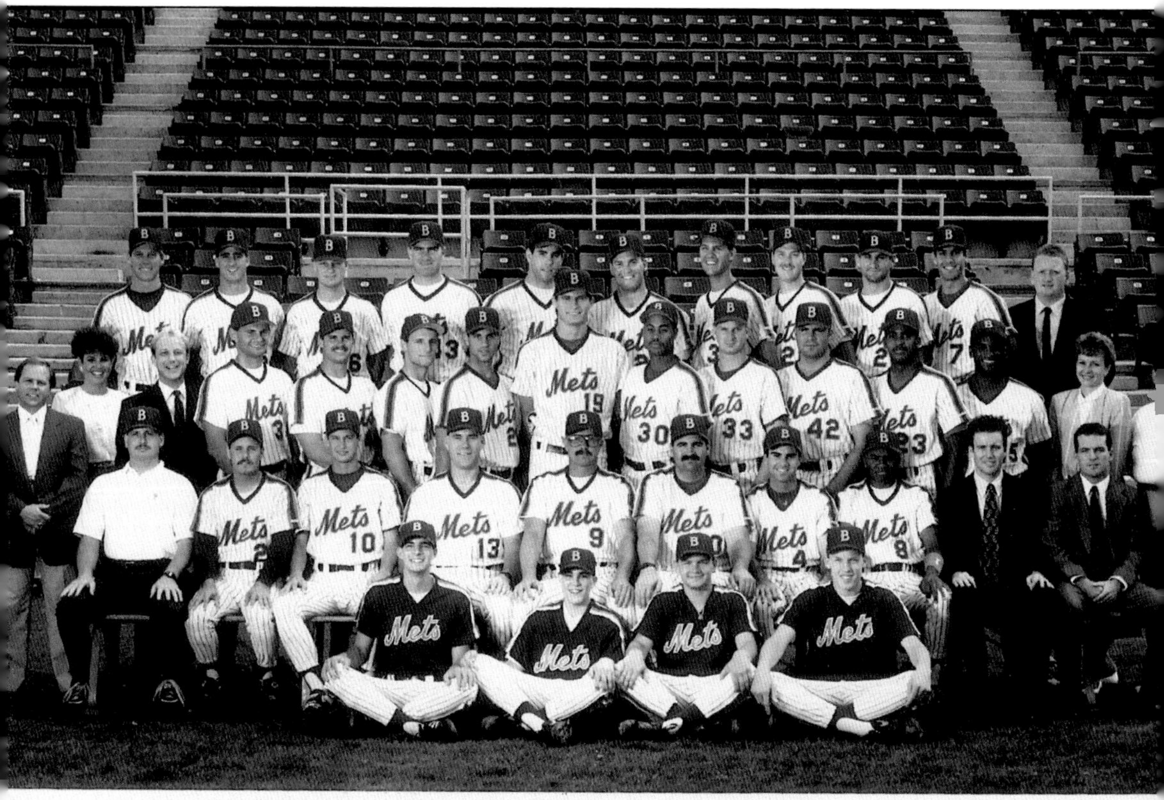

1992 BINGHAMTON METS

First Row: Andy Thompson, Emmet Gaube, Mike Dorrington, Bob Hollenbeck (Bat Boys)

Second Row: R.C. Reuteman (GM), Joe Hawkins (Trainer), Sean Fenton (BP Catcher), Tom Allison, Ron Gideon (Coach), Steve Swisher (Mgr.), Randy Niemann (Coach), Rob Katzaroff, Mark White (Asst. GM), Joe Barr (Admin. Asst.)

Third Row: Meghan Molnar (Mktg. Dir.), Charles Carlson (Oper. Dir.), Andy Dziadkowiec, Mike White, Dennis Harriger, Joe Delli Carri, Joe Vitko, Bert Hunter, Andy Reich, David Proctor Martinez, Curtis Pride, Ann Morris (Bus. Mgr.), Tony Cleary (Equip. Mgr.)

Fourth Row: Chris Butterfield, Brook Fordyce, Todd Douma, Bobby Jones, John Johnstone, Gregg Langbehn, Jamie Hoffner, Chris Dorn, Doug Saunders, Alan Zinter, Scott Decosse (Ad

Photo by Ed Aswad ©

This is the remarkable B-Mets team that won the Eastern League title in its first year. The team batting average of .245 was second lowest in the league and has proven to be the worst in the franchise's brief history. They also hit the least home runs in the league (77), and their 63 stolen bases were their worst ever. Pitching saved them—especially the 3.12 ERA that no Eastern League team has ever equaled.

Joe Vitko pitched the first home game ever for the Binghamton Mets in 1992 and made it special by hurling a shutout. He and Bobby Jones also won playoff games that year. The two hurlers led the staff with 12 wins each, and both had four complete games. Vitko got to appear in three games for the New York Mets that year but, unlike Jones, failed to impress.

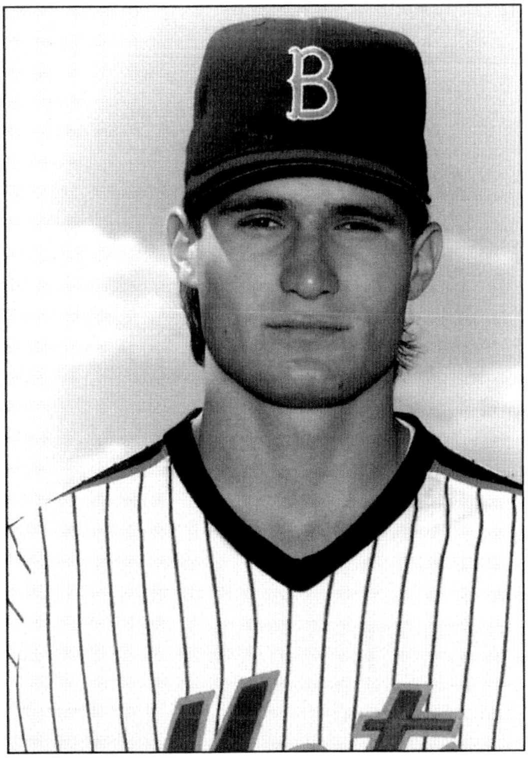

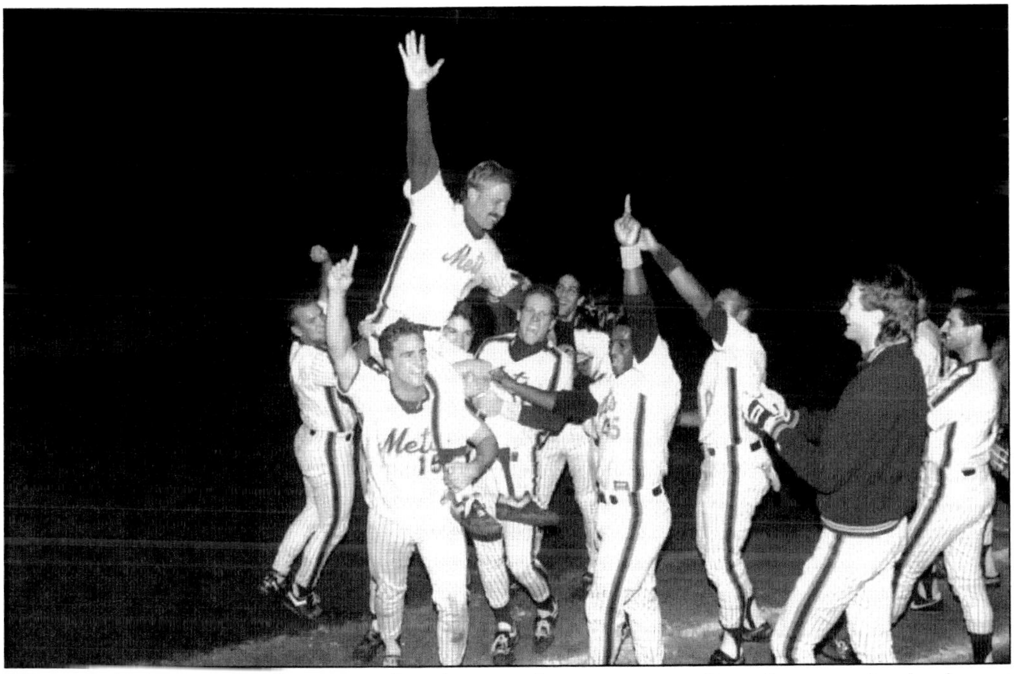

What could be sweeter for a new franchise, under new ownership, than to win the league championship in its first try? Manager Steve Swisher, being hoisted here by his exuberant players, enjoys such a moment. They had finished in second place by only one game during the regular season but won it all in the playoffs.

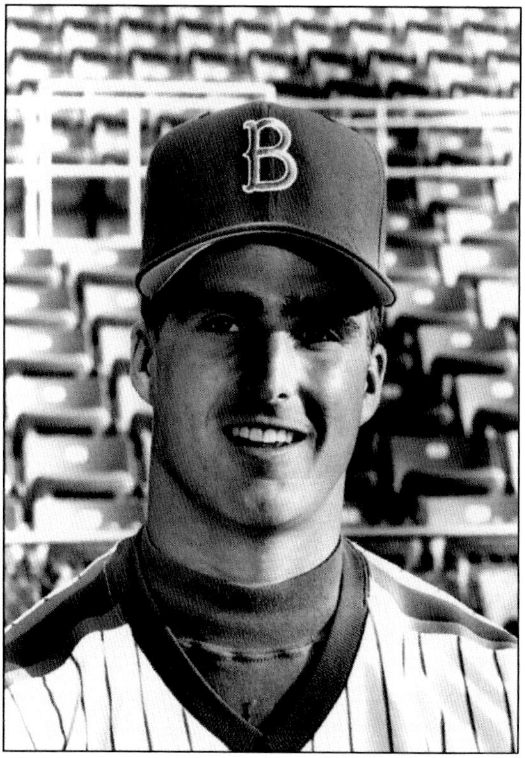

Brook Fordyce, now with the Baltimore Orioles, was an overwhelming choice as the catcher on the B-Mets 10th anniversary All-Star team. In the club's initial year, 1992, he had hit .278, led the team with 30 doubles, and handled the young pitching staff so well that it recorded a 3.12 ERA that has not been equaled since.

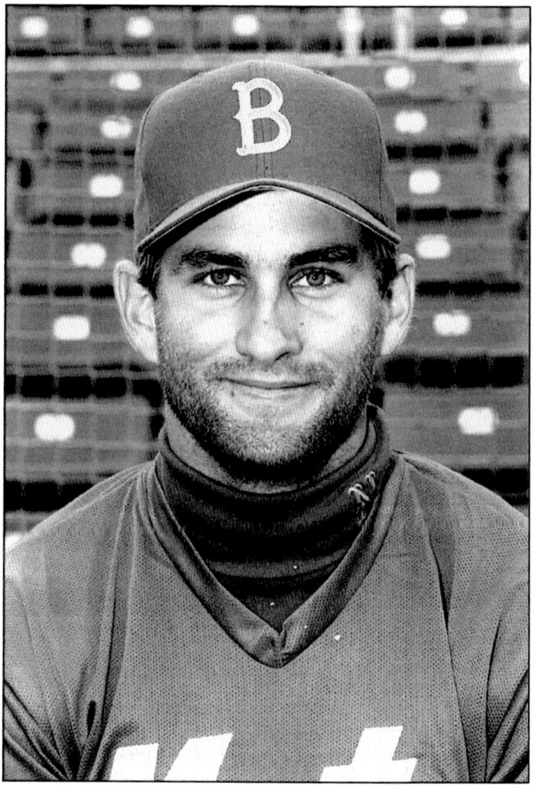

Doug Saunders spent the seasons of 1992 and 1994 with the B-Mets. What makes this unusual is that he spent 1993 in the major leagues as an infielder for the New York Mets. At age 23, he got into 27 games for that last-place team. He hit only .209, but Double-A pitching looked a lot easier to him after that experience. After hitting only .248 in 1992, he batted .294 in 1994.

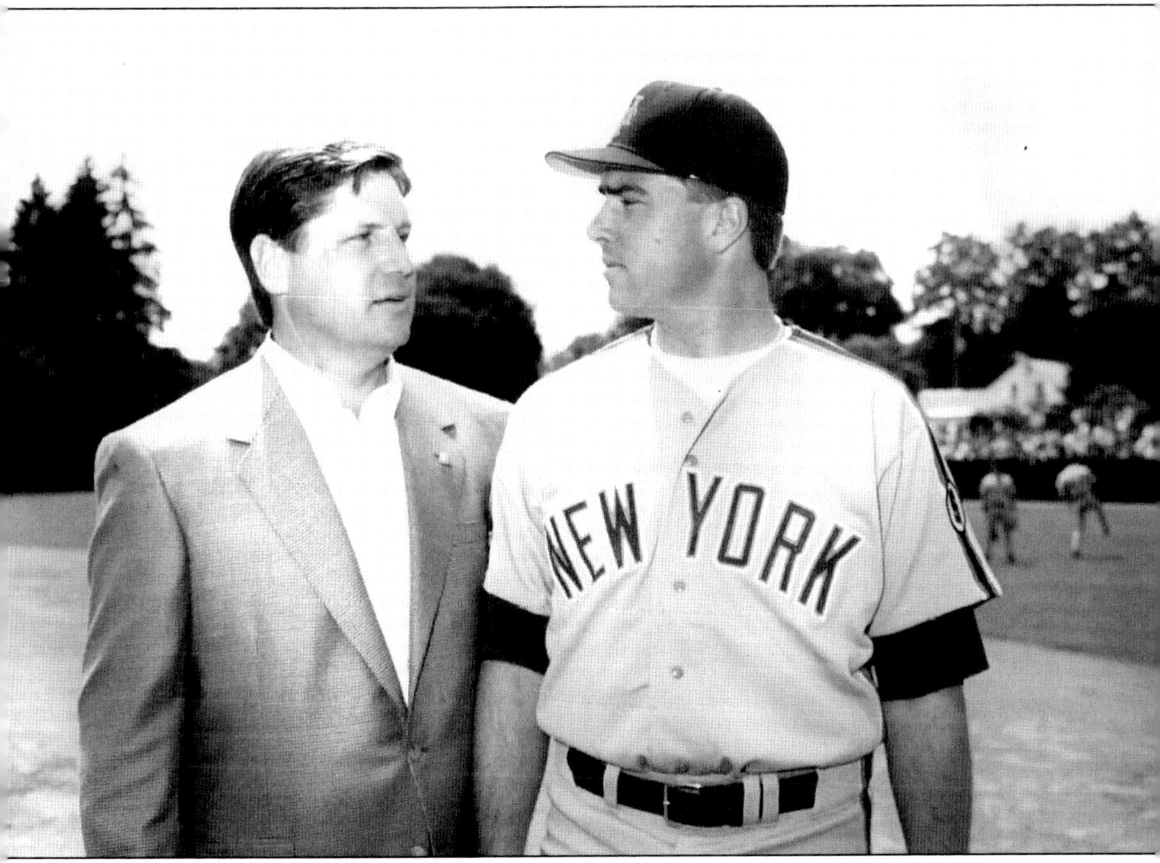

Bobby Jones (right), who had been the pitching leader for the 1992 B-Mets in their inaugural year championship drive, listens carefully to Hall of Famer Tom Seaver. Could Jones have had a better mentor? "Tom Terrific," as Seaver was known, won 311 games during a 20-year Hall of Fame career. During that time, he struck out 3,640 batters, threw 61 shutouts, and had an ERA of 2.86.

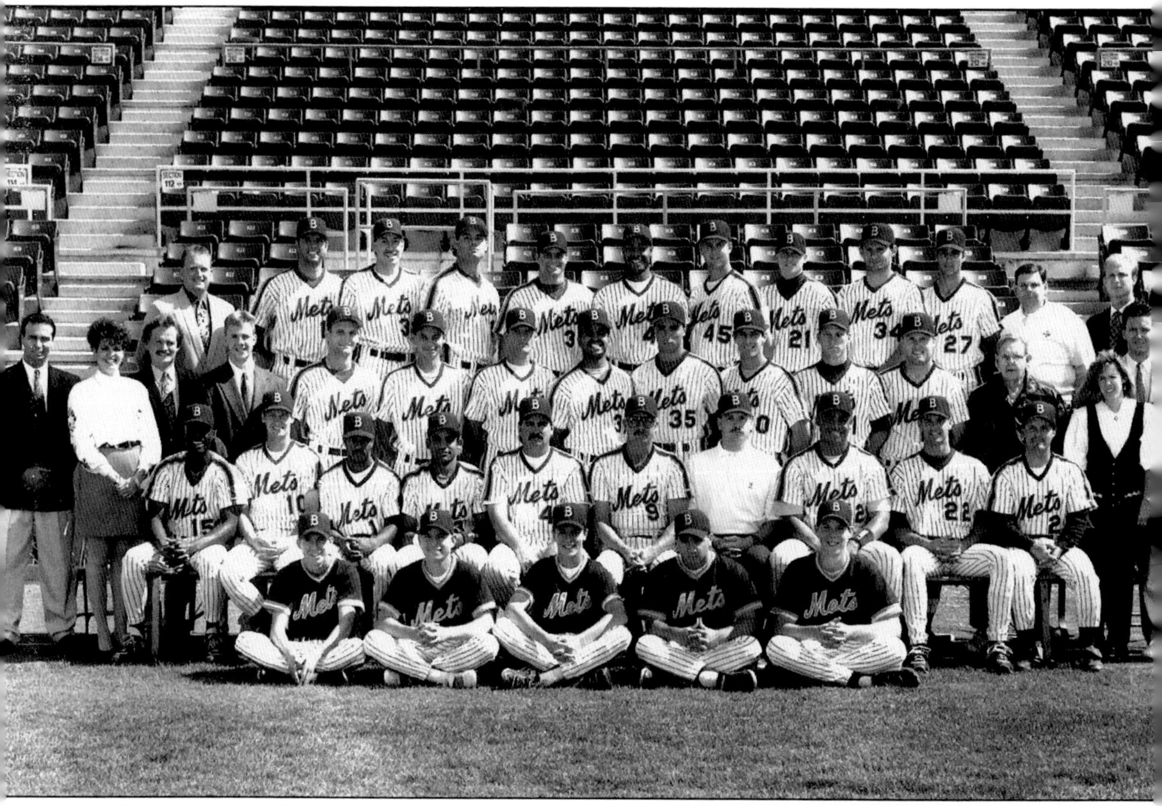

Things got a little rougher for former major-leaguer, and now manager, Steve Swisher and his B-Mets in 1993. The team finished fifth, missing the playoffs completely. A poor start, 15 wins in their first 48 games, ruined their season. On the bright side, four B-Mets made the Eastern League All-Star squad: Butch Huskey, Alan Zinter, Quilvio Veras, and Dennis Harriger. Harriger had the best ERA in the league, 2.95.

Butch Huskey won the William J. McGowan Award in 1993 as the team's Most Valuable Player. This award is special because the players themselves do the voting. Huskey certainly deserved it. In 526 at-bats, he racked up 232 total bases, with 25 home runs, and 98 RBIs. Those were all team-leading records for the year.

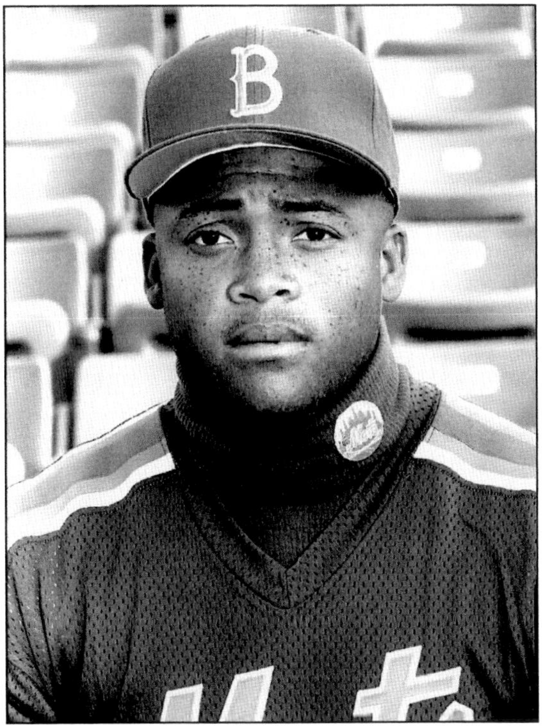

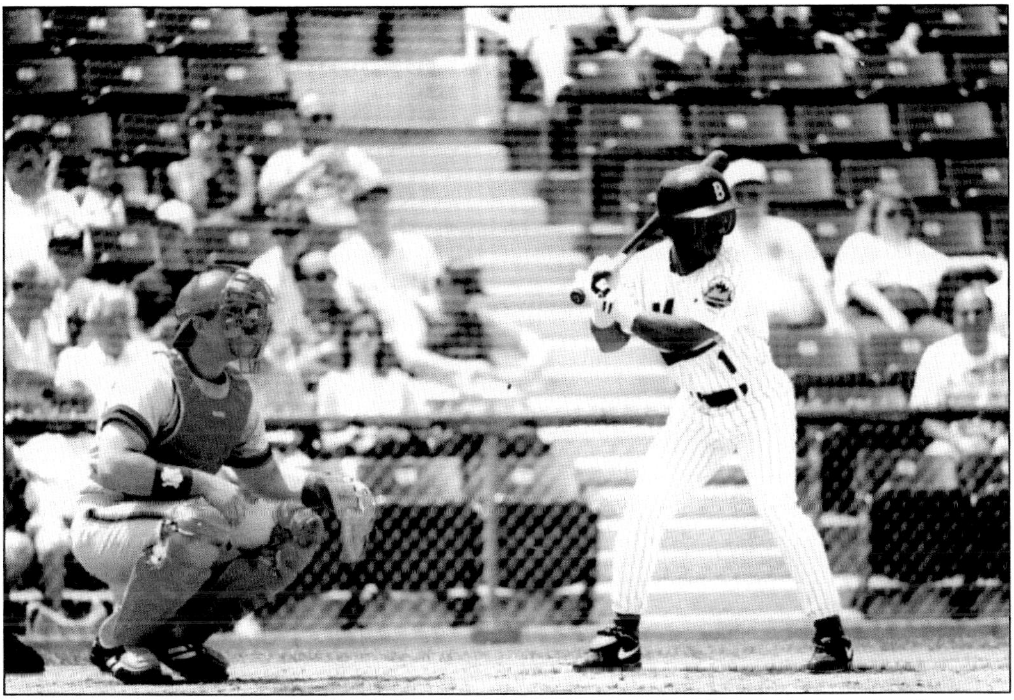

Ricky Otero was the speedy leadoff hitter for the B-Mets in 1993 and 1994. In his first year, he batted .264 and led the club in triples with 10. For the Eastern League champion B-Mets of 1994, he led the club once more in triples (9), as well as in hits (156), runs (96), and stolen bases (33). He was promoted to the New York Mets in 1995.

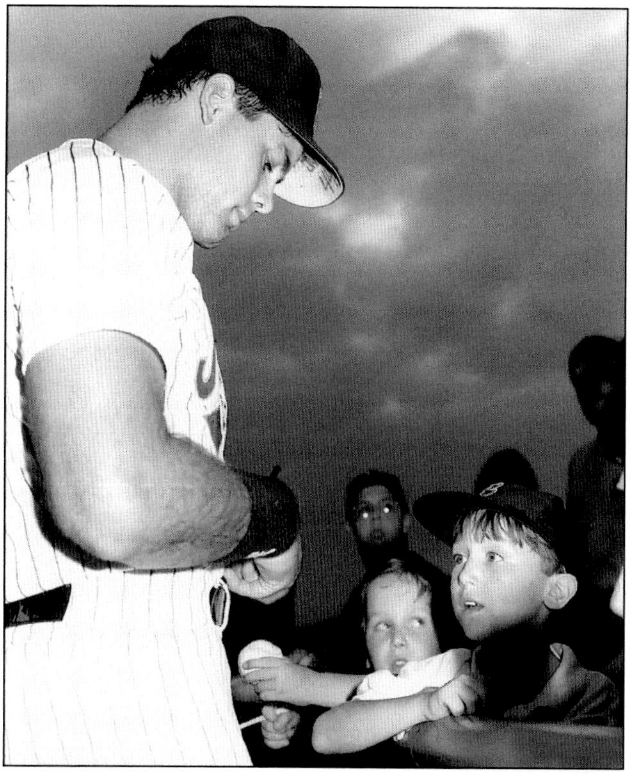

Frank Jacobs signs an autograph for an awed fan. The burly first baseman spent three seasons with the B-Mets (1993–1995). He hit .269 in his first year, then improved to .285 and .294 in 1994 and 1995. Frank was among the top five B-Mets in single-year batting average and doubles for the franchise's first four years.

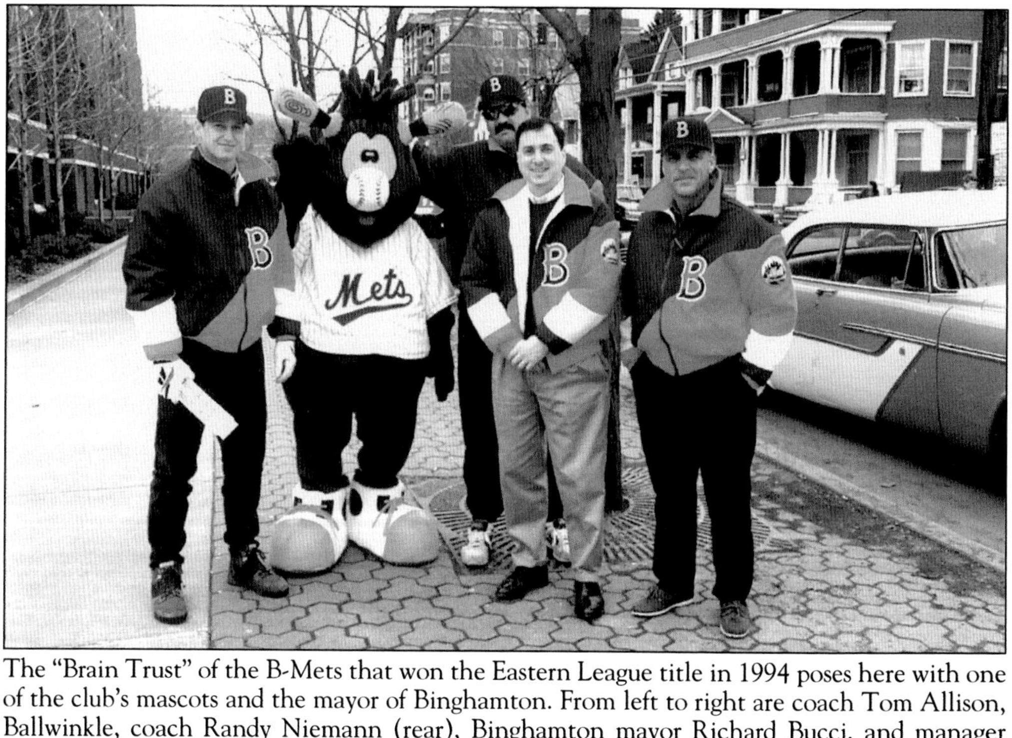

The "Brain Trust" of the B-Mets that won the Eastern League title in 1994 poses here with one of the club's mascots and the mayor of Binghamton. From left to right are coach Tom Allison, Ballwinkle, coach Randy Niemann (rear), Binghamton mayor Richard Bucci, and manager John Tamargo. It was the B-Mets' second championship in only its third year of existence.

In 1937, Al Reiss pitched a no-hitter for Wilkes-Barre in a playoff game. Unfortunately, Elmira won the championship anyway. Fifty-seven years later, the second no-hitter in the playoff history of the Eastern League was thrown by Bill Pulsipher. This one came in the second game of the championship series and helped the Binghamton Mets to win it all in 1994.

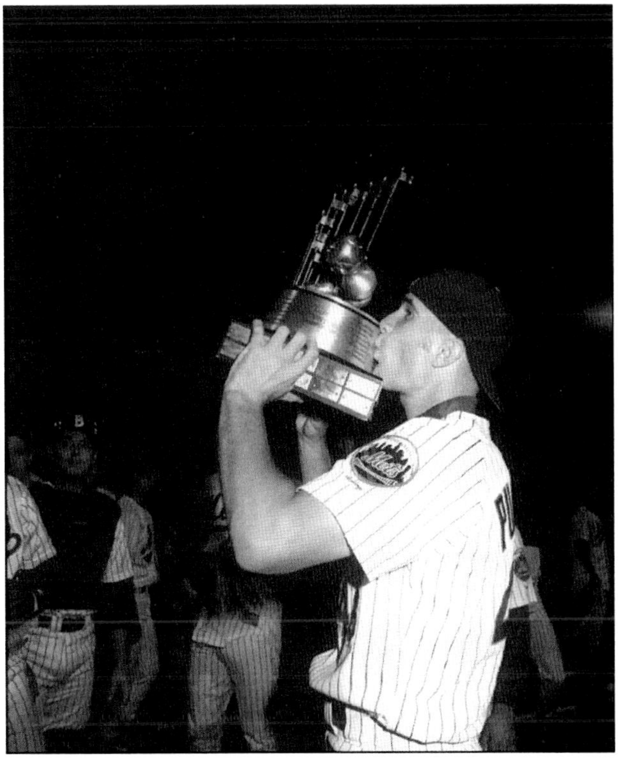

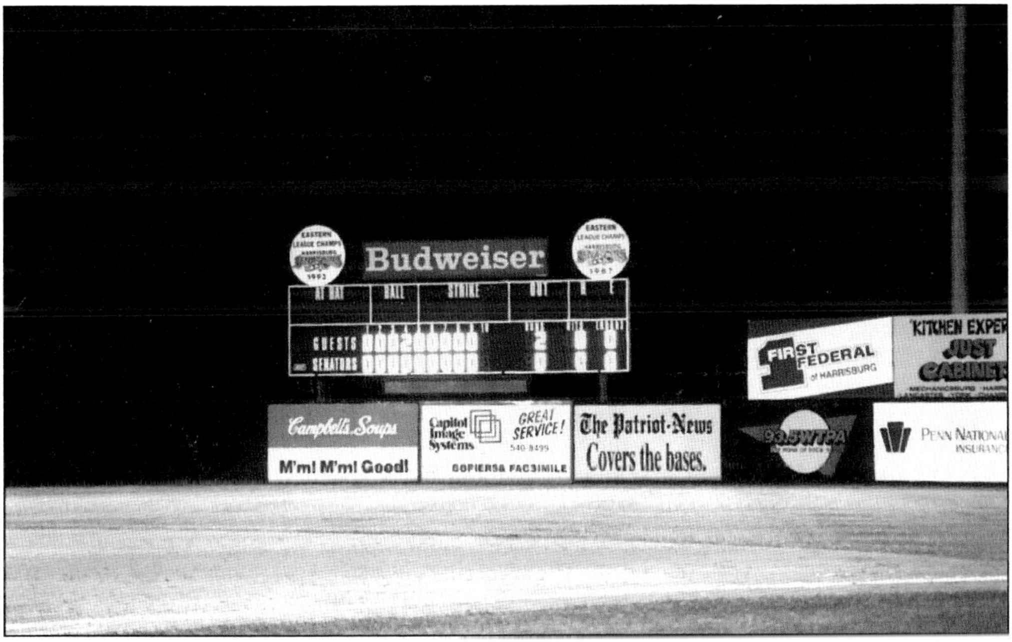

One of the greatest thrills that a fan can experience is being present when a no-hitter is thrown. The tension mounts, inning by inning, for everyone in the stadium and on the field. It then reaches a peak in the ninth inning. The experience is even more intense when it happens in a playoff game. The scoreboard on September 12, 1994, records the achievement of Bill Pulsipher in the second game of the championship finals in Harrisburg.

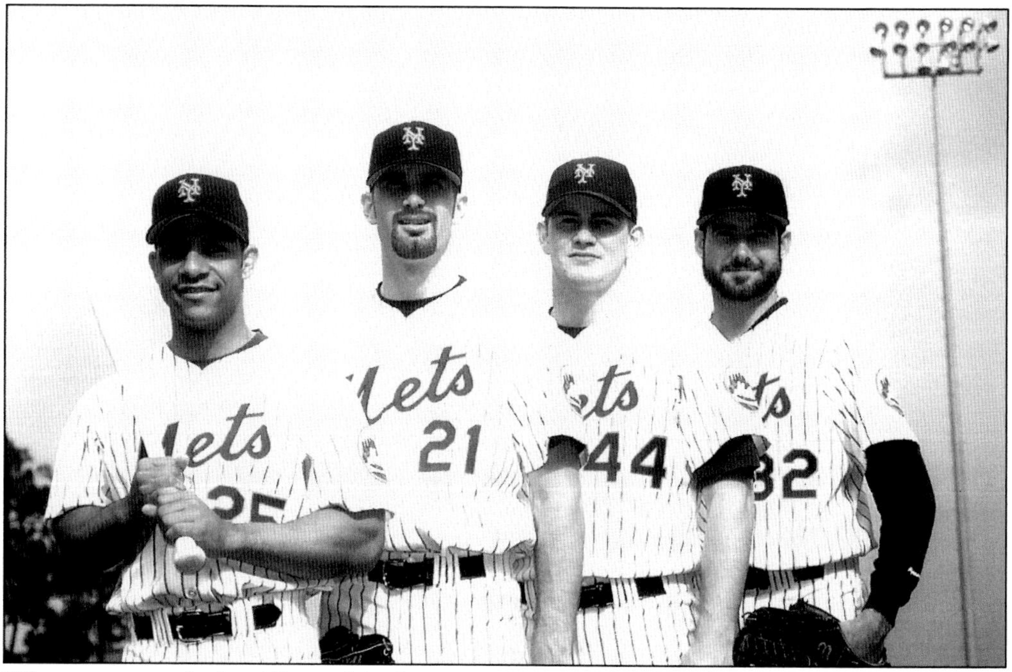

What a quartet of talent! Four of the best prospects ever developed for a parent club pose here. They are, from left to right, Jay Payton, Bill Pulsipher, Jason Isringhausen, and Paul Wilson. All four are currently in the major leagues, although not with the Mets. Was Payton holding a bat so that no one would mistake him for a pitcher?

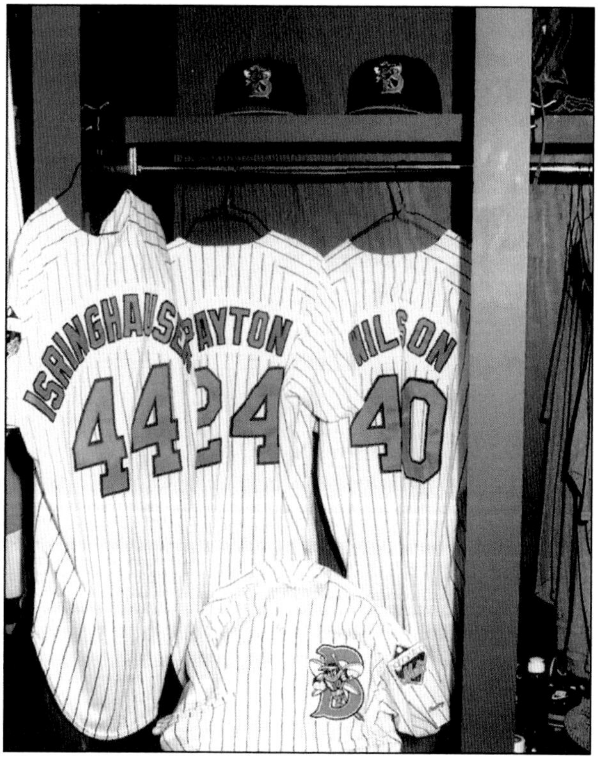

The jerseys of future stars Jason Isringhausen, Jay Payton, and Paul Wilson are displayed here. Isringhausen, a B-Met in 1994–1995, went to the Mets and now stars as a reliever for St. Louis. Payton was a B-Met from 1994 to 1996 and currently patrols the outfield for the Colorado Rockies. Wilson, despite many physical setbacks since going to the Mets in 1996, is with Cincinnati.

The B-Mets got their first look at Joe Crawford for a brief 14 innings in 1994. They liked what they saw, and Crawford returned to go 7-2 in 1995. After posting a 5-1 mark in 50 innings in 1996, Crawford had made his point. His ERA that year was a miniscule 1.45. Not surprisingly, Crawford was on the New York Mets roster in 1997.

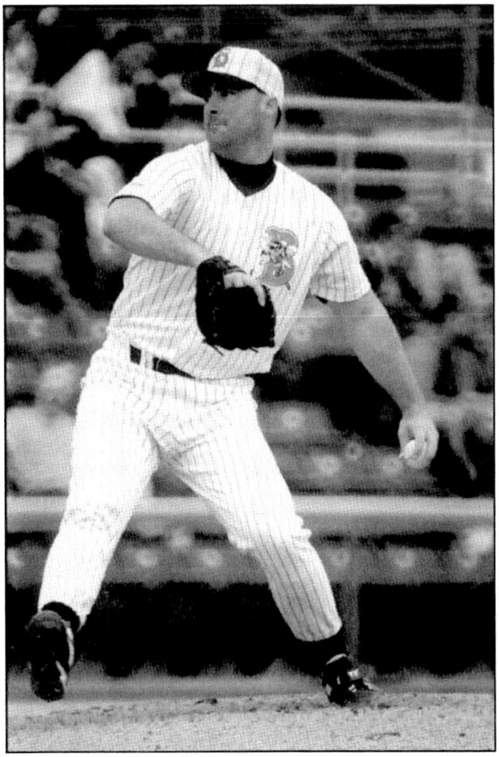

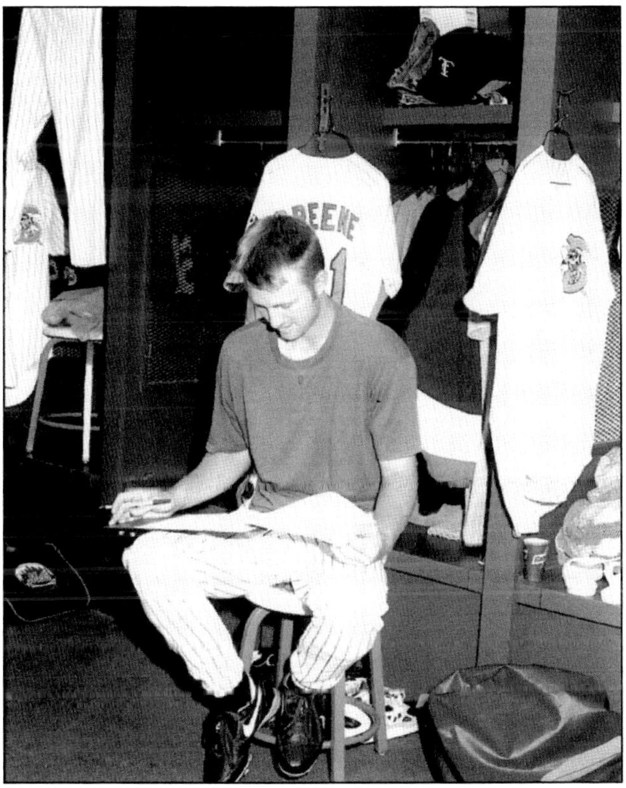

Most fans are aware of the physical beating that catchers take over the course of a season. However, it is easy to forget that a lot of studying is required for a catcher to be successful. He must know not only his own pitchers' strengths and weaknesses but also those of all of the opposing team's hitters. Here, B-Mets catcher Charlie Greene, who was with the club from 1994 to 1996, does his homework.

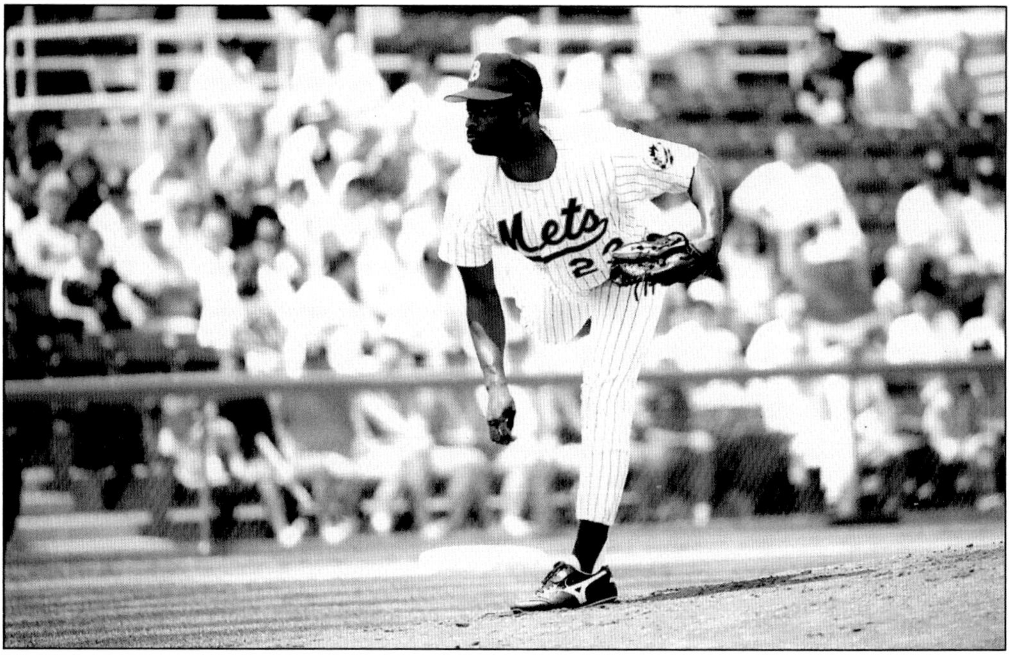

The Mets acquired Robert Person from the Florida Marlins in 1994 and assigned him to the B-Mets. In 1993, he had struck out 107 batters in 28 games for the High Desert club in the California League. Person struck out 130 batters for Binghamton and had two shutouts, while compiling a 9-6 record. After only 67 innings of pitching in 1995, he was called up by the New York Mets.

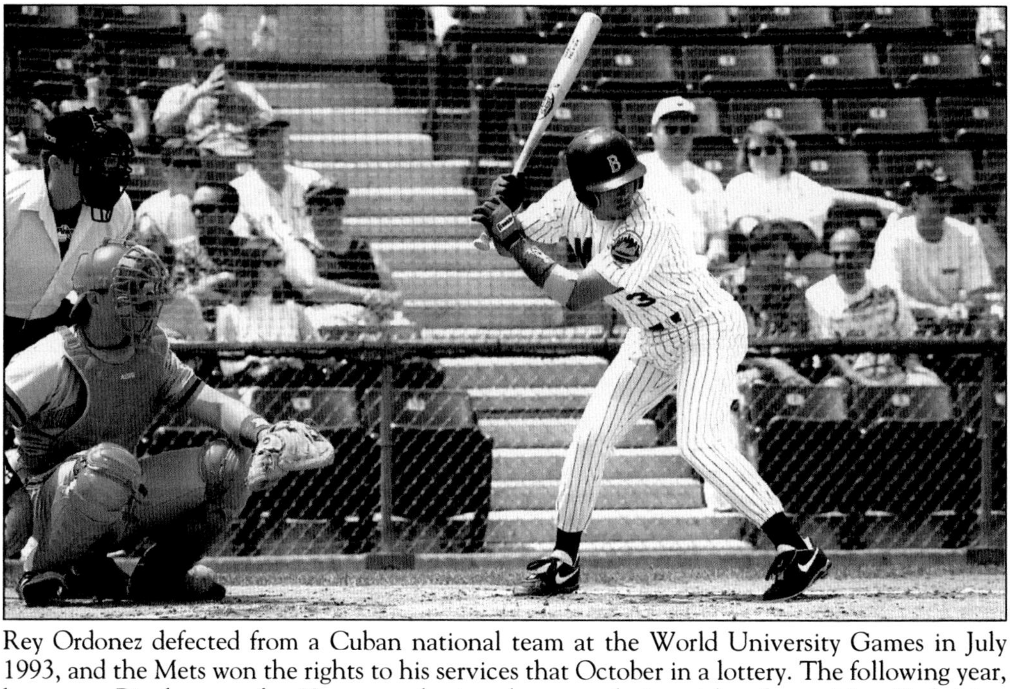

Rey Ordonez defected from a Cuban national team at the World University Games in July 1993, and the Mets won the rights to his services that October in a lottery. The following year, he was at Binghamton for 48 games, sharing shortstop duties with a future New York Mets teammate, Edgardo Alfonzo. By June 2003, Ordonez was with Tampa Bay and hitting .316.

In 1995, the Binghamton Mets introduced a new mascot: Buddy the Bee. The outfit was designed by Guy Gilchrist, best known for his creation of the Muppets comic strip for Jim Henson. Buddy quickly became a fan favorite, as well as a popular symbol of the organization. He is shown here in a promotion with the millionth fan, Bob Kutz.

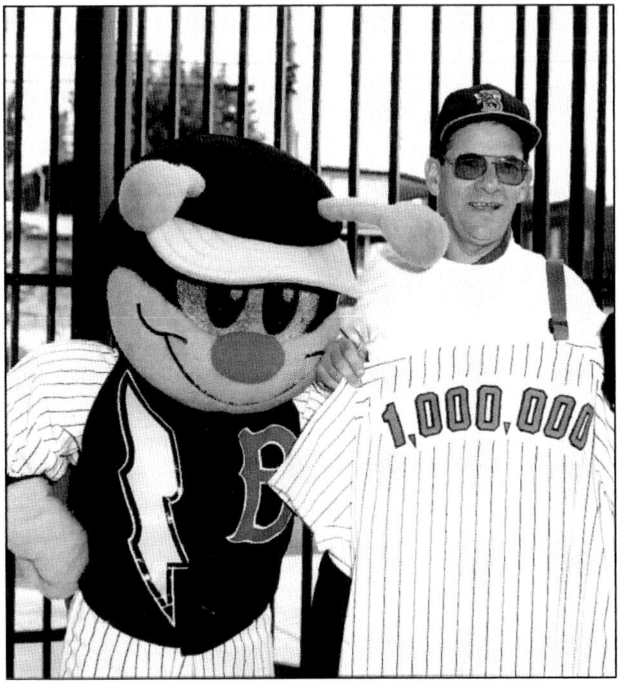

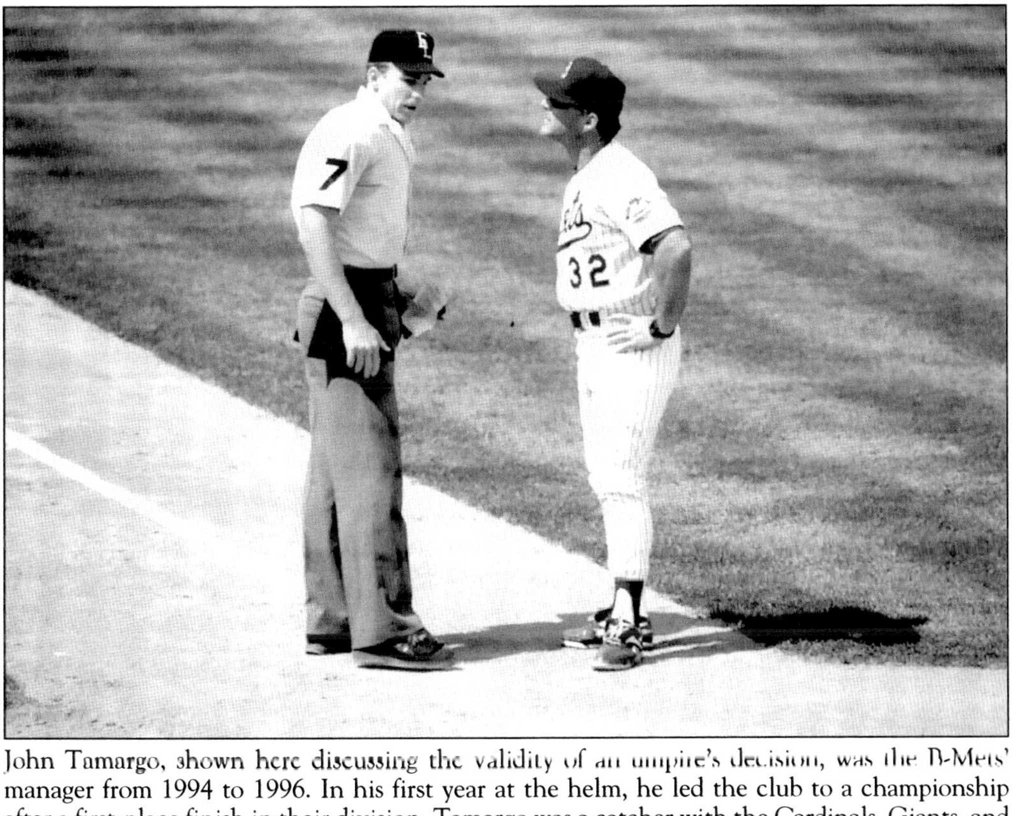

John Tamargo, shown here discussing the validity of an umpire's decision, was the B-Mets' manager from 1994 to 1996. In his first year at the helm, he led the club to a championship after a first-place finish in their division. Tamargo was a catcher with the Cardinals, Giants, and Expos. He was hitting .275 when a finger injury cut short his major-league career in 1980.

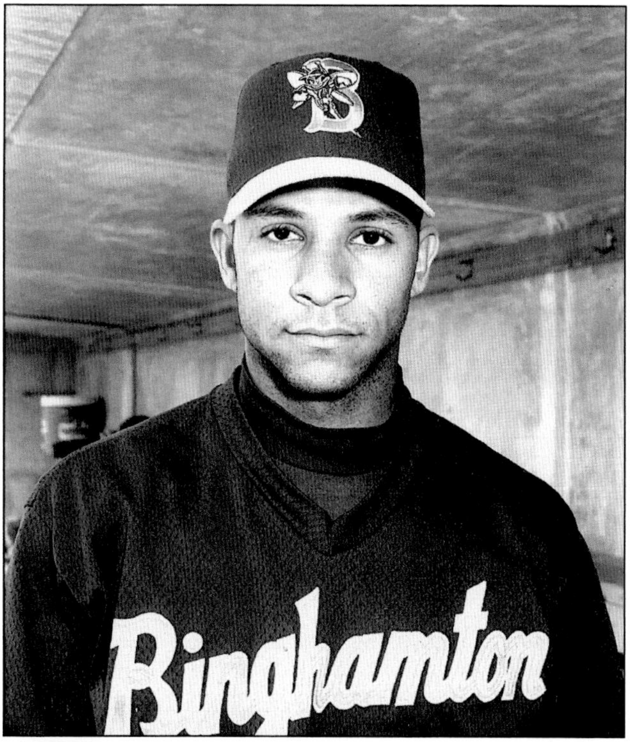

Jay Payton joined the Mets organization after starring at Georgia Tech. In 1995, after hitting a B-Mets franchise record .345, slamming 14 homers, and driving in 54 runs in only 85 games, he was quickly promoted to Norfolk. That performance earned him the unusual combination of Most Valuable Player and Rookie of the Year honors in the Eastern League for that year.

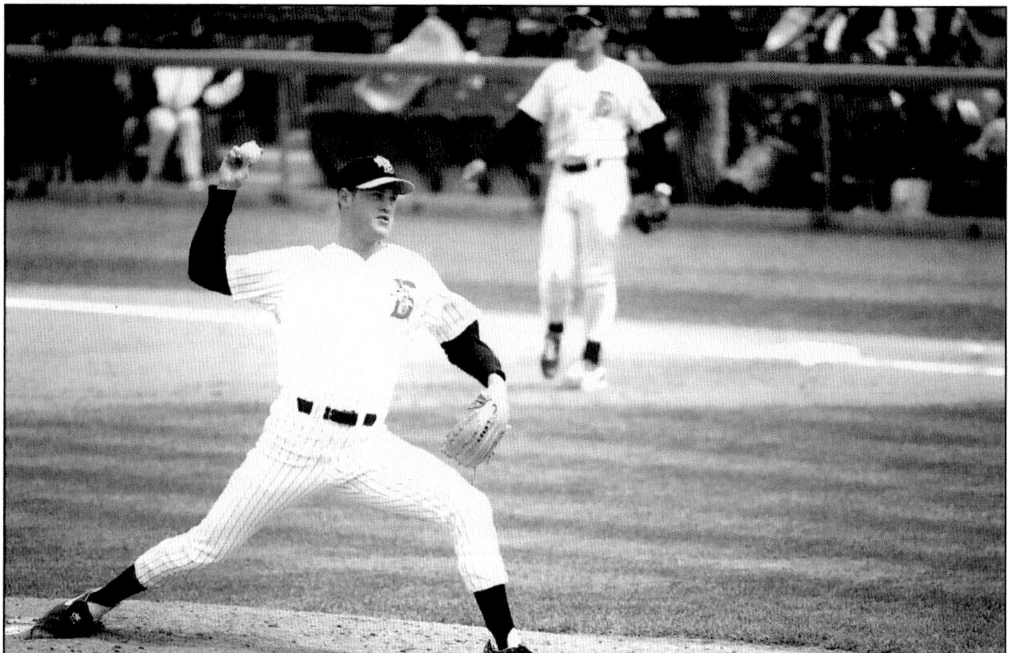

Erik Ludwick joined the B-Mets in 1995 and immediately established himself as a premier pitcher. He led the club in wins (12), complete games (3), and shutouts (2). Considering that Paul Wilson and Jason Isringhausen were on that staff, the competition was fierce. By 1996, Ludwick was a St. Louis Cardinal.

In the 1995 *Mets Magazine*, 10 top prospects were featured. Benny Agbajani was not one of them. He had hit only .251 for Pittsfield in the New York–Penn League in 1993. However, his .280 batting average in 1994 with St. Lucie got him a look from the B-Mets. He hit a quiet .275, with 60 RBIs, in 88 games. Agbajani's talent, however, was obvious, and in 1998, he was wearing a New York Mets uniform.

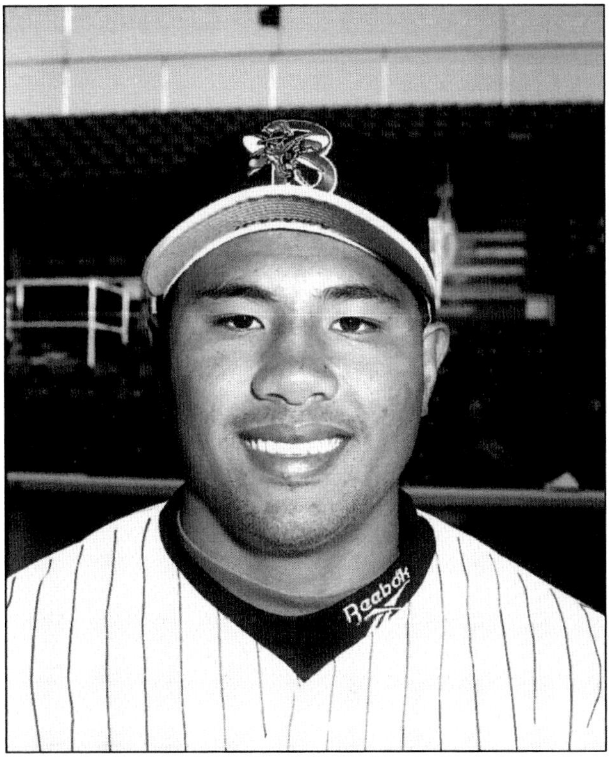

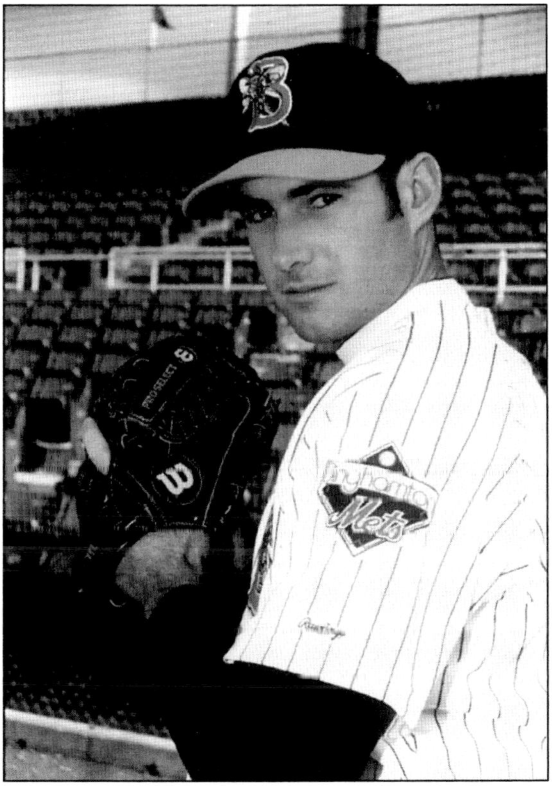

After being the pitching ace of Team USA in 1993, Paul Wilson was the Mets' No. 1 pick in the 1994 draft. In his first year with the B-Mets, 1995, he led the staff with a 2.17 ERA. He struck out 120 batters and finished with a 6-3 record. By the following year, he had been promoted and is now a highly regarded major-league hurler for the Cincinnati Reds.

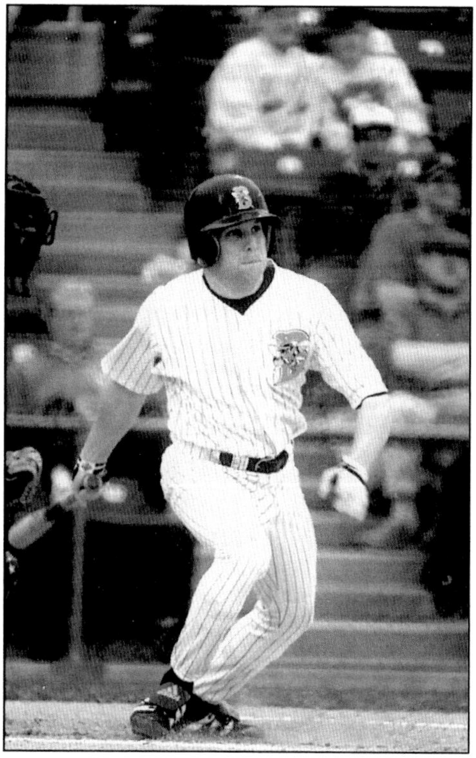

Jason Hardkte, obtained by the Mets organization from San Diego, had a .292 batting average after five years in the lower minors. In his three years with the B-Mets (1995–1997), the scrappy second baseman hit .286, .263, and .385, respectively. The last average is misleading since he was used in only six games. Hardkte had his moment in 1996, when he went to the Mets in September.

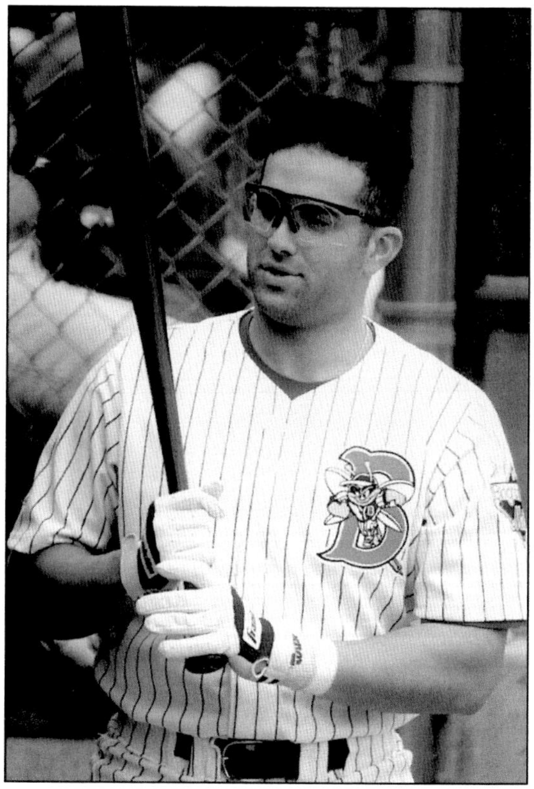

Pedro Grifol was known to be a strong defensive catcher. He also got to Binghamton in 1996 after five years in the lower minors. Grifol hit only .238, with seven homers. After hitting only .223 in 114 games in 1998, his future was definitely shaky. The arrival of some hard-hitting catching prospects in Binghamton in 1999 effectively ended the hopes of this Florida State athlete.

Dwight Maness was a fan favorite during his three seasons at Binghamton (1996–1998). However, he hit only .243 in 122 games that first year and was even worse in 1997 with a .189. Given one more chance in 1998, the speedy outfielder could muster only a .237 batting average in 25 games. That kind of performance does not get you to the next level.

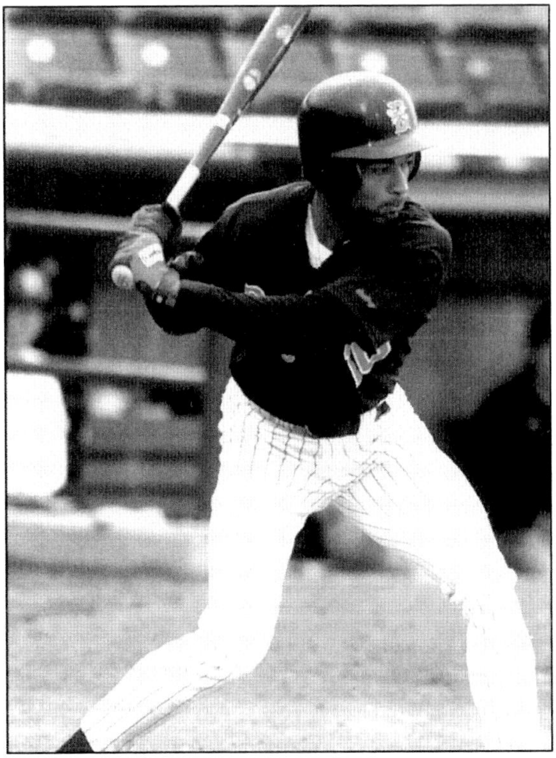

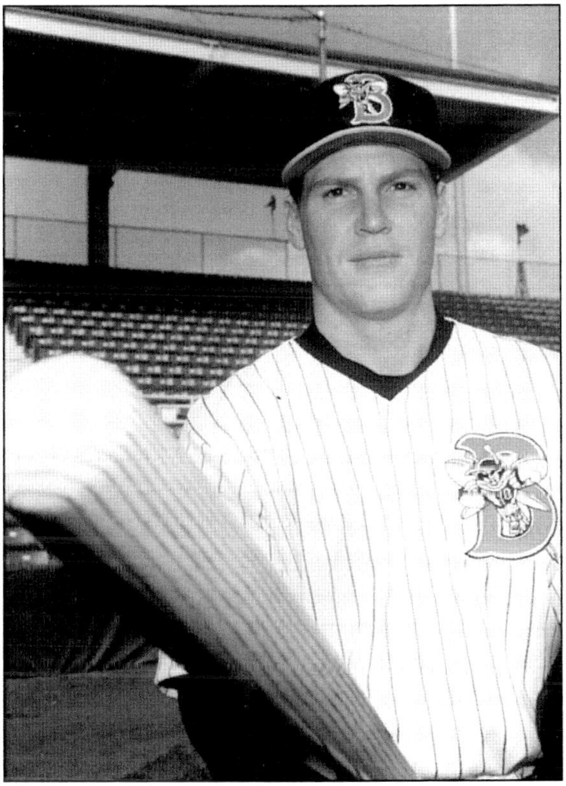

Chris Saunders always swung a big bat for the B-Mets. A third baseman with the club from 1994 to 1997, he hit .269 in his first year and then had his breakout year in 1996. That season, he led the club not only in batting average but also in hits (152), runs (82), total bases (236), doubles (27), and RBIs (105).

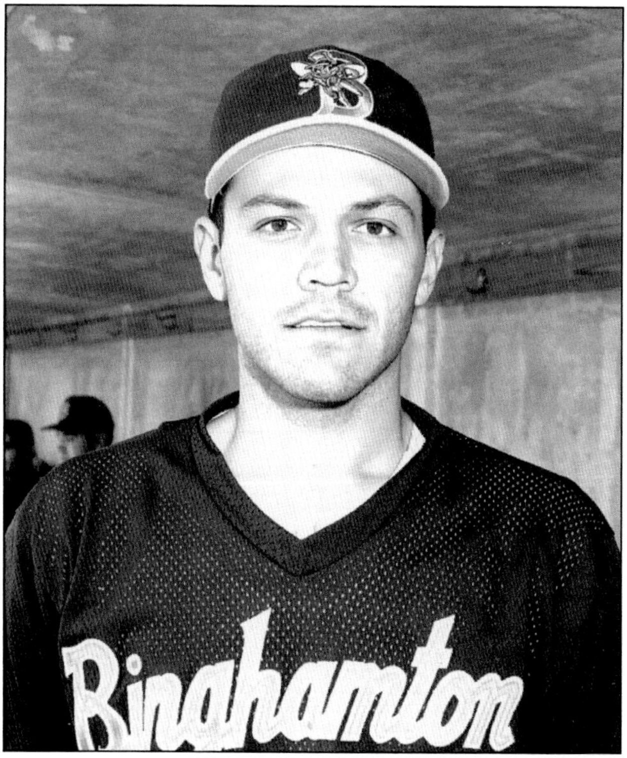

First base was a power base for the B-Mets in 1995–1996, with Brian Daubach handling the position. The future major-league slugger had 148 RBIs in those two years. In 1996, he hit .296 and led the club with 22 home runs. Daubach made his major-league debut with the Florida Marlins in 1998. In 2003, he was with the Chicago White Sox.

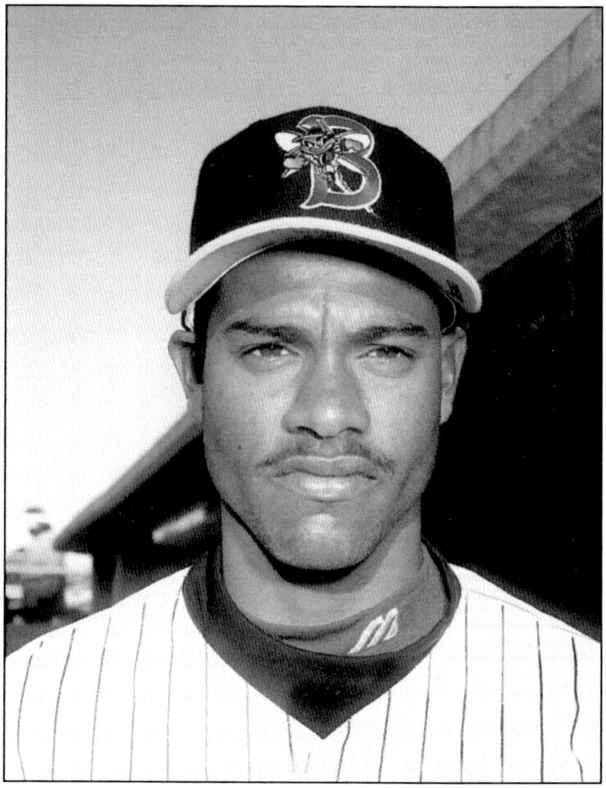

Rafael Roque was 0-4 with a 7.27 ERA in 1996, his first year with the B-Mets. He was not much better in 1997. In 26 innings of hurling, he had a 1-1 mark with a 6.84 ERA. However, somebody saw some potential in Roque. He was purchased by the Milwaukee Brewers and brought to the major leagues in 1998.

Corey Lidle became an instant star upon arriving in Binghamton in 1996. He led the pitching staff with 14 wins, matching Bill Pulsipher's club record, pitched the most innings (190), led in strikeouts (141), and had the most complete games (6). Corey might have been overlooked for the Eastern League All-Star team, but the following year he was with the New York Mets. In 2003, he was pitching for Toronto.

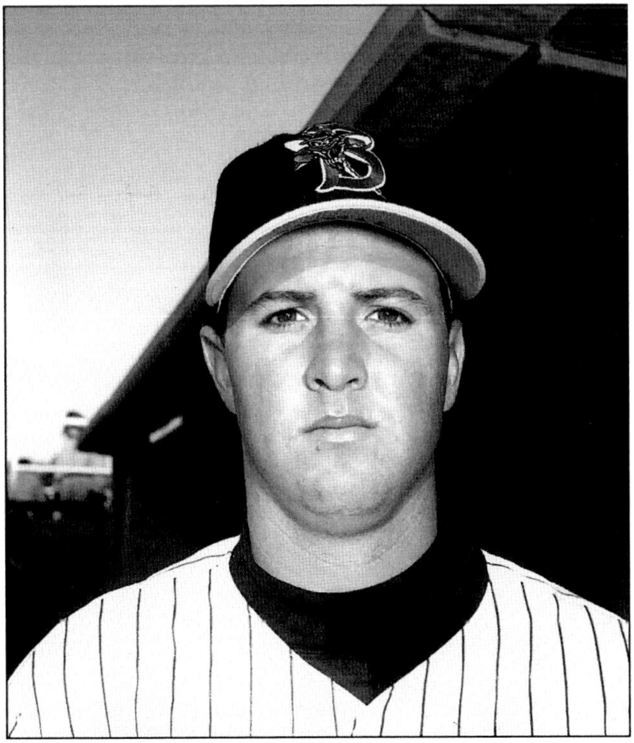

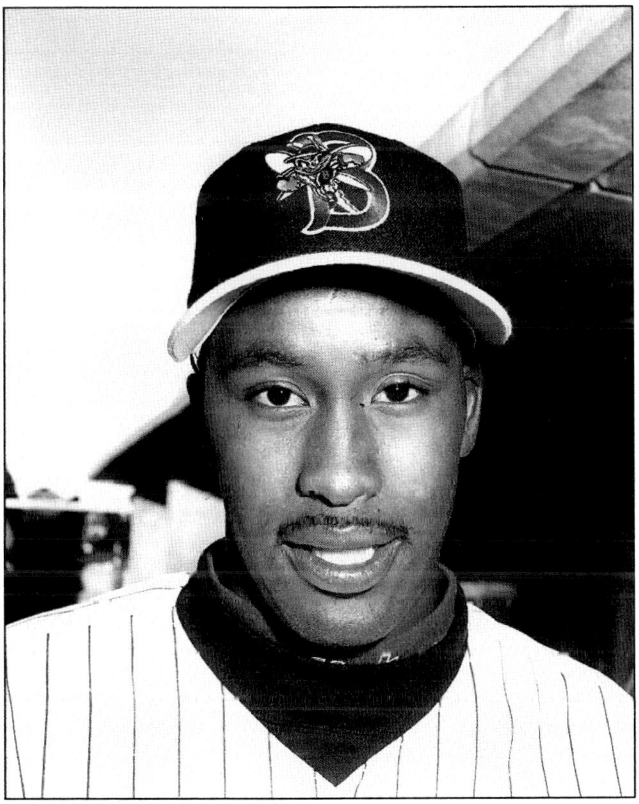

Terrell Lowery was in the outfield for the B-Mets in 1996. In 53 games, he hit .275 to lead the other seven outfield prospects. Scouts noticed, and in 1997, Terrell was roaming the ivied outfield of Wrigley Field as a Chicago Cub.

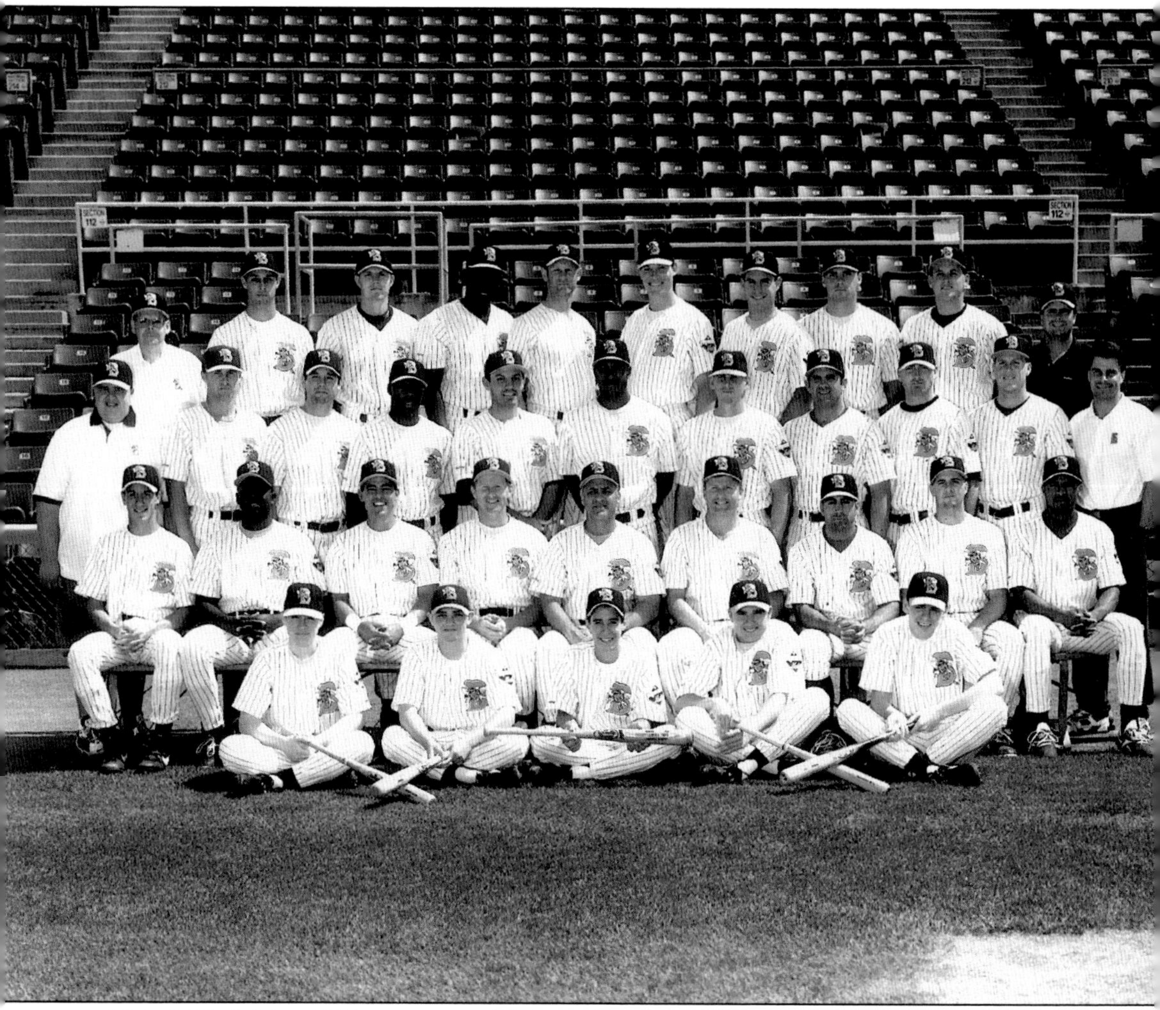

This 1997 club hit 182 home runs—70 more than in any previous season. Matt Raleigh led the power surge with 37. Unfortunately, the team also set a franchise high in strikeouts with 1,097. The pitching staff faltered too. Jesus Sanchez won 13 games, but Gooch, Sauerbach, Roberts, and Figueroa all lost more than they won. Not surprisingly, the B-Mets finished with the eighth worst won-lost record in the 10-team league.

Preston Wilson joined his former B-Mets teammate Jay Payton on the Colorado Rockies in 2003. By June, Wilson was among the leaders in the National League with 15 home runs. His breakout season with the B-Mets in 1997 led to him becoming a Met the very next year. His power surge should have come as no surprise. In 1995, with a Mets affiliate, the Capital City Bombers, he blasted 20 home runs.

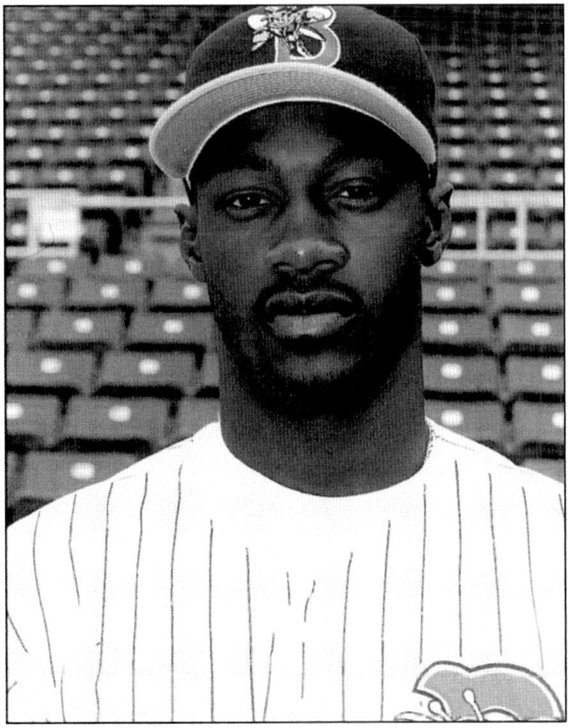

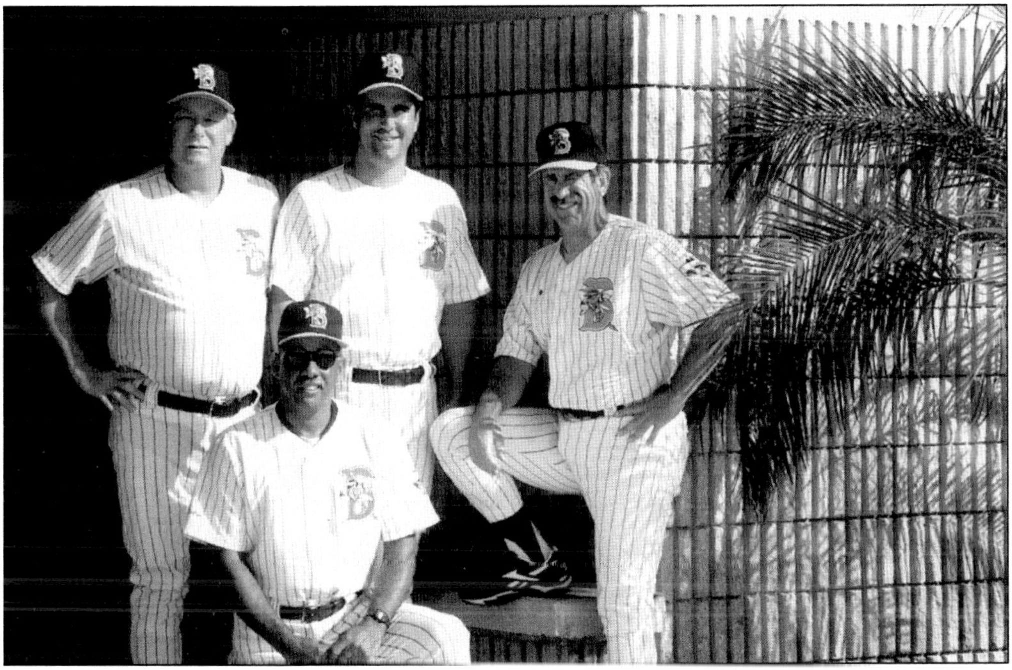

The B-Mets began the 1997 season with a new brain trust. Pictured here are coach Juan Lopez (kneeling), coaches Billy Champion (standing, left) and Howie Freiling (standing, center), and the new manager, Rick Sweet. After a second-place finish in their division in 1996, the club had high hopes for 1997. However, despite setting a team record with 182 home runs, they finished 10 games under .500 and missed the playoffs. Four years later, Freiling was the manager.

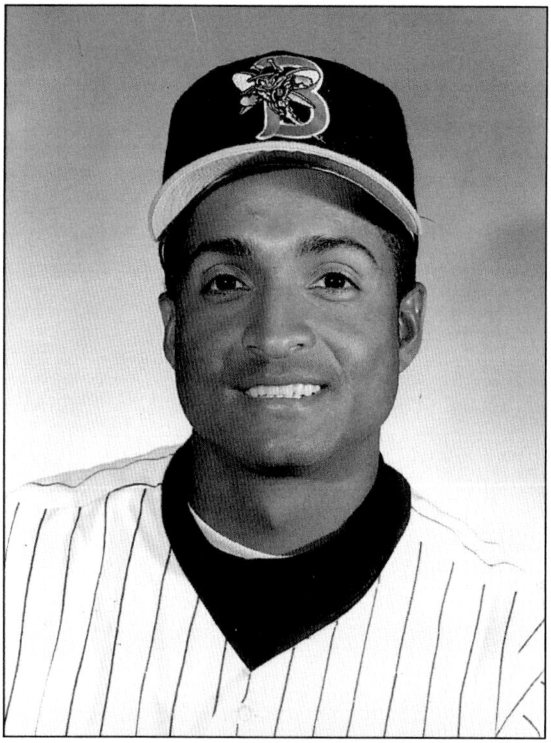

Venezuelan-born Carlos Mendoza showed the Mets organization early on that he could hit. He hit .350 in the Dominican League in 1994 and followed that with a .328 at Kingsport in the Appalachian League. After a .337 in 1996 with Capital City, Mendoza arrived in Binghamton the following year. He hit .382 in 46 games. Not surprisingly, the New York Mets sent for him that year.

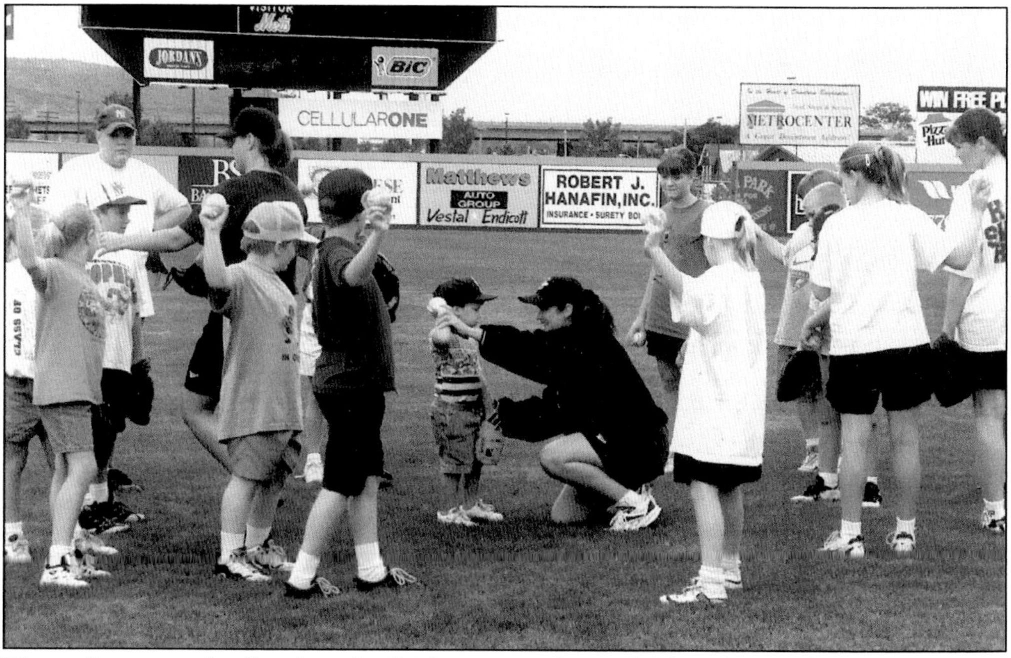

The stadium is rarely idle when the B-Mets are on the road. The Silver Bullets, a professional women's team, practiced there in August 1997. After practice, kids of all ages were invited onto the field for instruction. Clearly, girls were inspired to participate, as was the little guy getting individual throwing tips from Alyson Hebetz. Hall of Famer Phil Niekro was the Silver Bullets' manager.

Trying to work your way through a minor-league system in hopes of getting to the big show can be an exhausting and frustrating experience. However, baseball can be fun too. Pitcher Barry Short personifies the fun part here. He was 2-0 for the B-Mets with a fine 2.61 ERA in 1997. In 1999, his 0-5 record was no laughing matter.

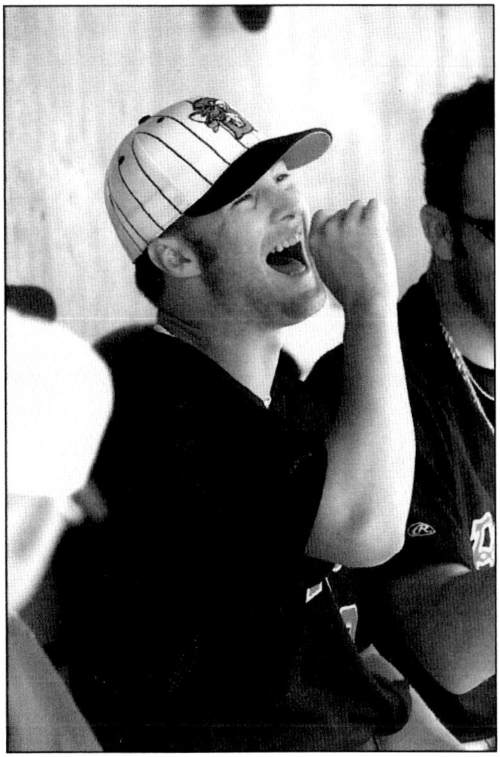

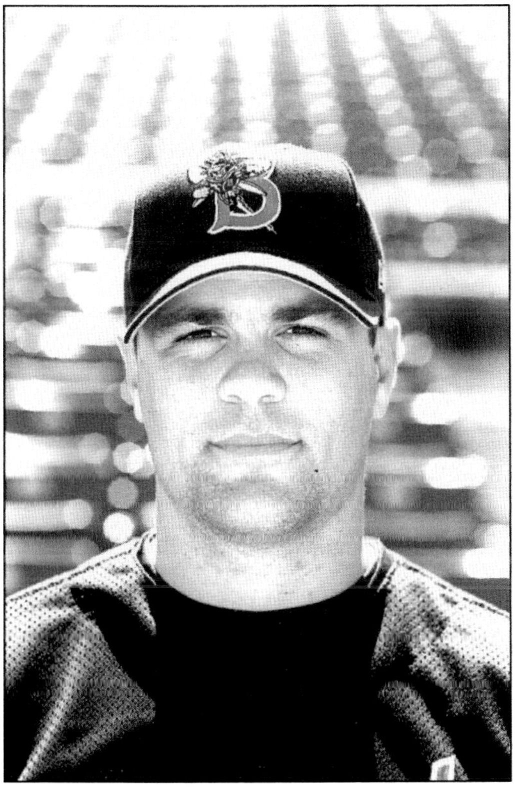

Scott Hunter played high school football with New York Giants fullback Charles Way. That may explain the aggressiveness that led to him breaking two ribs and bruising a lung diving for a ball in 1997. Known for his clutch hitting, Hunter spent four seasons with the B-Mets (1997, 1998, 2001, and 2002). His best year was 1998, when he hit .314, stole 39 bases, and was an Eastern League All-Star.

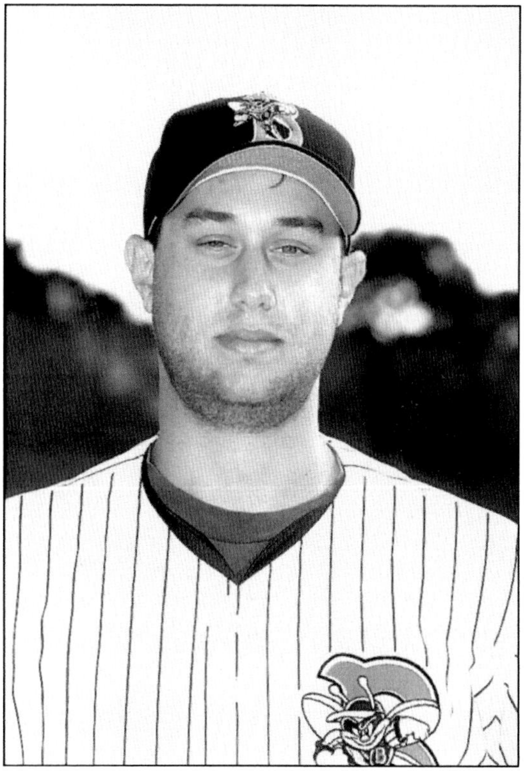

Southpaw Ed Yarnall was a Florida State League All-Star in 1996 and appeared in five games for the B-Mets the following season. Given a good look in 1998, he responded with a 7-0 record that included a remarkable ERA of 0.39 in 47 innings. Unfortunately, that made him trade bait, and he was grabbed by Florida for a fellow named Mike Piazza.

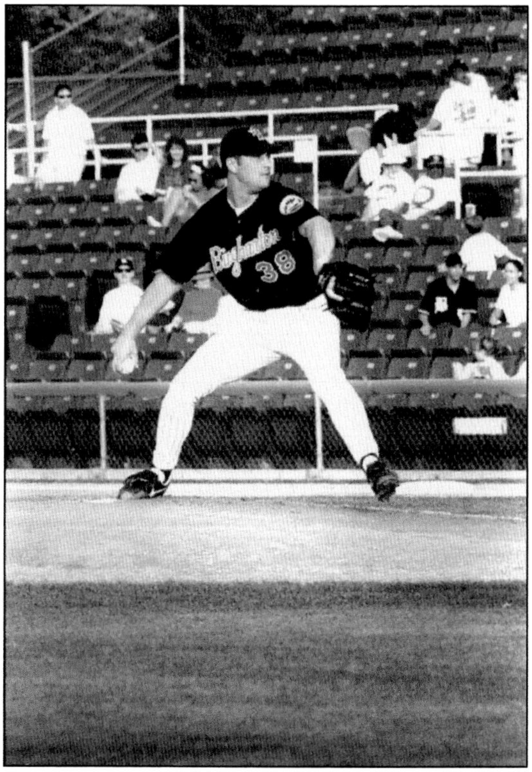

Dan Murray was just what B-Mets manager John Gibbons needed in 1998. Despite losing three of its best pitchers by the end of June, the club had the best July in its history (20-9). Murray was part of the reason for that streak. Moving from the bullpen to the starting rotation, he posted an 11-6 record, had 159 strikeouts, and gave up only 54 walks for the year.

Todd Landry was a three-time Most Valuable Player of the World Youth Classic, an annual Binghamton tournament that features mostly American Legion players. After five years in the lower minors, from Helena, Montana, to El Paso, Texas, he returned here in 1998. Landry hit a solid .274 in 89 games, but bad knees kept him hobbled for much of the season. He was not back in 1999.

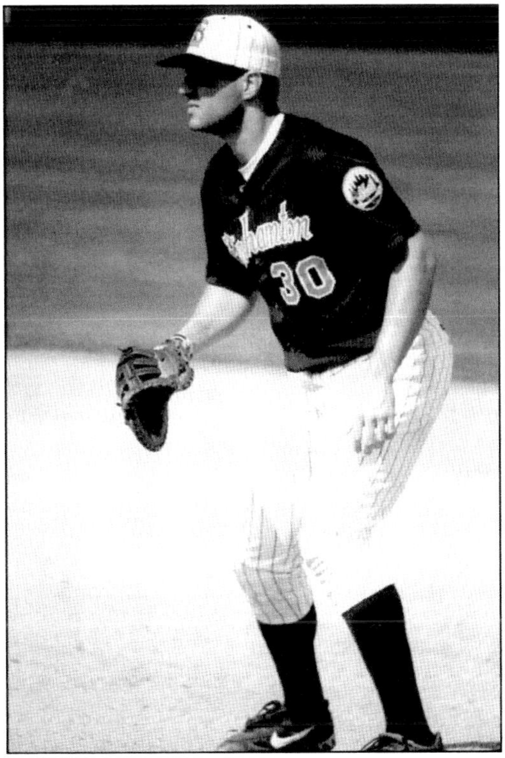

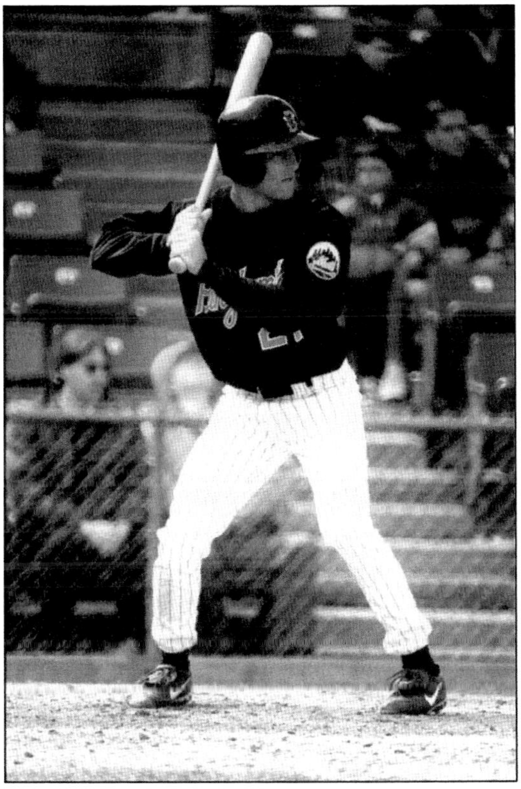

One has to wonder about the criteria that major-league teams sometimes use to evaluate players. Common sense dictates that putting up good numbers over two consecutive seasons should prove something. Garrett Neubart did just that. In 1998, the speedy outfielder hit .275 in 95 games. The following year, he hit .288. Still, we have yet to see his name in a major-league box score.

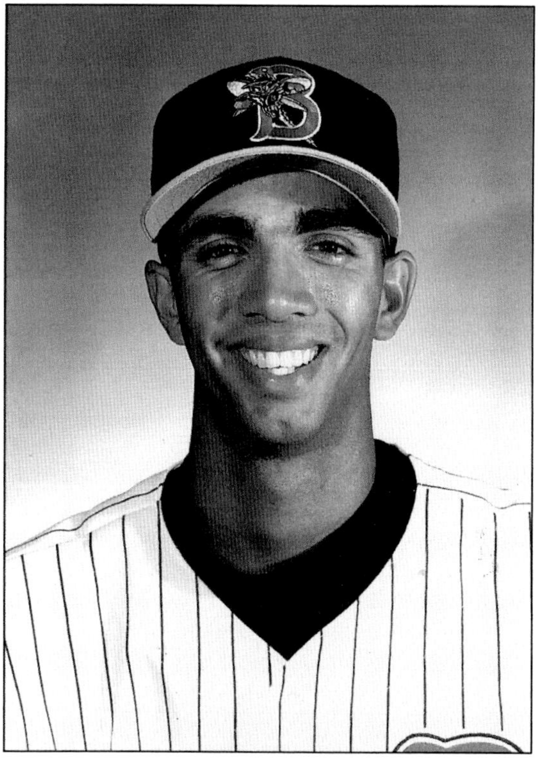

Nelson Figueroa, while with Capital City in 1996, dominated batters on the Class-A level. His 200 strikeouts, 14-7 record, 2.04 ERA, and four shutouts in 185 innings were outstanding. Double A was not as easy. In 1997, with the B-Mets, he was 5-11, with a 4.34 ERA. However, Nelson turned it around in 1998 with an excellent 12-3 mark. The result was a trade to Arizona.

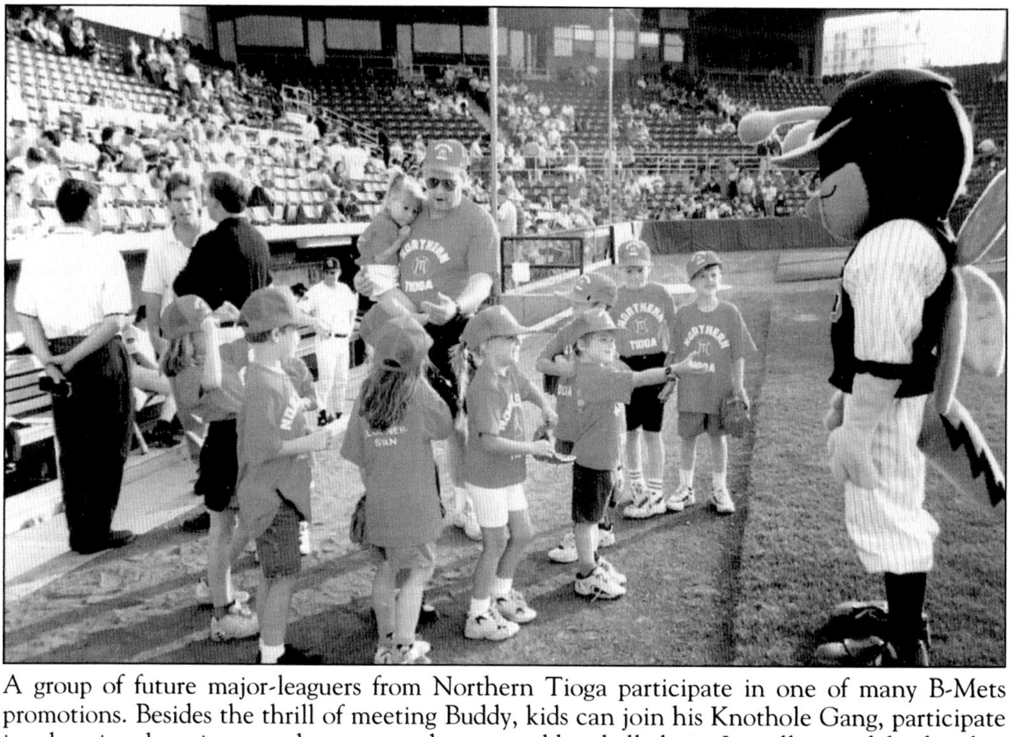

A group of future major-leaguers from Northern Tioga participate in one of many B-Mets promotions. Besides the thrill of meeting Buddy, kids can join his Knothole Gang, participate in educational seminars, and even attend an annual baseball clinic. It is all part of the fun that the ownership provides every day during the season.

Vance Wilson established himself as a major-league catcher with the New York Mets in 2003, when Mike Piazza went down with an injury. Wilson was the B-Mets' regular catcher in 1997. He hit a respectable .276 in 91 games and led the club in two-base hits with 17. Six years later, his potential is being realized.

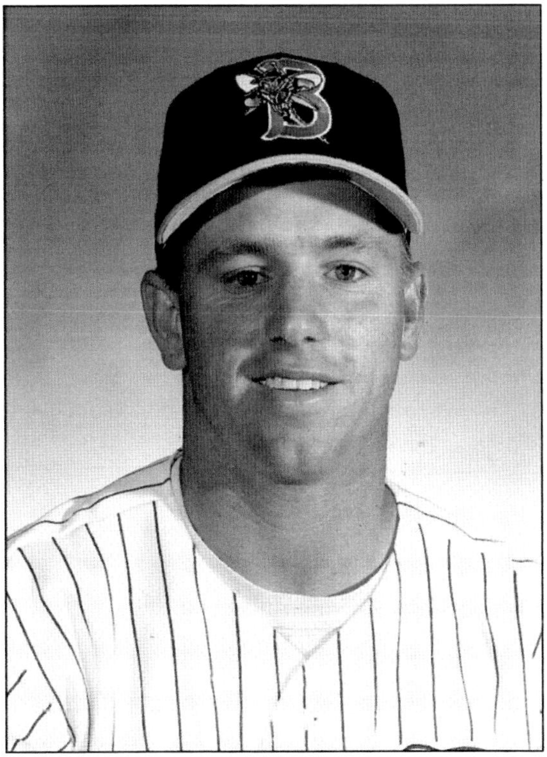

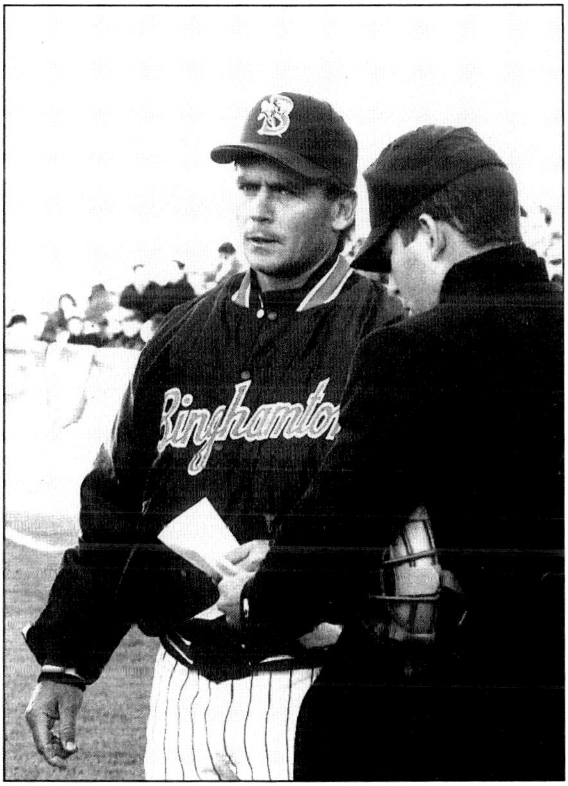

John Gibbons accomplished a managerial feat in 1998. Although his team was eliminated in the first round of the playoffs, he was still voted the league's Manager of the Year. Being able to take a club to the playoffs at all when it hit the least home runs (96) in the Eastern League and lost its best pitchers midway through the season may help to explain the honor.

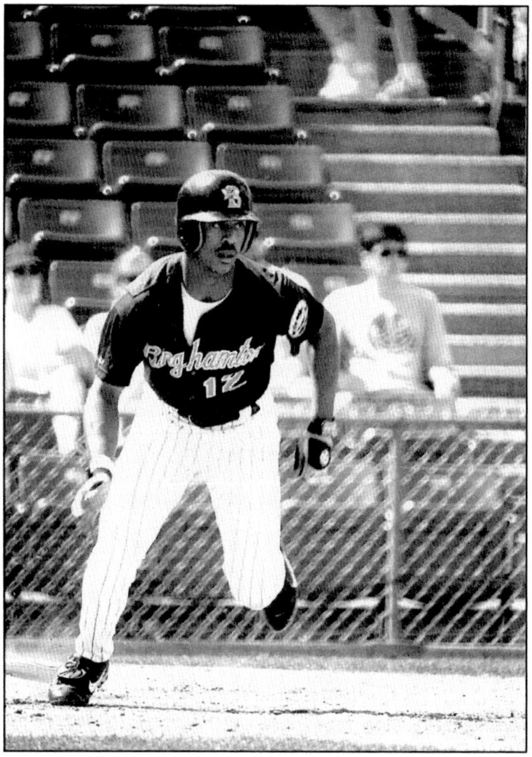

Mets player development director Jim Duquette once compared Terrence Long to Barry Bonds. Considering that Long had never hit .300 or collected more than 12 home runs in any of his four previous seasons, Duquette must have seen a lot of potential. In 1998, Long proved Duquette's ability to spot talent. He led the B-Mets with 16 homers, 10 triples, and 62 bases on balls. The following year, he was at Shea.

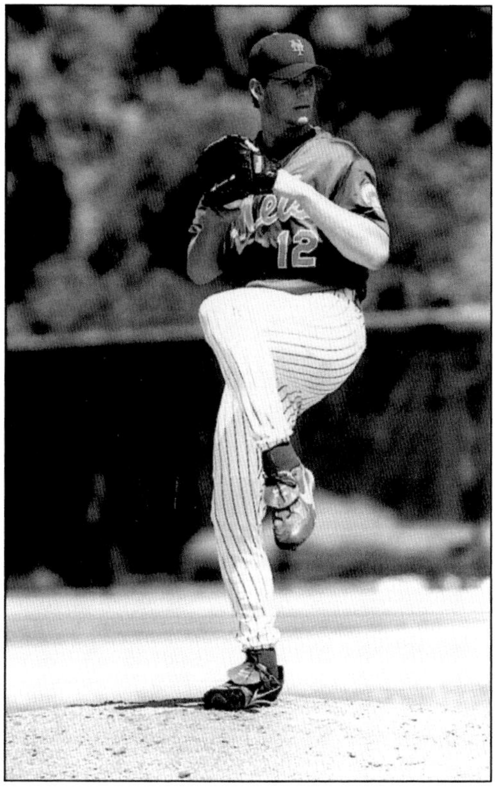

Grant Roberts threw 131 innings for the last-place 1999 B-Mets, who lost a franchise-record 88 games. His seven wins tied him for the team lead in that category with Mark Corey. Roberts's talent was obvious, and he made his Mets debut the following year. He is currently a rising star in the New York Mets bullpen.

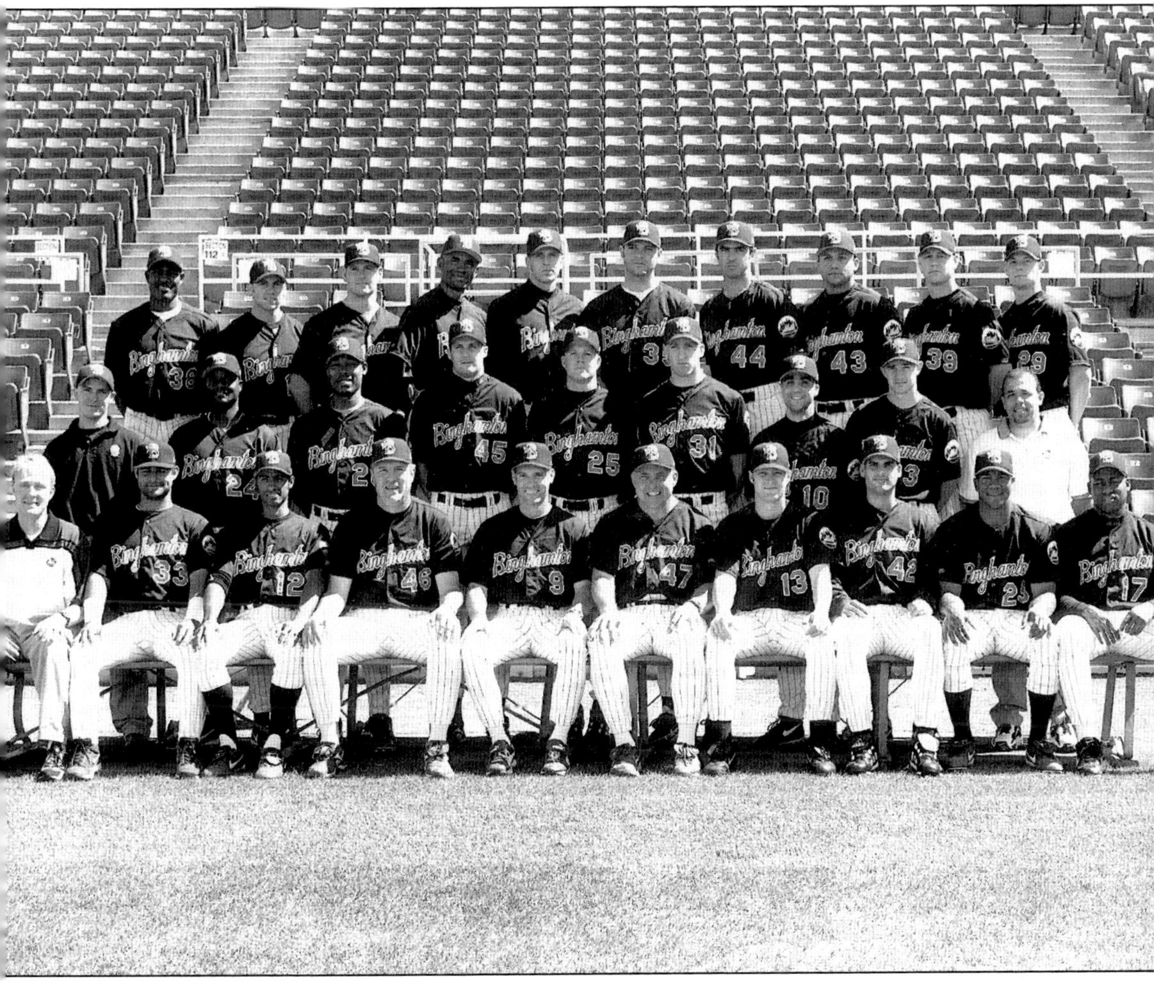

A 1999 season that opened with much promise ended with a devastating 88 losses. That happened to be the most losses for any minor-league team anywhere that year. The club finished 38 games behind Trenton. Manager Doug Davis, given another opportunity the following year, proved his worth by leading the B-Mets from the cellar to first place.

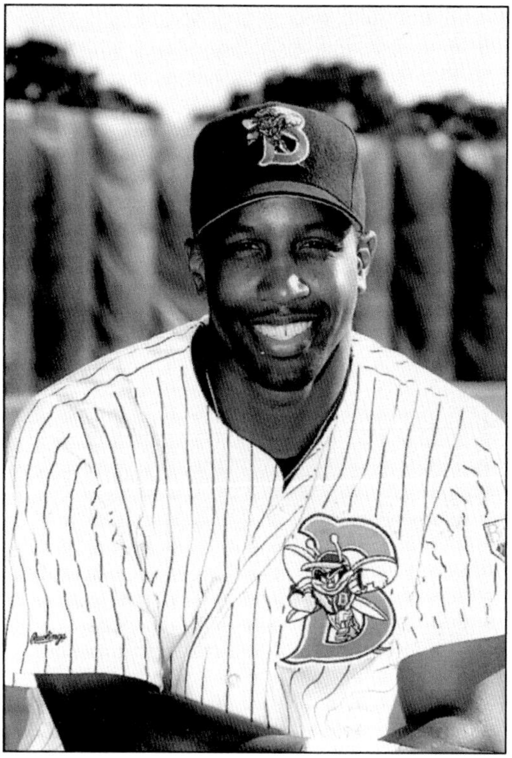

Moving up to Double-A ball can be a difficult adjustment for some. Many fall by the wayside, while others steadily improve. An example of the latter was Allen Dina. In 1999, his first year with the B-Mets, Dina hit only .229 in 48 games. He improved to .258 in 2000 and was hitting .275 in 2001, when he was promoted to Triple A.

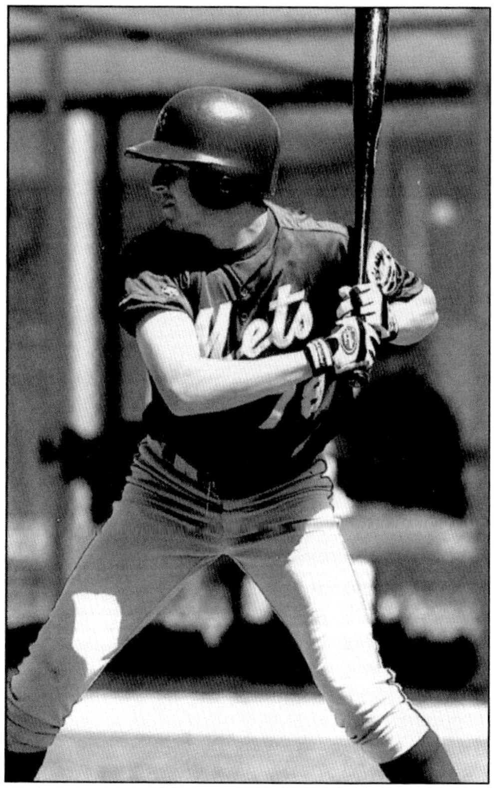

That bleak year of 1999 had one bright spot—the consistent hitting and hustle of Jason Tyner. He led the team in batting (.313), hits (162), runs (91), walks (62), and stolen bases (49). Not surprisingly, he is now in the major leagues as a Tampa Bay Devil Ray.

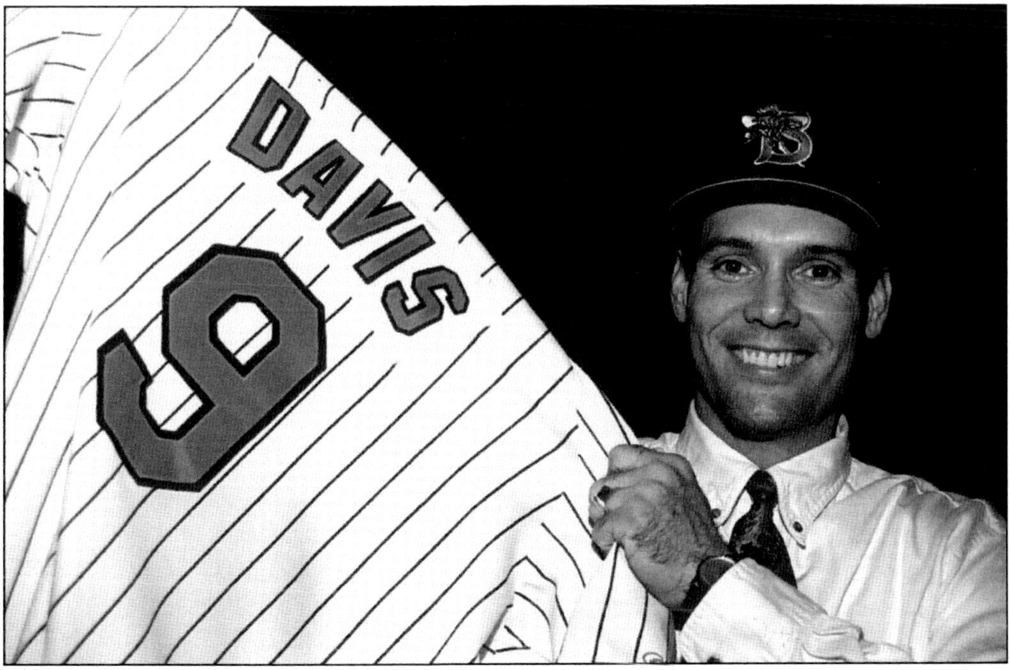

Doug Davis joyfully displays his uniform upon being introduced as manager of the B-Mets in 1999. He was not quite as cheerful at season's end, when the club finished last with 88 losses. Davis never lost his enthusiasm and was probably the least surprised person in the organization when the club rebounded to a first-place finish in 2000.

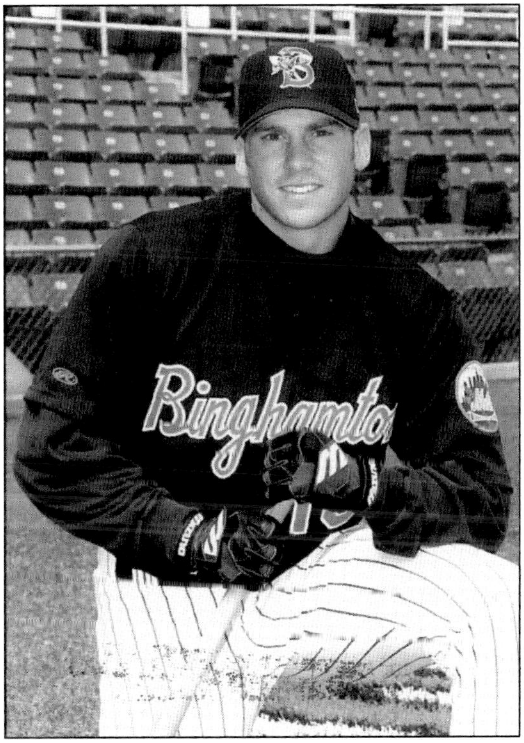

B.J. Huff was a popular B-Met during his three years with them (1999–2001). Starting with the last-place B-Mets in 1999, he hit .249 as an outfielder in 55 games. In the 2000 season, when the club finished first in its division, Huff hit only .212. Although he was on the roster in 2001, he was used in only four games. Outfielders are expected to be hitters.

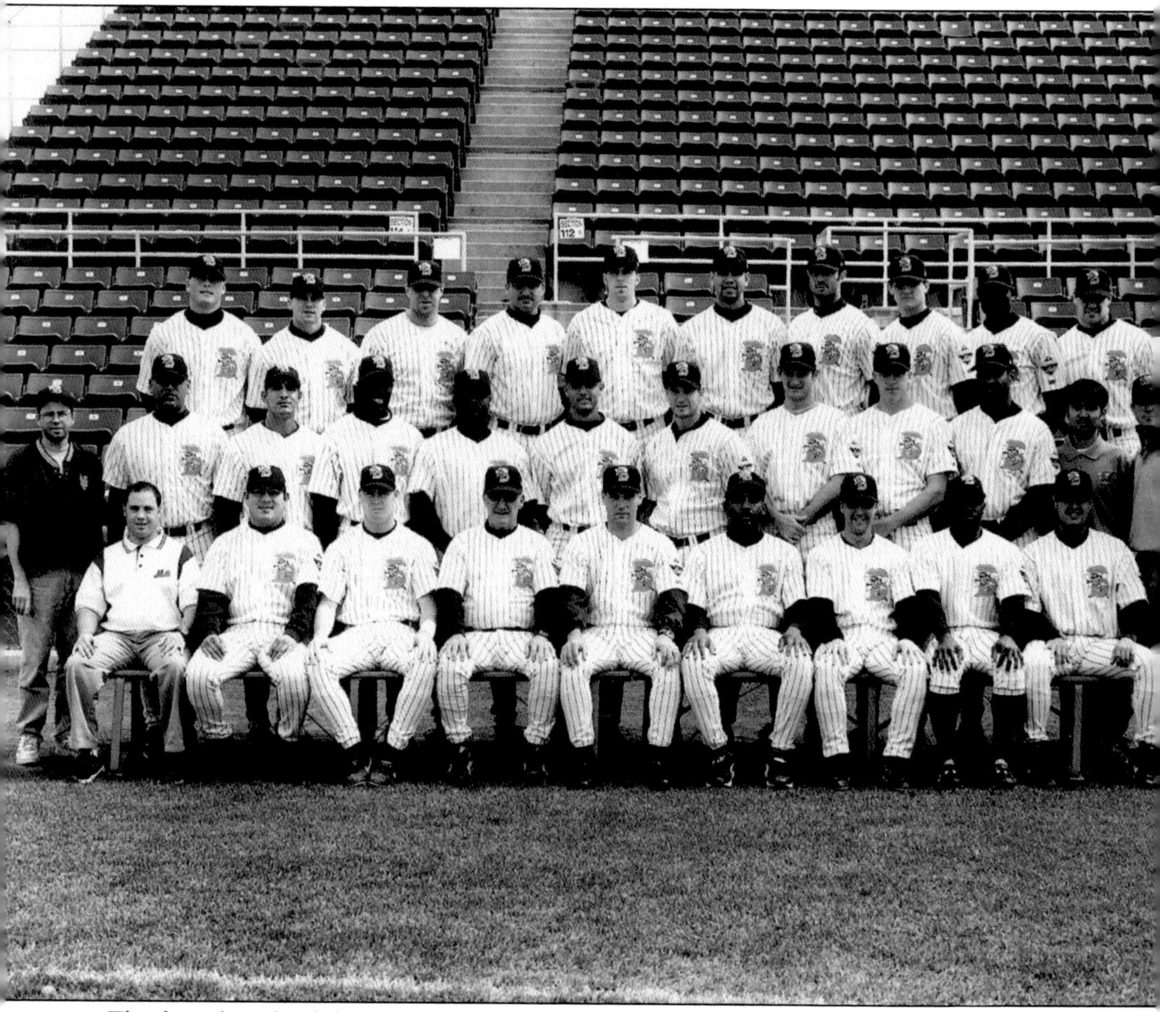

The first-place finish by the B-Mets in 2000 was no fluke. Jerrod Riggan showed the form that has made him an outstanding major-league relief pitcher. He achieved his 28th save of the season on the day that the club clinched the pennant and helped to create the club's turnaround from 88 losses in 1999 to 82 wins in 2000. Alex Escobar, Eastern League Rookie of the Year, and Dan Held, voted Most Valuable Player by his teammates, also contributed mightily to the improvement.

Those 28 saves by Jerrod Riggan (shown here) broke the Eastern League record formerly held by Mike Welch. Even more remarkable is the fact that Riggan never blew a single save opportunity. A high point had to be the last save. It not only clinched the Northern Division title for his club but also, for that one day, gave the B-Mets the best won-lost percentage of any team in the major leagues, Double A, or Triple A.

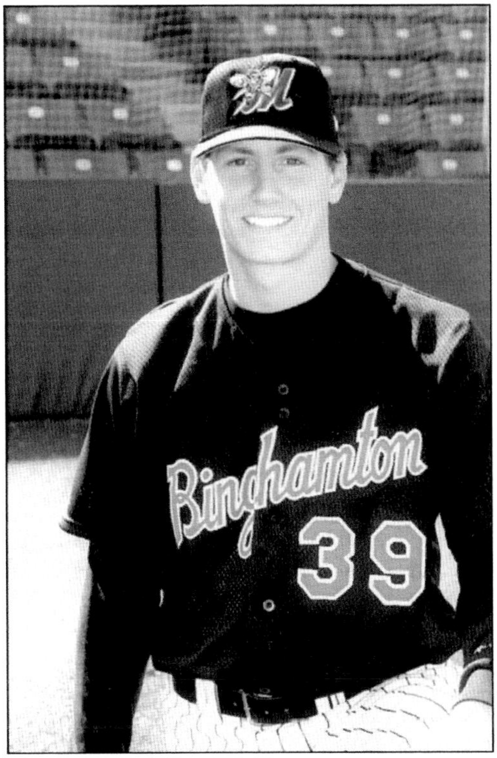

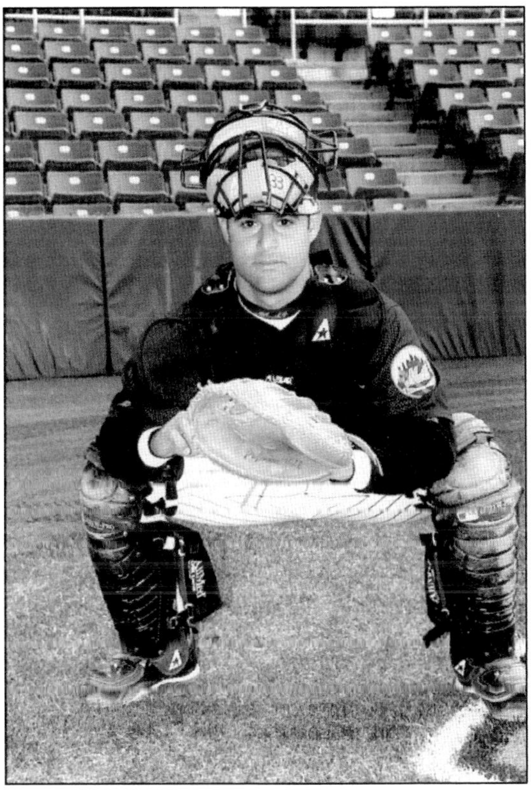

Sammy Rodriguez certainly paid his minor-league dues. From 1995 to 1998, he caught 144 games in places such as Butte, Pittsfield, and St. Lucie before coming to the B-Mets. He remained in Binghamton through 2001, catching over 100 games. Unfortunately, his hitting never exceeded .250 during those three years. Catchers have to be able to swing the bat too.

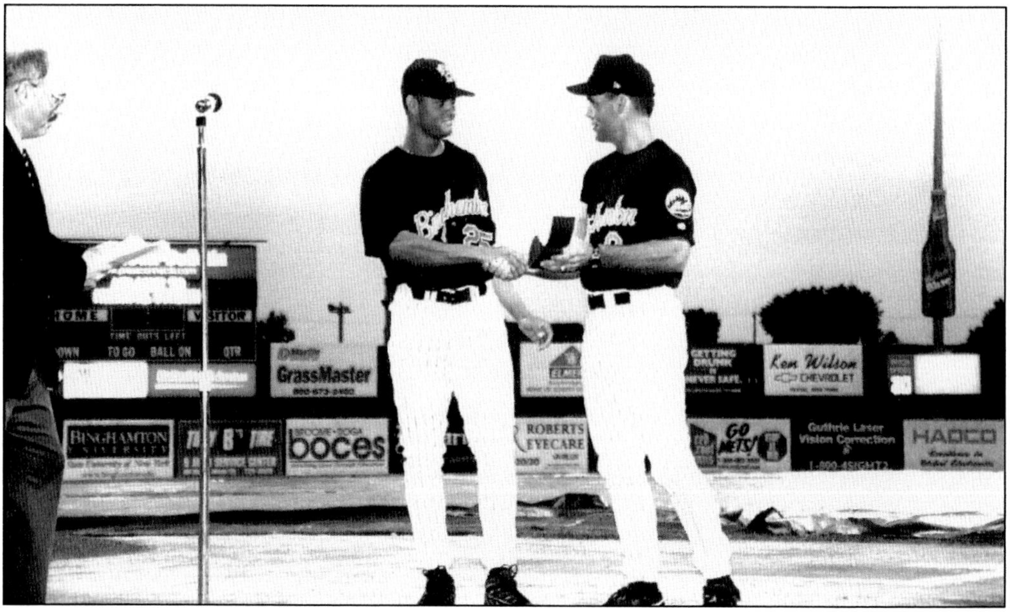

Manager Doug Davis (right) congratulates Alex Escobar for earning a Player of the Month award. Escobar was picked in 2000 for the Eastern League All-Star team and as one of the top prospects of the decade. Injuries held him back, but his combination of speed and power could not be denied. By 2001, he was on the roster of the New York Mets.

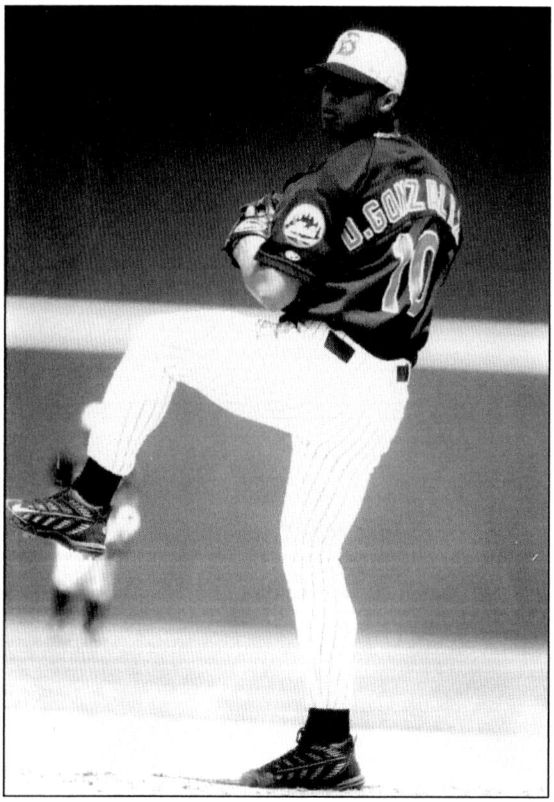

Dicky Gonzalez had a 14-9 record at St. Lucie in 1999, with a fine 2.83 ERA. The brass was impressed and let Gonzalez bypass Binghamton to pitch a game for Norfolk. Wiser heads soon prevailed, and in 2000, he got his needed year of seasoning with the B-Mets. Gonzalez led the staff with a 13-5 record and 138 strikeouts. Now he was ready to join the New York Mets, and the following year, he did.

In 2000, Mike Kinkade, now with the Dodgers, was leading the B-Mets with a .366 batting average. Suddenly, on July 21, he became part of a deal between the Mets and the Baltimore Orioles. Kinkade was sent to the Bowie Baysox, where he finished the season as the Eastern League batting champion with a .358 average. Later that year, he was part of Tom Lasorda's gold-medal-winning Olympic baseball team.

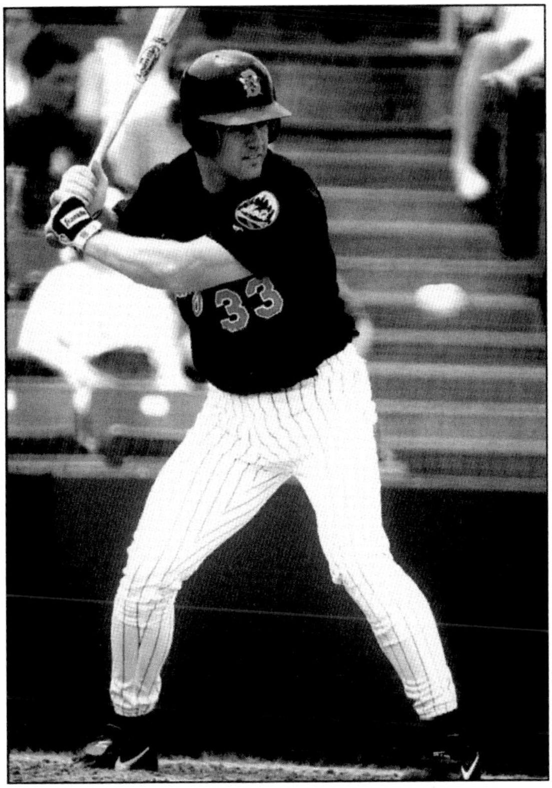

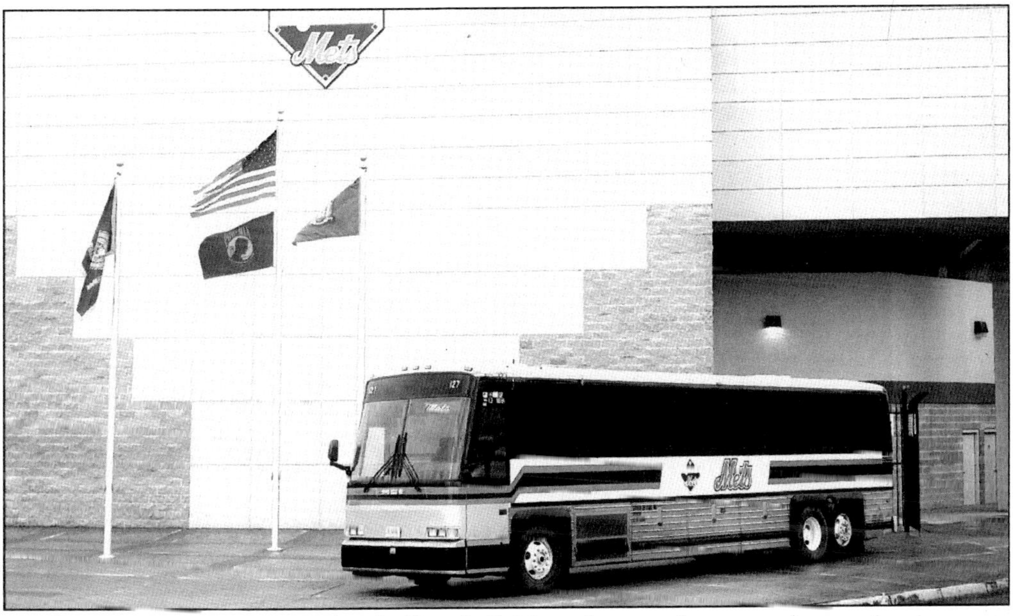

Road trips are tiresome on any level of baseball. Major-leaguers hop onto the team's private jets when they travel, and although the players are lavishly wined and dined, they can grow weary of the travel. Things are a little different on the Double-A level. However, the B-Mets do their best by providing the most comfortable air-conditioned bus available. No problem with "fear of flying" here.

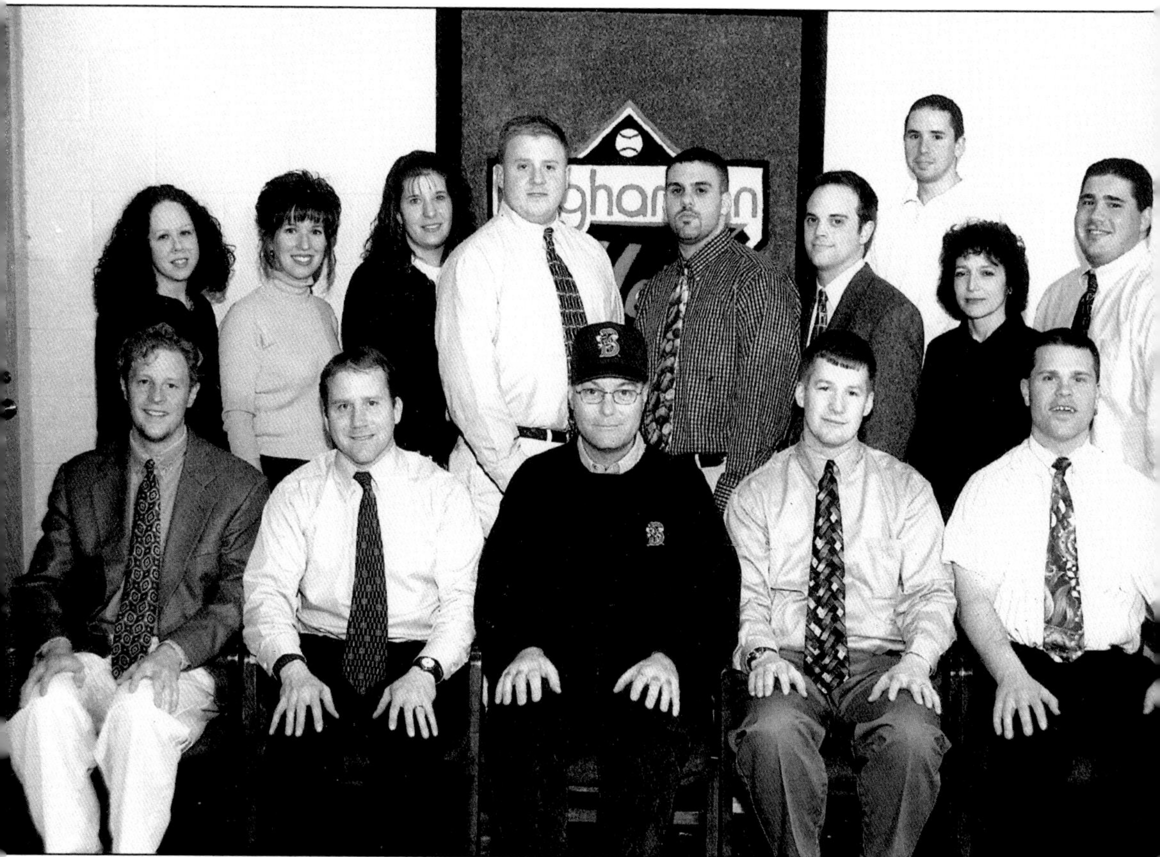

Hillary Clinton has written that "it takes a village to raise a child." Running a baseball club, by comparison, should require a metropolis. The staff, shown here, somehow manages to make a tremendously complicated task look easy. The great baseball enjoyed by Binghamton Mets fans is the direct result of the staff's hard work. From left to right are the following: (front row) Bob O'Brien, Scott Brown, Bill Terlecky, Kevin Mahoney, and Richard Tylicki; (back row) Jennifer McMahon, Rebecca Brown, Lisa Shattuck, Jim Weed, Chad Efron, Josh Whetzel, Chris Edmonds, Karen Micalizzi, and Mike Catalano.

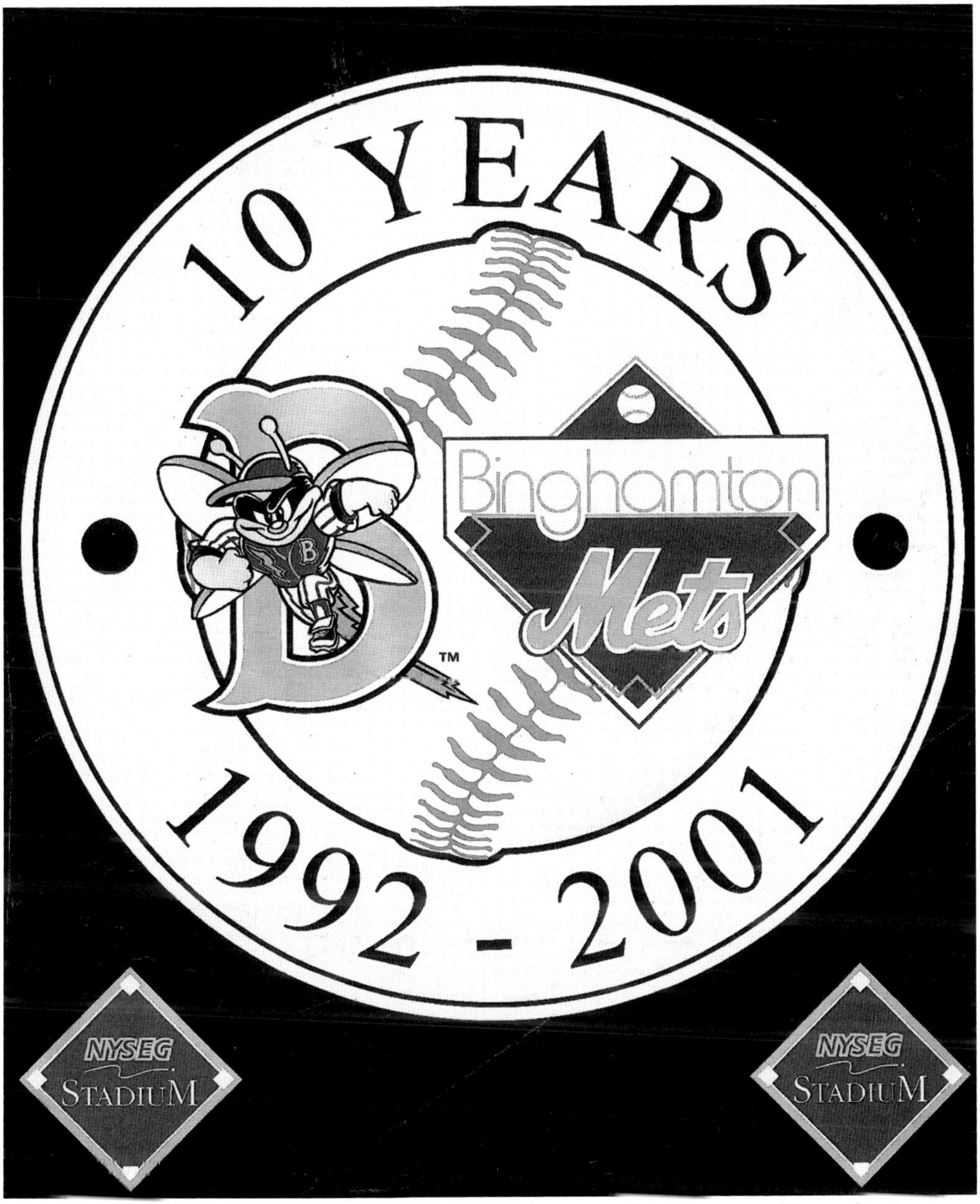

The B-Mets celebrated their 10th anniversary in this special publication. Howie Freiling was the new manager and had the distinction of being the team's first leader who had not been a catcher. He was also the first left-handed manager since Phil Page, who had led the Triplets to their best winning season in 1953. Despite these positive omens, the club finished out of the playoffs.

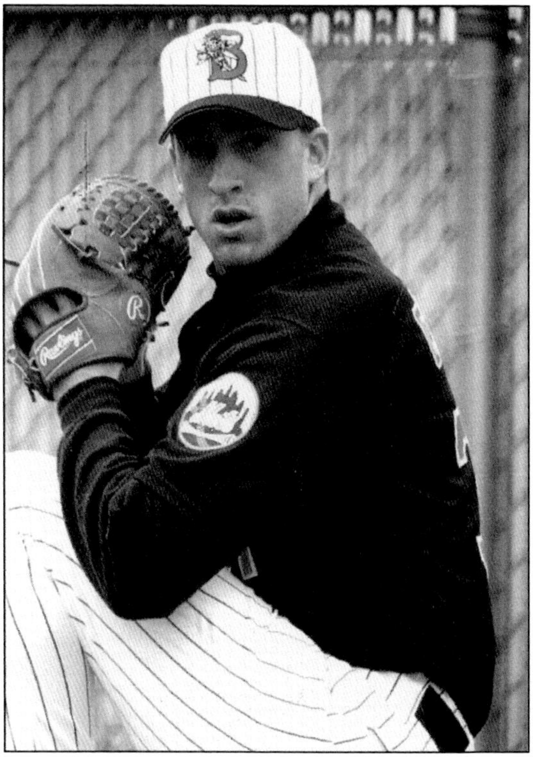

Mark Corey was 7-13 with a 5.40 ERA in 1999. He threw for only 26 innings in 2000, and very little was expected of him in 2001. However, after being converted to a relief pitcher, Corey found his niche. Before being promoted to Norfolk in July, he already had a league-leading 17 saves and a 1.80 ERA. Corey continued to dominate at the Triple-A level and spent September with the Mets.

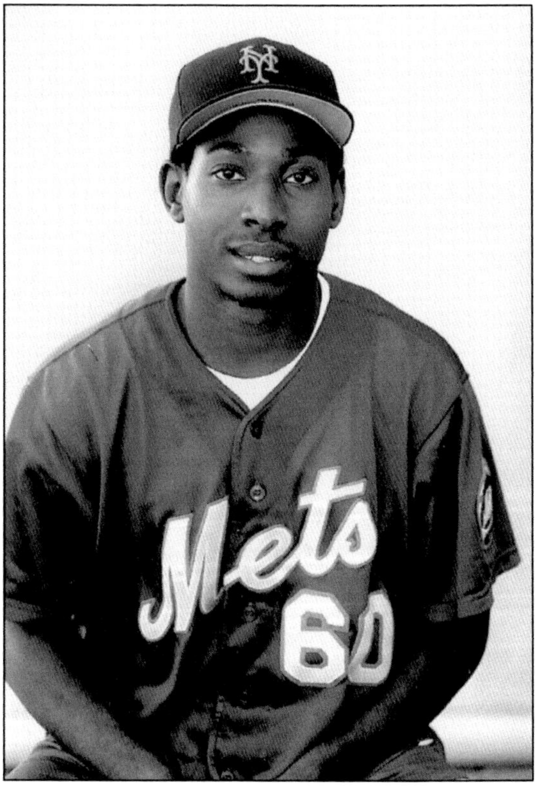

Tragedy struck the Mets organization when Brian Cole was killed in an automobile accident just two days before he was to return to the B-Mets for the 2001 season. Cole was a highly rated prospect, already touted as the fastest base runner in the entire Mets system. In addition to his skills as a leadoff man and center fielder, he was one of the most popular players on the club. His smile and ability are sorely missed.

In 2001, Rob Stratton exemplified the best and the worst that a free-swinging slugger can bring to the table. He led the club in at-bats (483), hits (120), runs scored (70), total bases (239), doubles (30), homers (29), and RBIs (83). On the other hand, he struck out 201 times to set a new Eastern League record in that undesirable category.

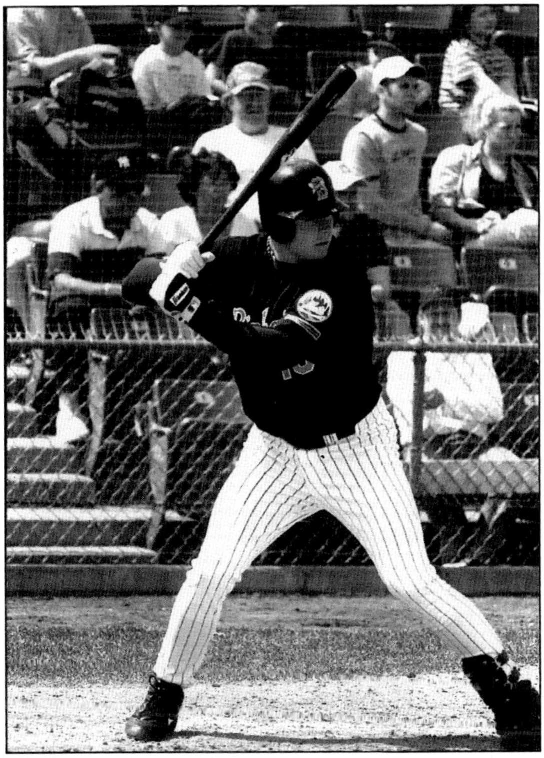

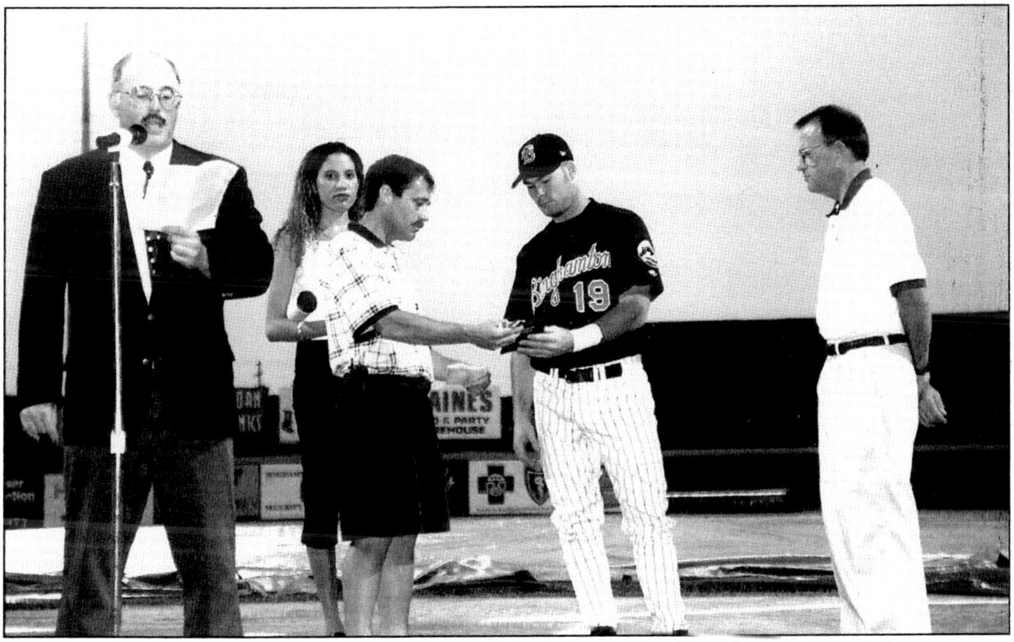

With Roger Neal at the microphone, Ty Wigginton receives his Player of the Month award as club president Mike Urda (right) looks on. Wigginton arrived in Binghamton in 2000 as a second baseman. The Mets' decision to switch the rugged youngster to third base was a good one. He adjusted quickly, and the combination of his good batting eye plus power got him called up to the Mets in 2002. He is thriving in 2003 as their regular third baseman.

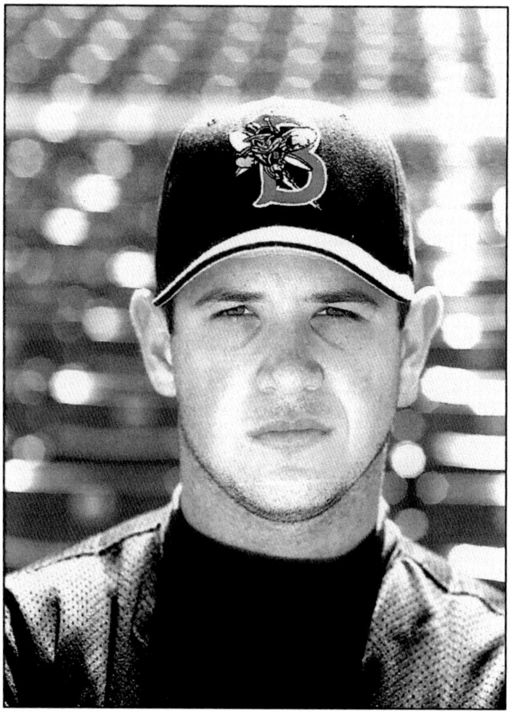

Pat Strange joined the B-Mets' pitching staff in 2000. In 55 innings, he had a 4-3 record, with a 4.55 ERA. The following year, he became the ace of the staff. His 11-6 mark in 153 innings pitched was three wins higher than anyone else. The New York Mets sent for him in 2002.

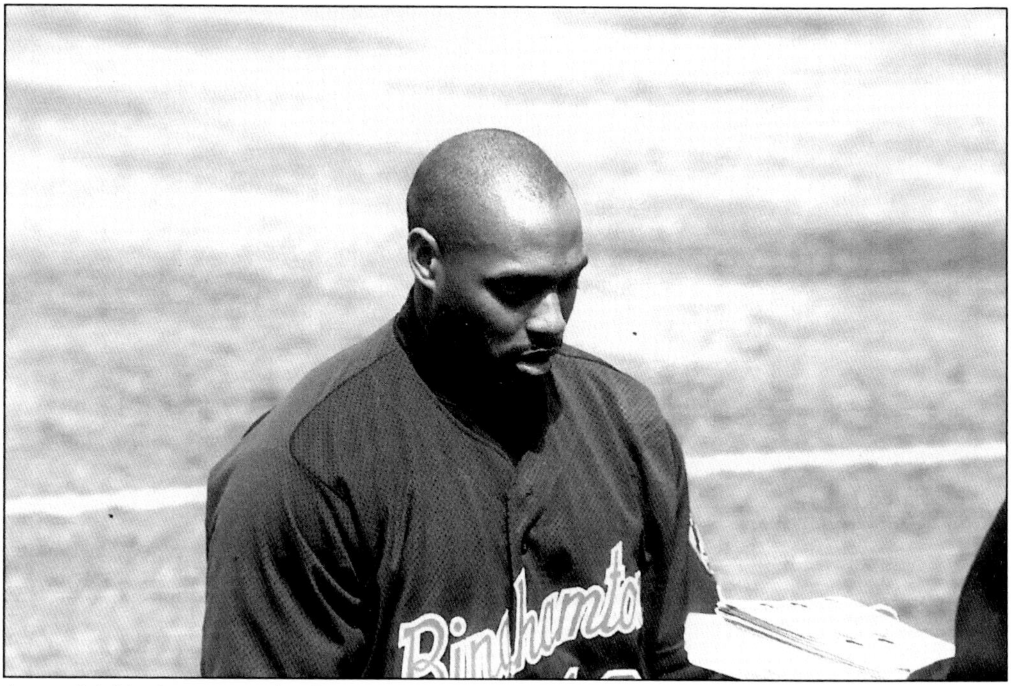

Aaron McNeal came to the B-Mets in 2001, when the first base position was owned by Earl Snyder, a .281 hitter. McNeal had a rough first year, barely eking out a .201 percentage. However, when Snyder's contract was bought by the Cleveland Indians in 2002, Aaron got his chance. He made the most of it by leading the club in batting average (.299), home runs (19), and RBIs (67).

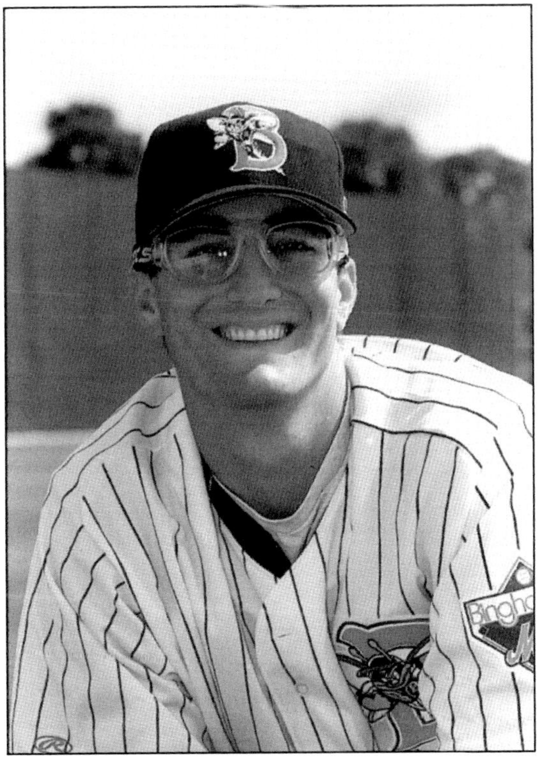

Jason Phillips, now playing first base for the New York Mets in 2003, did something rare for a Double-A player in 2001. He got called up directly to the Mets during the season, bypassing the usual stopover in Triple-A. His stay did not last long, but the man described by his B-Mets manager as "the toughest out in the league" is finally getting his chance and making the most of it.

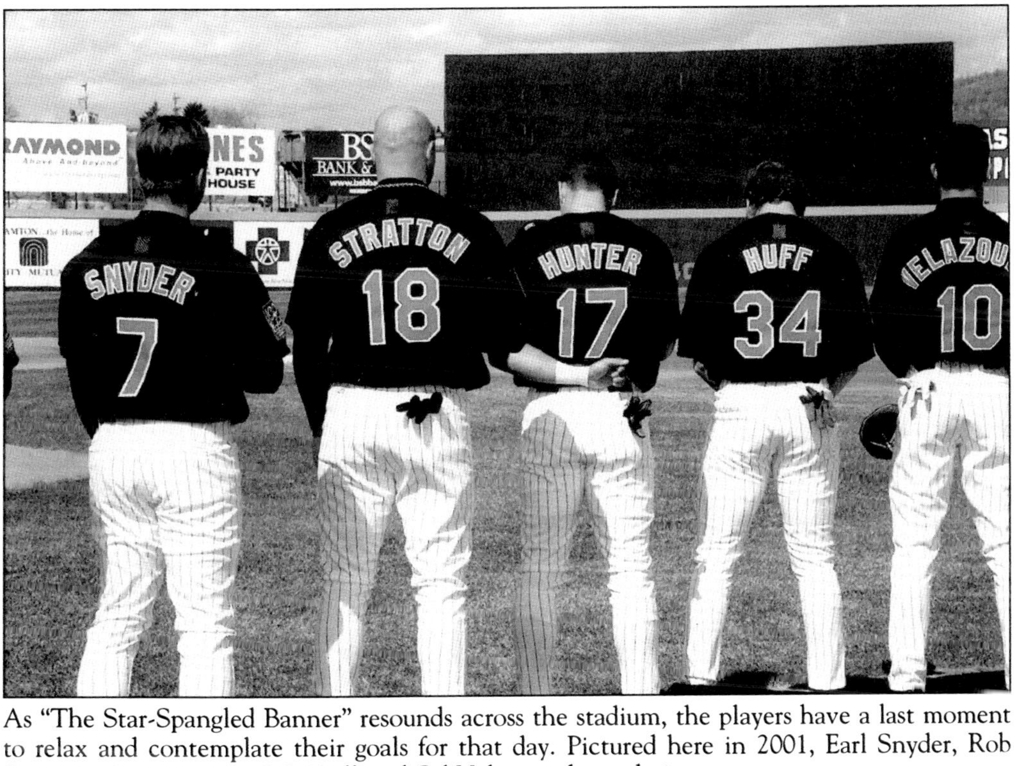

As "The Star-Spangled Banner" resounds across the stadium, the players have a last moment to relax and contemplate their goals for that day. Pictured here in 2001, Earl Snyder, Rob Stratton, Scott Hunter, B.J. Huff, and Gil Velasquez have their moment.

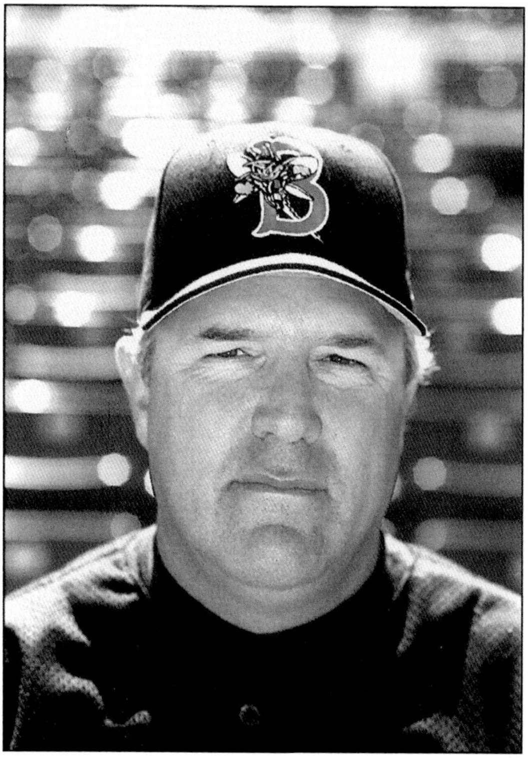

B-Mets pitching coach Bob Stanley had the dubious distinction of being on the mound for the Red Sox when Mookie Wilson's ground ball skipped under Bill Buckner's glove in the sixth game of the 1986 World Series. The Mets went on to win, thus continuing the "curse of the bambino" that Boston fans seem fated to suffer. Many people forget that Stanley pitched $6^1/_3$ innings in that series without giving up an earned run.

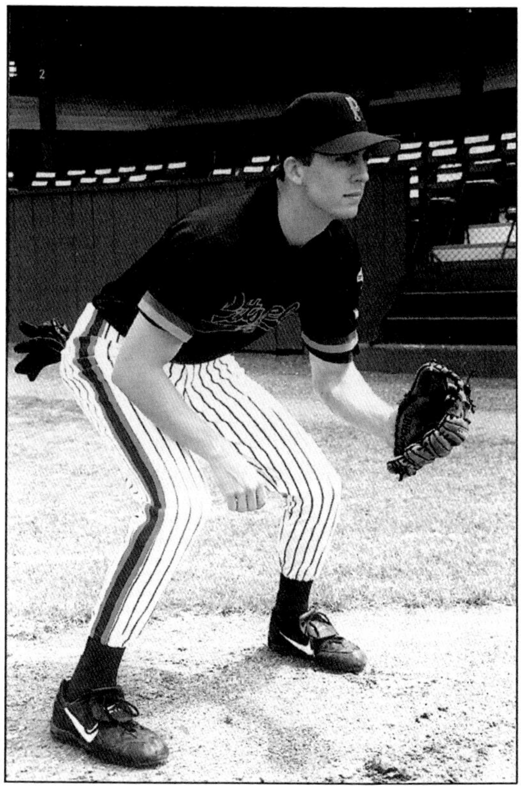

Shortstop Chris Basak opened some eyes in the Mets organization when he hit .372 in 13 games with the B-Mets in 2001. That got him to Triple-A Norfolk in 2002. Chris hit only .217 in 17 games for them and was returned to Binghamton. With Jose Reyes apparently installed as the Mets' future shortstop, Basak, hitting .275 midway through 2003, will probably need a trade to make it to the majors.

Earl Snyder was known for his consistency, both in the field and at the plate. In 2001, he was the B-Mets' lone entry on the Eastern League All-Star squad. His .281 batting average, 20 homers, and 75 RBIs placed him among the league's top 10 hitters. Snyder did not go unnoticed. When the Mets craved Roberto Alomar, Cleveland wisely insisted that Snyder be part of the deal.

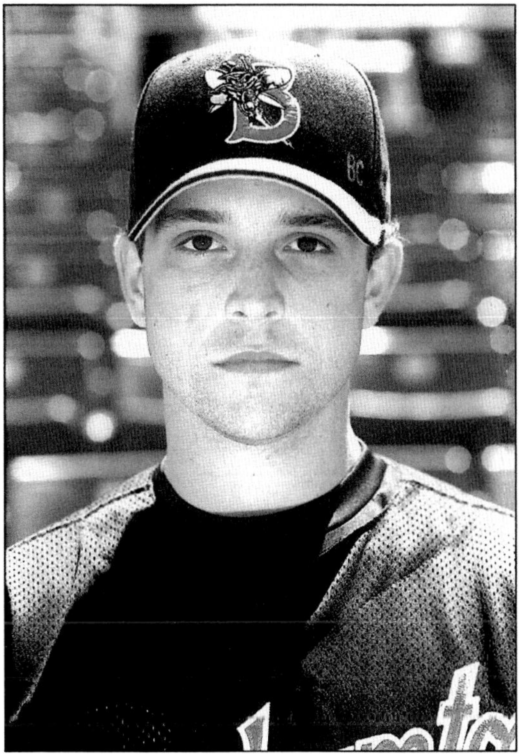

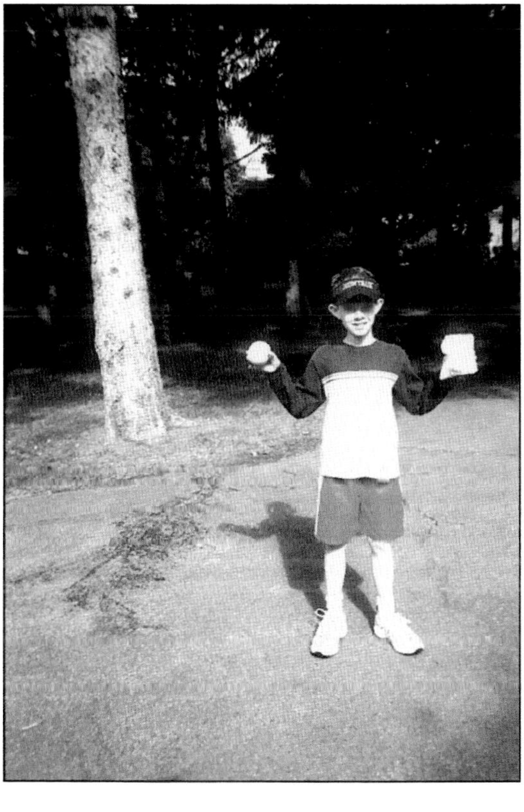

The stadium comes to life and the air becomes electric during every B-Mets home game when T-shirts and soft baseballs are tossed randomly into the stands between innings. The noise level rises to a fever pitch as screaming youngsters jockey for position, while pleading for something to be thrown their way. Sometimes, a lucky fan catches both souvenirs at one game. That happened to Alex Bufi, shown here posing happily after the game with his treasures.

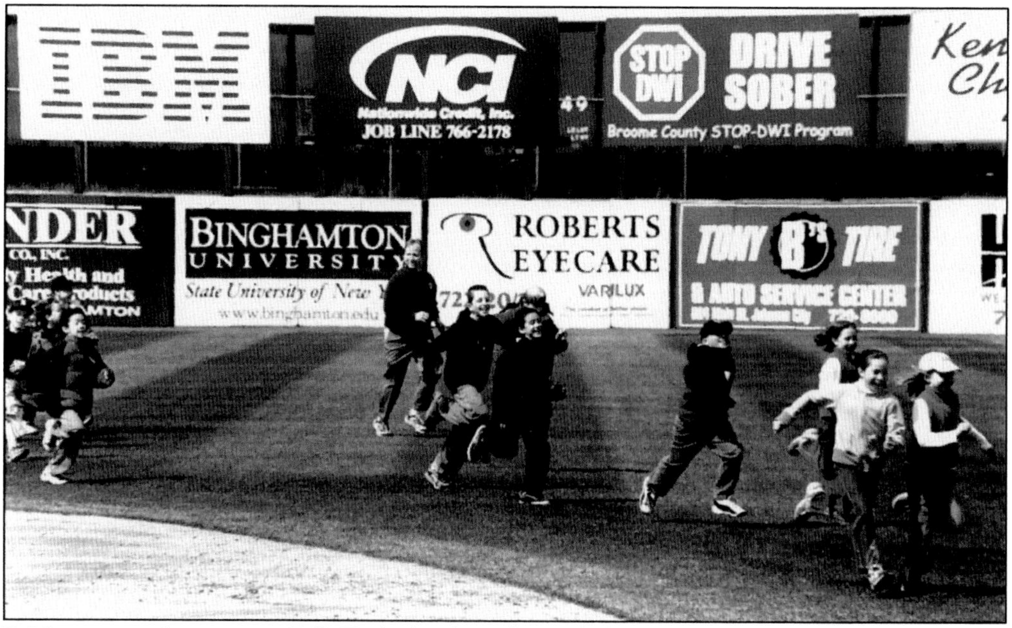

B-Mets general manager Bill Terlecky brought a feeling of fun and excitement to the organization. One of his first decisions, after convincing the groundskeepers that the turf could survive, was to give kids attending games the opportunity to run across the field. It has become a staple of the entertainment provided at every home game. Here, assistant general manager Scott Brown directs traffic as scores of happy faces race by.

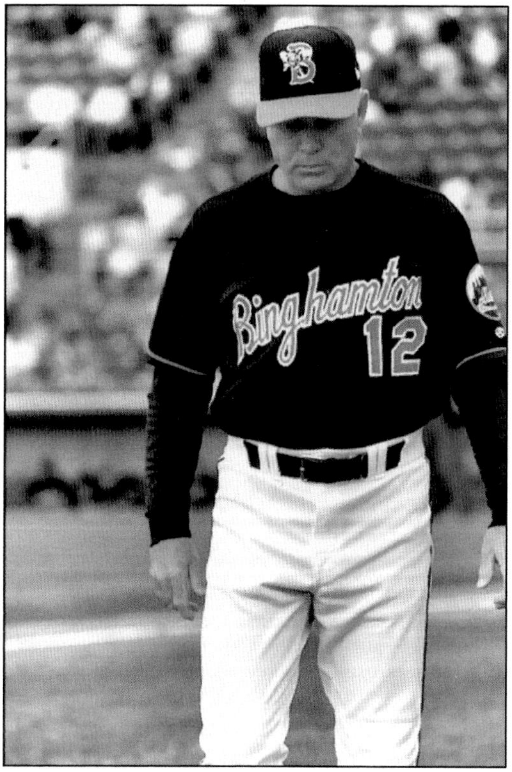

The B-Mets manager in 2003 was John Stearns. Already the seventh manager in the team's 12-year history, he was known for his intensity as a major-league catcher. For example, in the 1980s, he tackled the Atlanta Braves mascot for taunting his teammates. A four-time National League All-Star during his time with the New York Mets (1975–1984), Stearns has a lot to offer for those smart enough to listen.

The Binghamton Baseball Shrine was established in 1993 to pay tribute to those who made a significant contribution to baseball in the Southern Tier of New York. Shown in June 2000 are former former Triplets Clete Boyer (left) and Ralph Terry (right). Both later starred for the Yankees. Co-author Mike McCann is pictured between them.

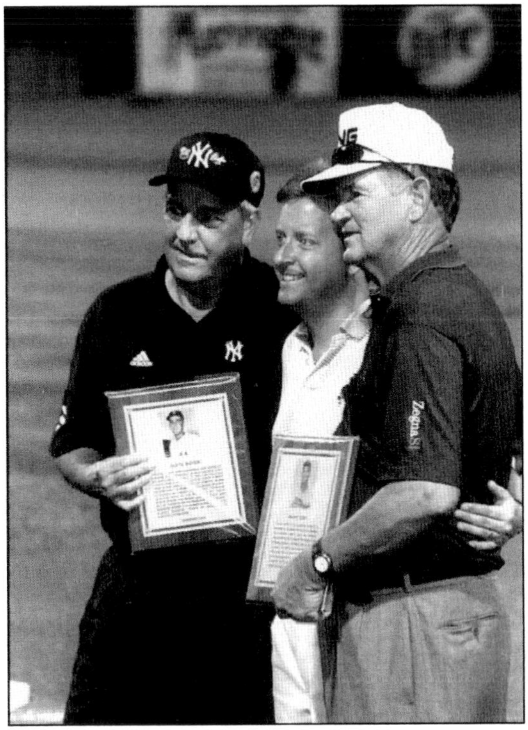

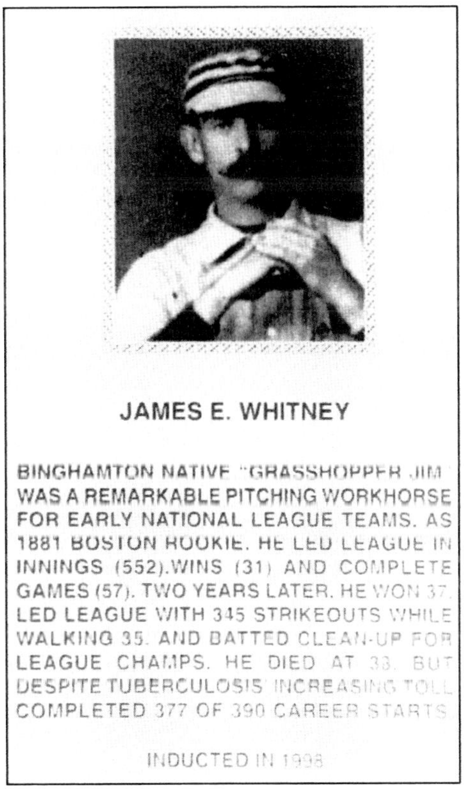

James Evans Whitney, known as "Grasshopper Jim" because of his unusual gait, grew up in Binghamton in the years following the Civil War. Whitney was with the Binghamton Crickets in 1878 and eventually played for Boston, Kansas City, Indianapolis, and Washington in the National League from 1881 to 1889. He led Boston to the league championship in 1883 by winning 37 games and striking out 345 batters. Whitney died in Binghamton in 1891 and is an honored member of the Binghamton Baseball Shrine.

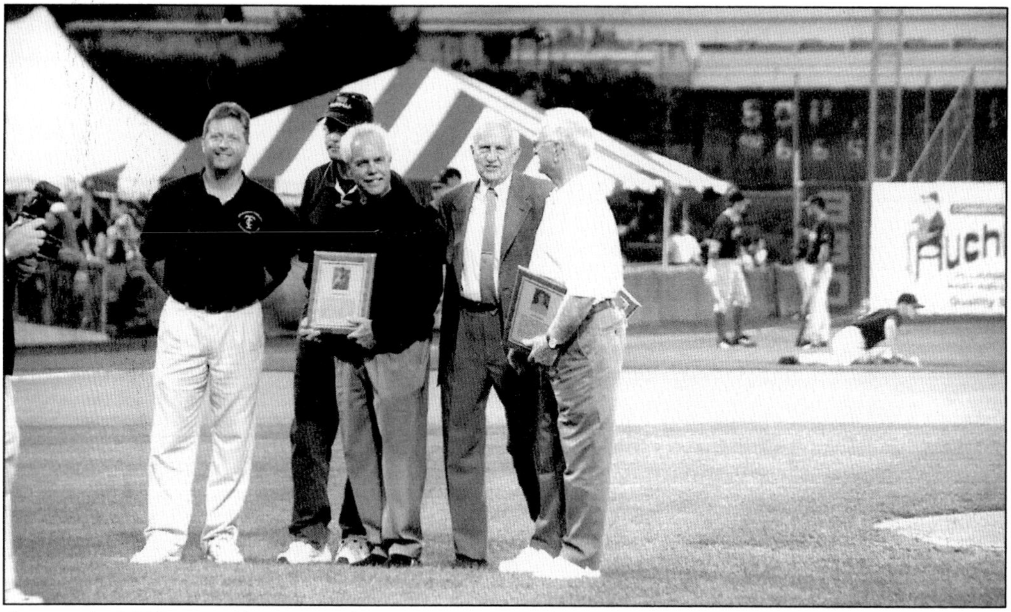

August 1, 2003, was Shrine Night at NYSEG Stadium. Fred Norman is shown here proudly displaying his plaque after being inducted into the Binghamton Baseball Shrine. He is flanked by (from left to right) Mike McCann, B-Mets general manager Bill Terlecky, well-known sportswriter John Fox, and Joe McCann.

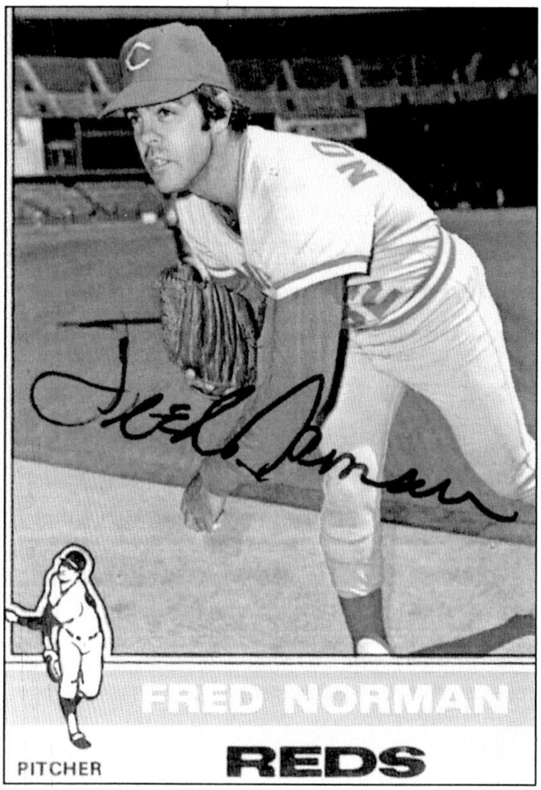

Fred Norman had a 19-year career in the major leagues, but nothing could equal the sensational season that he had with the Triplets in 1963. At age 21, the southpaw struck out 258 batters to set an Eastern League record that will probably never be broken. He went on to strike out 1,303 major-leaguers, mostly as a member of Cincinnati's "Big Red" machine from 1973 to 1979.